Studies in Renaissance Literature

Volume 26

THE ENGLISH CLOWN TRADITION FROM THE MIDDLE AGES TO SHAKESPEARE

Studies in Renaissance Literature

ISSN 1465–6310

General Editors
David Colclough
Raphael Lyne
Sean Keilen

Studies in Renaissance Literature offers investigations of topics in English literature focussed in the sixteenth and seventeenth centuries; its scope extends from early Tudor writing, including works reflecting medieval concerns, to the Restoration period. Studies exploring the interplay between the literature of the English Renaissance and its cultural history are particularly welcomed.

Proposals or queries should be sent in the first instance to the editors, or to the publisher, at the addresses given below; all submissions receive prompt and informed consideration.

Dr David Colclough, School of English and Drama, Queen Mary, University of London, Mile End Road, London, E1 4NS

Dr Raphael Lyne, Murray Edwards College, Cambridge, CB3 0DF

Professor Sean Keilen, University of California Santa Cruz, Santa Cruz, CA 95060, USA

Boydell & Brewer Limited, PO Box 9, Woodbridge, Suffolk, IP12 3DF

Previously published volumes in this series are listed at the back of this volume

THE ENGLISH CLOWN TRADITION FROM THE MIDDLE AGES TO SHAKESPEARE

Robert Hornback

D. S. BREWER

First published 2009
D. S. Brewer, Cambridge
Paperback edition 2013

ISBN 978 1 84384 200 2 hardback
ISBN 978 1 84384 356 6 paperback

Transferred to digital printing

D. S. Brewer is an imprint of Boydell & Brewer Ltd
PO Box 9, Woodbridge, Suffolk IP12 3DF, UK
and of Boydell & Brewer Inc.
668 Mt Hope Avenue, Rochester, NY 14620–2731, USA
website: www.boydellandbrewer.com

A catalogue record for this title is available
from the British Library

The publisher has no responsibility for the continued existence or
accuracy of URLs for external or third-party internet websites referred to
in this book, and does not guarantee that any content on such websites
is, or will remain, accurate or appropriate

This publication is printed on acid-free paper

For Jeanne,
and in memory of Vernon T. (Ted) Hornback Jr,
who loved to laugh

CONTENTS

LIST OF ILLUSTRATIONS

ACKNOWLEDGMENTS

I trace the conception and development of *Clown Traditions* to research completed at the Folger Shakespeare Library during multiple yearly pilgrimages and long-term stays between 2003 and 2008. The digging I did there, often near the crypt of the Folgers themselves and the replica grave monument to Shakespeare, led to unexpected finds. I especially wish to thank the Folger for a three-month fellowship, awarded in 2007–8, which allowed me to complete this project. (Thanks as well to the Huntington Library, which also contributed a short-term fellowship in 2007–8.) I want to thank the entire staff of the Folger and do not wish to single any one individual out ... except that I must; Carol Brobeck's graciousness and wit have helped to make the Folger feel like a (better) home away from home, as have the friends and colleagues with whom I have had the great pleasure of sharing ideas and conversation there, among them especially Sean Keilen, Paula Blank, Palmeira Brumell, Kent Cartwright, and Sarah Werner. Many others have offered helpful advice, feedback, support, or encouragement at various stages, including Chris Ames, David Bevington, Stephen Booth, A.R. Braunmuller, Oscar Brockett, Susan Ceresano, Greg Chaplin, Alan Dessen, Carolyn Couson-Grigsby, Chris Holcomb, Arthur Kinney, Matt Kozusko, Brian Levack, Meg Powers Livingston, Stephen Longstaffe, Eric Mallin, Leah Marcus, Joe Navitsky, Helen Ostovich, Elizabeth Richmond-Garza, Andy Strycharski, Karen Sawyer-Marsalek, Virginia Mason Vaughan, Paul Whitfield White, Dolora Chappelle Wojciehowski, and Susan Zimmerman. Many of the arguments here were first aired and then refined in response to presentations of the arguments at the Sixteenth Century Studies Conference in 2002, the Second Blackfriars Conference in 2003, the National Conference of the Popular Culture Association in 2003, the Third Blackfriars Conference in 2005, and the Elective Affinities Conference at the University of Pennsylvania in 2005. Similarly, previous incarnations or portions of some of the chapters here have also appeared over the last few years in journals, and subsequent response here too has helped with dramatically reconceiving chapters and the conclusions of the project as a whole: Chapter 1 appeared in an earlier form as "The Folly of Racism: Enslaving Blackface and the 'Natural' Fool Tradition," *Medieval and Renaissance Drama in England* 20 (2007): 46–84; much of Chapter 2 appeared as "The Reasons of Misrule Revisited: Evangelical Appropriations of Carnival in Tudor Revels," *Early Theatre* 10.1 (summer 2007): 35–65; an early version of Chapter 3 had its first incarnation as "'Verie Devout Asses': The Stupid Puritan Clown," *Renaissance and Reformation/ Renaissance et Réforme* 28.3 (summer 2004): 95–132; and Chapter 4 appeared in its first form as "The Fool in Quarto and Folio *King Lear*," *English Literary Renaissance* 34.2 (autumn, 2004): 306–38. I am grateful to the many editors at these journals, not least for copyright permission to reproduce portions or revisions of the articles, as well as to anonymous readers. In addition to Caroline Palmer at Boydell & Brewer, one anonymous reader there merits special mention for offering some of the most helpful and insightful advice I have ever received; the feedback he/she provided allowed me to clarify and reshape my arguments in significant ways. Many played a role, then, in shaping and revising this project.

A special thank you is due to the Huntington Library, the British Library, the Folger Shakespeare Library, and the Bodleian Library for the permission to use the images reproduced here; the staff in each case were incredibly gracious, particularly Jean-Robert Durbin of the Huntington, who was extraordinarily helpful.

I am likewise thankful to many in the theatre who have furthered my work since I arrived at Oglethorpe University in 2000, thereby advancing my understanding of the comic in performance. Here, I refer to all those at Georgia Shakespeare, especially actors Chris Kayser, Carolyn Cook, and Chris Ensweiler, Artistic Director Richard Garner, and Education Director Allen O'Reilly; all those affiliated with the Blackfriars Theatre/American Shakespeare Center/the Mary Baldwin M.Litt program, especially Ralph Cohen, Paul Menzer, Sarah Enloe, and scholar-actors Rick Blunt, Patrick Bentley, Rob Smith, and James Mainard-O'Connell. I also need to thank Patrick Spottiswode of the Globe Theatre and the International Shakespeare Centre for his generous encouragement.

I am grateful to Oglethorpe University, which provided numerous faculty development and summer research grants that enabled research at the Folger, the British Library, and the Bibliothèque Nationale, Paris. The outstanding students at Oglethorpe University on whom I tried out ideas have also been very helpful in their feedback; among them are Laura Braddick, Kristy Clodfelter, Dan Cohl, Geoff Heatherington, Stephanie Laubscher, Amy Lester, Lollie Lott, Allison Martin, Kelly Poor, Chelcie Rowell, Jenna Sardella, Jack Storz, Megan Van Doren, Greg Wallace, and the entire class of the Oxford Shakespeare in Performance Class from the summer of 2008.

Finally, on a personal note, I want to express my deep gratitude to my family, especially my late father, my mother, my brothers Ted and Jim, and my uncle Jerry (better known as Bert). Above all, I need to thank my wife, friend, and colleague, Jeanne McCarthy, who has seen these ideas through from first to last. Without her intellect, insight, interest, patience, and encouragement I would never have finished this book. Of course, however, I alone am responsible for the flaws therein.

Introduction

UNEARTHING YORICKS: LITERARY ARCHEOLOGY AND THE IDEOLOGIES OF EARLY ENGLISH CLOWNING

A S THIS introduction's invocation of Hamlet's discovery of the jester Yorick's skull obliquely hints, this book attempts a kind of literary archeology. Unearthing major, however largely obscured, clown traditions of the late medieval period through the Renaissance, it aims to recover some understanding of their former import. Its focus is how theatrical clowns came to carry ideological significance and then, finally, to have it stripped from them, sometimes violently. By the close of the Renaissance, the famed "license" associated with fooling, whether in the context of the court fool or the clown in the drama, would no longer be countenanced, for reasons both political and aesthetic. This study, then, attempts to reclaim and thereby revalue an ideological dimension of late medieval, Tudor, and Stuart English comedy that has remained unacknowledged by either the critical tradition or recent scholarship. In particular, it aims to bring to light clowns' roles in a tradition of early religious and political theatrical satire. In so doing, the project not only aims to recover a sense of the power of theatrical satire in the early English theatrical tradition but also to suggest some of its long-term cultural impact. When we examine clowns in this light, a rich history of underlying traditions, tactics, and conventions emerges, as do the stakes involved in changing aesthetic tastes. This work, in short, offers a significant rethinking of early English clown traditions and their impact on their culture.

To be clear, the term "clown" here encompasses several meanings in both modern and Renaissance usage, all of which are relevant to this

1

re-examination. These include the general, still familiar sense expressed in *The Oxford English Dictionary* of "A fool or jester, as a stage character" (*OED* 3) and even, more commonly, in *Webster's Collegiate Dictionary* 3a of "a fool, jester, or comedian in an entertainment (as a play)." I employ as well the specialized, historical senses of the term outlined by David Wiles as referring to the "principal comedian" at a playhouse.[1] When the word appears in scripts it "is a technical playhouse term"; Shakespeare, for instance, was "second only to [Thomas] Heywood in the consistency with which he specifies 'the clown' in stage directions."[2] At the same time, to the audience, "the clown" is also "recognizable … as a special category of player." As a result, the word "*refers both to a particular type of part*," that of the clown or fool, and also to "*the particular actor whose job it was to take that part in the company's repertoire.*"[3] That is why Robert Armin, famous for playing Shakespearean "fool" parts, referred to himself as "Clonnico de Curtainio," the clown of the Curtain Theatre, and as "Clonnico del Mondo," the clown of the Globe. That is likewise the reason that, in "the stage directions of the First Folio, the term 'clown' is used throughout to denote Touchstone, Feste, and Lavatch."[4]

Further complicating our desire for rigid notions of terminology, the Shakespearean actor Will Kemp, known for his rustic clowns, refers to himself in his *Nine Daies Wonder* (1600) as a "fool" not a "clown," since the ancient, less specialized sense of the former was then dominant in everyday use.[5] We see the same conflation in Hamlet's censorious demands for players: "[L]et those that play your clowns speak no more than is set down for them. … That's villainous, and shows a most pitiful ambition in the fool that uses it" (3.2, 38–45). Thus, I do not restrict my use of the term clown to its perhaps most familiar sense in Renaissance studies, that of a "rustic," low-class, "boorish person," but consider so-called fools as well. Such broadened understandings inform excavations of the root traditions, contemporary conventions, and ideological

---

1   David Wiles, *Shakespeare's Clown: Actor and Text in the Elizabethan Playhouse* (Cambridge, 1987), 12.
2   Ibid., 64–5, 67.
3   Ibid., 65; emphasis added.
4   Ibid., 65, 66.
5   Ibid., 68, 69.

underpinnings governing clowns in Tudor morality plays and inter ludes, court and university entertainments, playhouse play-texts featuring rustic clowns and other fool types, as well as the repertoire of several principal comedians of the public stage.

Qualifications also attend my use of the term "literary archeology." I make no pretense to using scientific method (e.g., sampling or statistics) in what follows but rather simply to use archeology here as an analogy that captures what may distinguish my approach. While I do not employ scientific method, I do share with "historical archeologists" (as opposed to "prehistoric archeologists" who examine cultures with no form of writing) their willingness to analyze words and images, an interest in surveying previously unknown and little understood "sites" for explora-tion, discovery, recovery, typology, analysis, and interpretation, and a skepticism of received theories and narratives as weighed against uncov-ered evidence.

This venture into a literary archeology arises, above all, out of a deep and abiding sense that something has been lost, that "the comic" (i.e., in the sense of the comical, not just the professional comedian) has been grossly underestimated both by recent literary theory and in the critical tradition, that of the Renaissance more than most and of the era's clowns perhaps above all. Among other things, the work of unearthing "Yoricks" undertaken here reflects a broader effort to understand why English comedy as a genre, a subject typically overlooked in high-brow Renaissance studies, advanced so much more rapidly – and arguably further – than did tragedy, while also forming a more distinctively English contribution to literature. Whereas Cambridge University dons, for instance, included Roman comedy in the curriculum as early as 1510–11, when a Terentian play was performed in Latin, Roman tragedy (also produced in Latin) would have to wait until Westminster Grammar School's mid-1540s' production of Seneca's *Hippolytus* to enter the English curriculum.[6] At Cambridge, tragedy seems not to have appeared until the 1550s, when titles such as "Medea," "Oedipus," and "Hecuba" appear in the records[7] – likely Seneca's *Medea, Oedipus,* and

---

6   Bruce R. Smith, *Ancient Scripts and Modern Experience on the English Stage 1500–1700* (Princeton, NJ, 1988), 3.
7   Ibid., 205.

Trojan Women. Even so, Seneca never achieved quite the place in the grammar school and university curriculum that Terence and Plautus held. The notion of the tragic also held an ambiguous verbal status through much of the Tudor period; in terms of the English court, Greg Walker notes in his study of drama under Henry VIII, the word "tragedy" in the late medieval period denoted "any narrative charting a fall from prosperity and happiness," not a play proper.[8] By contrast, comedy appeared among Henry's circle at least as early as 1519 when an unnamed company performed "a goodly comedy of Plautus" and again in 1526–7, when Plautus's *Menaechmi*, still in Latin, appeared at Wolsey's York Place.[9] We do not yet fully understand why comedy in the vernacular likewise developed more rapidly than tragedy, why it long held so much more respect among academics and intellectuals, nor why, as M. C. Bradbrook noted half a century ago, "comedies outnumber tragedies on the Elizabethan stage by nearly *three to one*,"[10] so that comedy was *the* national genre.

Whereas moderns tend to hold the comic in low esteem, that attitude did not really become influential *on stage* until well into the Jacobean period. The comic – and the clown – in the Elizabethan theatre was something else entirely, less like neoclassical tragedy as "caviare to the general" (*Hamlet*, 2.2, 433) and more, to strain the gustatory metaphor, like oysters for everybody, an affordable delicacy widely coveted by high and low. As absurd as such a comparison might initially sound, like the once plentiful bi-valves consumed in the cellars of New York City during the nineteenth-century oyster boom, comedy was once avidly sought by rich and poor alike, in close proximity.[11] The contrasting alignment of a "purer" form of theatrical genre with an elite group distinguishing between high and low tastes, arguably the goal of the imported neoclassical revaluing of comedy, did not really find strong footing in the professional theatre until, not coincidentally, the

---

8 Greg Walker, *Plays of Persuasion: Drama and Politics at the Court of Henry VIII* (Cambridge, 1991), 21.
9 W. R. Streitberger, *Court Revels, 1485–1559* (Toronto, 1994), 122–3, 101, 124, 266.
10 M. C. Bradbrook, *The Growth and Structure of Elizabethan Comedy* (London, 1955), 3; emphasis mine.
11 Mark Kurlansky, *The Big Oyster: History on the Half Shell* (New York, 2006).

retirement not just of Shakespeare but of the clown Armin, *c.* 1613. Clowns like Tarlton, Kemp, and Armin had much to do with maintaining the previous status of comedy among intellectuals and elites. Tarlton would famously perform at Oxford; Kemp would appear as a fictional character in the third part of the Cambridge *Parnassus* trilogy (*c.* 1601–2); and as late as 1608, Armin could still dedicate a work to young intellectuals: "To the youthful and rightly compleat in all good gifts and graces, the generous Gentlemen of Oxenford, Cambridge, and the Inns of Court."[12] Benefiting from the Humanist embrace of folly, their appeal to intellectuals was also partly due to the fact that the stakes involved in clowning could once be extraordinarily high, incorporating heady moral, religious, political, philosophical, and educative concerns. Furthermore, clowns were not simply satiric but they also played a considerable role in articulating the ideologies of their age, encompassing, I will argue, the place of humor in the rise of racism, uses of the comic in both early Reformation and then later anti-puritan polemic, and the role of the clown in terms of aesthetic trends. Ultimately, one of the central arguments of this book will be that religious, political, and ideological elements were indeed often an, if not *the*, animating spark in the comic repertoire of much Renaissance clowning. The project of unearthing Yoricks is thus, in the end, a recovery of the extent to which the supposedly low or indecorous Renaissance English habit of mingling clowns and politics offered both satiric depth and thoughtfulness which the neoclassical decorum that came to dominate thereafter could neither sound nor ascend.

BEYOND NECROMANCY, BEAR-BAITING AND SUBVERSION

Given my stated goal of unearthing a number of buried Yoricks, perhaps I should hasten to add the following disclaimer: I do *not* mean to suggest that I too "begin with the desire to speak with the dead," as Stephen Greenblatt dramatically did, twenty years ago now, in the opening sentence of his *Shakespearean Negotiations,* a seminal work of the New

---

12 *A Nest of Ninnies and Other English Jestbooks of the Seventeenth Century,* ed. P. M. Zall (Lincoln, NE, 1970), 17.

Historicism. This project of literary archeology is far less romantic than any imagined conversation with the dead, although the results are, at least occasionally, nonetheless weightier. Though ideology and even politics (broadly defined) undoubtedly form an interest of the following study, as they did for the New Historicism, my goals, scope, approach, and methodology diverge fundamentally from previous practice in ways that I expect will become readily apparent, not just in terms of depth of focus or rigor but notably in my relative lack of interest in an elevated political mode that presumes hierarchical, top-down power structures. Nor would I embrace Greenblatt's provocative insistence that "what we call ideology ... Renaissance England called poetry";[14] I have no wish to impose a quest for ideology on all scholars and all subjects but have rather noted its presence in the Renaissance comic because the evidence has proven so insistent. Considering the comic in varied animating cultural contexts to recover its potential to be remarkably consequential is the only sort of unearthing that I have in mind, but I believe that the results of this rational digging should be enough to mitigate the need for either necromancy or the paranormal. I am, then, it must be said before proceeding, most definitely not hoping to disinter and revivify the moribund New Historicism or any brand of "New New Historicism."[15]

After all, such an approach to history was only slightly less damaging than neoclassicism to the comic through its reductive, sweepingly dismissive "subversion-containment" dynamic. This model allowed for too little interpretation as everything was made to fit into the same universalizing dynamic: the comic and the clown were always subversive and therefore low, and presumed subversion was always contained in the end, thereby bolstering the power of elites. In this sense, the New Historicists echoed the old-school forerunners they ostensibly rejected; Stephen Longstaffe has demonstrated, for instance, that New Historicism effectively reiterated the Tillyard–Campbell old historicists' assessment of an orthodox/conservative Shakespeare working to uphold

---

13 Stephen Greenblatt, *Shakespearean Negotiations* (Berkeley, CA, 1988), 1.
14 Stephen Greenblatt, *Hamlet in Purgatory* (Princeton, NJ, 2001), 46.
15 Patricia Fumerton, "Introduction: A New New Historicism," in *Renaissance Culture and the Everyday*, ed. Patricia Fumerton and Simon Hunt (Philadelphia, 1999), 1–17; esp. 3.

official ideology and power.   Along the way, less compliant milieus, indeed much history itself, too often consequently was deemed irrelevant in favor of anecdotal, mystifying, sensational, or exoticized invocations of racy, attention-getting moments like Simon Forman's wet-dream about the aged Queen Elizabeth, an imposter Martin Guerre's "return" to a wife, cross-dressing, spontaneous sex change, New World encounters, the disastrous Essex Rebellion, exorcism, or animal abuse.

The results of the resort to racy anecdotes were, again, really not very different than those produced by a facile brand of old historicism which, trotting out sweeping generalizations about what people laughed at "back then," rendered much early comedy alien, simply different, and irretrievably remote, typically via sensational generalizations about widespread cruelty reflected in the popular culture. For example, David Ellis remarks that it "has been customary to point out major differences between Shakespeare's time and our own" when responding "to the charge of cruelty" in Shakespearean comic moments (e.g., in cases such as those of Malvolio in *Twelfth Night* or Williams in *Henry V*).[17] And so one critic asserted that Malvolio's humiliating imprisonment at the hands of Sir Toby, Fabian, Maria, and Sir Andrew and particularly his inquisition conducted by the fool, Feste, quite simply "is a bear-baiting," arguing that such blood-sport "actually occurred within the same auditorium" and, further, that the connections between theatre and bear-baiting were thus so "well established" that "the awareness of [such] connections would have governed the audience's experience of Malvolio."[18] Evoking similar associations after having played Malvolio, the actor Donald Sinden commented that "The play was written when

---

16 Stephen Longstaffe, "What Is the English History Play and Why Are They Saying Such Terrible Things About It?," *Renaissance Forum: An Electronic Journal of Early-Modern Literary and Historical Studies* 2.2 (autumn 1997); available online at www.hull.ac.uk/renforum/v2no2/longstaf.htm. By contrast, Longstaffe illustrates ways in which Shakespearean and non-Shakespearean history plays are hardly conservative in their effects. Stephen Longstaffe, " 'A Short Report and Not Otherwise': Jack Cade in *2 Henry VI*," in *Shakespeare and Carnival: After Bakhtin*, ed. Ronald Knowles (London, 1998), 13–35.
17 David Ellis, *Shakespeare's Practical Jokes: An Introduction to the Comic in His Work* (Lewisburg, 2007), 149.
18 Ralph Berry, "*Twelfth Night*: The Experience of the Audience," in *Shakespeare Survey* 34, ed. Stanley Wells (Cambridge, 2002): 111–20; 118.

bull- and bearbaiting were common sports, the pillory entertained jeering crowds, idiots were part of 'the public stock of harmless pleasures' and the populace thronged to public executions."[19] However much references to such supposed analogues in the culture in and outside the auditorium may or may not illuminate former audience attitudes toward – or experience of – the gulled Malvolio (and I would suggest that they have the potential to do so only minimally), they still have little to tell us about the laughter, feelings, aesthetic responses, and thought provoked by the figure of Feste, a clown governed by a host of specific, complex audience expectations, cultural traditions, and theatrical conventions of the artificial fool type. As Ellis concludes, then, "As far as comedy is concerned, the traditional role of historical scholarship has been to remind us that the Elizabethans laughed at things we no longer find at all funny."[20] (The effect is rather like reading a bad translation of a joke.) But I hope to show that such need hardly be the inevitable outcome of historically informed scholarship if we move away from the equally reductive thumbnail sketch or estranging anecdotal historicism.

In anticipation of the inevitable knee-jerk objection to a serious attempt to analyze the comic – i.e., that explaining the joke necessarily kills it – I am tempted merely to cite the recent film, *The Aristocrats* (2005), a documentary examining a dirty joke beloved by a subculture of comedians; here, the more the joke is analyzed, prodded, questioned, and re-told, the funnier it becomes. Resisting an extended examination of such a convenient contemporary precedent, however, I will rather observe that one certainly cannot have murdered humor that has long been dead and buried and that few have actually been "getting." To those scholars and directors who seem to find many of the Renaissance clowns discussed here at once obvious and tedious (e.g., often subject to cuts in performance or absented from serious studies of the drama), I would suggest that understanding the logic of wit, recognizing allusions, and being aware of the contexts for satire are all key to appreciating – and performing – much Renaissance stage clowning, and worth the

19 Donald Sinden, "Malvolio in *Twelfth Night*," in *Players of Shakespeare: Essays in Shakespearean Performance*, ed. Philip Brockback (Cambridge, 1985), 41–66; 63.
20 Ellis, *Shakespeare's Practical Jokes*, 78.

effort. While "explaining a joke" is almost always *said* not to make it laugh-worthy for one to whom the joke is explained, not only is that *not* the experience of many of us who have worked with the comic in the drama, particularly with students and actors, but, more importantly, such explaining does make it possible to get or perform the kind of joke in question next time, and that is surely a worthy goal of teaching or writing about the comic.

But leaving the goal of immediate laughter aside, on another level, some further understanding is essential to appreciating the degree to which Renaissance stage clowning often allowed for, even *required*, layers and ranges of audience response, encompassing not just laughter but delight and something very different, responses more intellectually, aesthetically, and emotionally challenging than the "mere farce" or "comic relief" critics have too often assumed clowns performed. My work thus shares assumptions with recent studies of the comic in David Ellis's *Shakespeare's Practical Jokes: An Introduction to the Comic in His Work* and Jeremy Lopez's *Theatrical Convention and Audience Response in Early Modern Drama*. Lopez recognizes, for instance, that comedy of the Elizabethan and Jacobean period "is terrifically complicated" partly because "seriousness and ridicule, artifice and reality, fixed representations and irony exist in [such] vital tension" as authors and actors sought "to indulge and delight in complexity."[21] I likewise embrace Ellis's challenge to reductive critical orthodoxies to eschew oversimplifying the comic in order to recover that characteristic "current of thoughtfulness" running beneath the laughter, that "intriguing blend of seriousness and laughter" that so often characterizes the comic in the Renaissance.[22]

"MINGLING KINGS AND CLOWNS": BEYOND NEOCLASSICAL COMIC RELIEF

An in-depth re-examination of import and nuance in early clowning aiming at a revaluing of the comic could do worse than to begin by confronting the famous remarks on clowns in *Hamlet*; Hamlet's words

---

21 Jeremy Lopez, *Theatrical Convention and Audience Response in Early Modern Drama* (Cambridge, 2003), 170, 192, 37, respectively.
22 Ellis, *Shakespeare's Practical Jokes*, 156, 172.

about clowns, both his nostalgic praise of the late jester Yorick and his haughty contempt for the improvisatory antics of stage clowns, continue to haunt the study of Renaissance clown traditions no less than does Sidney's related, oft-quoted neoclassical critique in his *Apology for Poetry* (printed 1595) of that typically English Renaissance practice of "mingling kings and clowns." Interjecting relatively new-fangled, foreign notions of the comic in his assessment of the plays of his countrymen in the professional theatres, Sidney had famously objected that,

> all their plays be neither right tragedies, nor right comedies, mingling kings and clowns not because the matter so carrieth it, but thrust in clowns by head and shoulders, to play a part in majestical matters, with neither decency nor discretion, so as neither the admiration and commiseration, nor the right sportfulness, is by their mongrel tragi-comedy obtained.[23]

Holding forth in his eponymous tragedy, the similarly *avant-garde*, cosmopolitan intellectual Hamlet speaks censoriously of stage clowns and, in this theatrical context at least, laughter generally, indeed invoking a chain of neoclassical associations rejecting "groundlings, who for the most part are capable of nothing but inexplicable dumb-shows and noise" (3.2, 11–12),[24] the laughter of "barren spectators" (l. 41), and the purportedly "unskillful laugh" (l. 26), again, of the groundling.[25] In his related commentary on stage fooling, Hamlet explicitly proscribes the stage clown from speaking anything impromptu not because the matter of the play requires it but solely in order to raise a laugh, "though in the mean time some necessary question of the play be then to be consider'd" (ll. 42–3). If the advice that the actor playing the clown should not distract from necessary questions of the play now sounds not only apt enough but obviously valid, it is

---

23 Philip Sidney, *Apology for Poetry*, ed. H. A. Needham (London, 1931), 54–5.
24 Unless otherwise specified, quotations from Shakespeares plays refer to *The Riverside Shakespeare*, ed. G. Blakemore Evans (Boston, 1997).
25 For the reader's reference, here is the famous quote to which I refer in full: "[L]et those that play your clowns speak no more than is set down for them; for there be them that will themselves laugh, to set some quantity of barren spectators to laugh too, though in the mean time some necessary question of the play be then to be consider'd. That's villainous, and shows a most pitiful ambition in the fool that uses it." (3.2, 38–45)

nonetheless true that in an age in which melancholia was associated with wit and fancy, the playwright's would-be neoclassical melancholic also betrays an appreciation and aptitude for skillful clowning at other moments that is at odds with neoclassical ideals.

Hamlet himself is, in fact, anything but consistent in his attitudes toward clowning around; in contrast to his expressed disdain for the supposed inherent lowness of clowning and the low regard for laughter he had shown in his advice to the actors, in 5.1, the graveyard scene, Hamlet recognizes and appreciates the wit – the "infinite jest" (l. 184) and "excellent fancy" (l. 185), that is, the imagination and witty invention – behind the seeming mere pranks of a jester that the grave-digger mistakenly calls a "whoreson mad fellow" and a "mad rogue" (ll. 176, 179). Yorick was, by this description, what Renaissance audiences would have recognized as a witty "artificial" fool, one whose folly and mad-cap clowning came by art (an art, increasingly, inspired by Humanist-derived Socratic and Stoic philosophy), not by nature (i.e., some impairment of his reason, such as the actual madness the gravedigger seems to suggest).

The lines further reveal that there was a method in Yorick's "gibes," "gambols," and "flashes of merriment" (ll. 189–90), and it is arguably just such method that similarly informs Hamlet's own "antic disposition" (1.5, 72) – his own pointed, artful appropriation of fooling as a stalking-horse – from the first. Ironically, the neoclassically posing Hamlet, thrust into the presence of a royal ghost and a usurper-king, effectively becomes one of the great witty fools of the English Renaissance. He is, in fact, an extension of Shakespeare's earlier experimentations with figures of a hybrid clown-hero, "[m]ingling vulgar Vice and worthy history," in the titular figure of *Richard III* [1592–93] and the Bastard, Faulconbridge, in *King John* [1594–96], both of which plays feature protagonists who are descendants of the Vice.[26] After all, Hamlet is frequently shown prompting "spectators to laugh," through improvisatory, quick-wit repartee, "though in the mean time some necessary question of the play be then to be consider'd." Contrary to Hamlet's espoused anti-comic acting theories, his own jesting scarcely distracts from the "necessary question[s]" of the

---

[26] Robert Weimann and Douglas Bruster, *Shakespeare and the Power of Performance: Stage and Page in the Elizabethan Theatre* (Cambridge, 2008), 59.

play but rather it asks the audience to view those questions in rich ways, from different angles. Hamlet's example, more so than the theory he avows but habitually violates, may therefore be worth keeping in mind in the analyses of more recognizable stage Yoricks that follow.

Too often, however, it has been to Hamlet's apparent disdain for clowns that modern readers have given the most weight, as if the prince of Denmark voices the playwright Shakespeare's aesthetic ideals. But Hamlet himself – like the play that bears his name – violates all the neoclassical decorum that he claims to favor. For all the plot parallels between Hamlet's situation and *The Murder of Gonzago* or the unpopular tragedy involving Phyrrus and Hecuba that the prince admired but described as "caviare to the general" (2.2, 433), these dry neoclassical works do not actually resemble the extraordinary aesthetics of *Hamlet*, which fuses tragedy and its expected eloquent poetry with elements that would be an affront to the neoclassical assumptions of a Hamlet as audience member: the protagonist's antic disposition, the serio-foolish Polonius, the foppish Osric, the clueless but compromised oafs Rosencrantz and Guildenstern (out of their depth), a literal-minded clownish grave-digger, and, especially enigmatically, the haunting evocation of the wit and merriments of Yorick. That critics have managed to take Hamlet wholly at his word in speaking against clowns, to the point of reading Hamlet's advice to the players as an uncomplicated rebuke of Shakespeare's former stage clown Will Kemp,[27] despite all the contradictory evidence in the play itself, demonstrates the degree to which neoclassicism ultimately helped to kill off Renaissance Yoricks.

The sometimes antic fictional prince's assertions suggesting any groundling's inability to focus at length on serious drama probably helped to rationalize the reflex foisting of that neoclassically inspired critical chimera of "comic relief" upon the English Renaissance, where it is all the more an anachronistic, mythical beast. It is, after all, a concept

---

27 On the passage in question, James P. Bednarz remarks, "That Shakespeare recognized the clown's potentially disastrous effect on the comprehension of his own densely rhetorical art is apparent in *Hamlet*, where (shortly after Kemp left the Lord Chamberlain's Men) the hero advises the players (who come to Elsinore without a clown)" to avoid improvisation. "William Kemp," in *Fools and Jesters in Literature, Art, and History: A Bio-Bibliographical Sourcebook*, ed. Vicki K. Janik (Westport, CT, 1998), 273–80; 277.

12

whose origins are remarkably late; the *Oxford English Dictionary* finds the earliest known use of the term/concept to be in 1825 in E. Fitzball's *Dramatic Author's Life*: "And the moment the point necessary for the plot is attained, the audience are always impatient for comic relief." Hamlet's construction of a clown's interference with a "necessary question of the play" seems to lie behind a reductive and dismissive sense of the comic as extraneous distraction from a "point necessary for the plot" – a shallow paraphrase of Hamlet. It was evidently that notorious deplorer of Shakespeare, George Bernard Shaw, who famously claimed that "With the single exception of Homer, there is no eminent writer … whom I can despise so entirely as I despise Shakespeare," who first applied the term to the playwright, in 1921, when he referred dismissively to "The Shakespearian-Dickensian consolation of laughter at mischief, accurately called comic relief." On Christmas day 1910, an article in the *New York Times* remarked that "George Bernard Shaw, who has devoted a large part of his time to whacking his fellow-dramatist William Shakespeare, once remarked that the indiscriminate eulogies of that poet filled him with an insane desire to dig Shakespeare's bones up and throw stones at them"[28] – hardly the sort of unearthing I would hope. Given Shaw's avid antipathy toward Shakespeare, his definition of the role of the comic in Shakespeare's plays hardly seems deserving of so much faith; as Claudius puts it, "So much for him" (1.2, 25), and so much for "comic relief." Clearly, we need a different vocabulary – and less anachronistic conceptions – to account for the comic in Shakespeare and in the Renaissance more generally.

"TARLETONIZING," OR, "CHRONICLING THE TIME"

If, as Hamlet also claims, the players were indeed "the abstract and brief chronicles of the time" so that "after your death you were better have a bad epitaph than their ill report while you live" (2.2, 524–6), we must recognize in what follows that the satirical clown was, in Shakespeare's

---

[28] "George Bernard Shaw Puts Shakespeare into His Latest Play; But the 'Bard of Avon' Is Scarcely a Hero in 'The Dark Lady of the Sonnets'," *New York Times*, December 25, 1910, SM6.

day, not just the most playful of players but also the brief chronicler whose traditionally licensed ill report one most needed to avoid. Thus, any study of early English clownage aimed in part at unearthing the significance of clowns' unique ability to chronicle the time must address the notoriety of a remarkable personage; Yorick himself is often said to constitute Shakespeare's tribute to the first and most famous professional stage clown of the English Renaissance, Richard "Dick" Tarlton (Figure 1). If Yorick did indeed honor the memory of Tarlton, the critical tradition's devaluing of the politics underlying much clowning seems all the odder, for Tarlton became famous both in plays like *The Famous Victories of Henry V* and at Elizabeth's court especially for the "mingling" of monarch and clown denounced by his friend Sir Philip Sidney. Moreover, the fact that a supposedly disapproving Sidney was godfather to the clown's son Philip suggests that Tarlton's talents had, for a time, trumped Sidney's own neoclassical ideals.

In any case, there was obviously something satirically topical about Tarlton's own comic line. Not long after the first extant reference to him as a stage actor appeared in *The Letter-Book of Gabriel Harvey* (1579), where Harvey alluded to his "extemporall faculty," Tarlton authored a religiously focused work for the Queen's Men, *The Seven Deadly Sins* (1585), which was likely the lost work that the puritan (thus anti-episcopal) satirist Martin Marprelate recalled in 1588, just months after Tarlton's death, in citing the stage clown's own mockery of London bishop John Whitgift as a precedent for his own satire: "I thinke Simonie be the bishops lacky. Tarleton tooke him not long since in Don John of Londons cellor."[29] In offering up an evidently topical commentary on the bishop's supposed spiritual profiteering, Tarlton was certainly "chronicling" the time. His take on Whitgift was successful enough that Harvey remarks that Tarlton's play was "not Dunstically botched-vp, but right-formally conueied."[30] In *Pierce Peniless* (1592) Martin's opponent satirist Thomas Nashe recounts another episode

29 Martin Marprelate [pseud.], *Oh read ouer D. Iohn Bridges ["The Epistle"]* (1588), in *The Marprelate Tracts [1588–1589]* (Leeds, 1967), 19. All subsequent Marprelate citations refer to this facsimile edition.
30 Edwin Nungezer, *A Dictionary of Actors and of Other Persons Associated with the Public Representation of Plays in England before 1642* (1929; rpt New York, 1968), 350.

Figure 1. Elizabethan clown Richard Tarlton amalgamated rustic, vice, and Lord of Misrule. *John Scottowe's Alphabet* (Norwich, after 1588). Harley 3885, fol. 19. By permission of the British Library.

involving *The Seven Deadly Sins*. When it was being performed before the learned audience of Oxford, a fact telling on its own, Nashe himself supposedly demanded of Tarlton

which of the seauen, was his owne deadlie sinne, [which] he bluntly aunswered after this manner: By God, the sinne of other Gentlemen, Lechery. Oh but that, M. Tarleton, is not your part vpon the stage: you are to blame, that dissemble, an other for your owne. I am somewhat of Doctor Pernes religion, quoth he: and abruptlie tooke his leaue.[31]

[31] Ibid.

15

Tarlton's (or Nashe's) jest depends here on the fact that Andrew Perne was infamous as a dissembling hypocrite and an apostate, noted especially for "the ambidexterity with which he responded to the drastic religious changes and reversals of successive Tudor regimes and reformations."[32] Contemporaries like Nashe and Marprelate thus attribute to Tarlton an impressive knowledge of contemporary and controversial religious figures.

Once regarded by the evangelical Protestant Edwardian regime as "one of themselves" and having been "close to the famous Strasbourg reformer Martin Bucer," it was Perne who "would, posthumously, play Judas" under Mary during "the macabre proceedings in which, in order to lift an interdict from the university church, the bones of Bucer … were exhumed and burnt in Cambridge market, following an oration in which Perne [himself] had denounced the great reformer and his doctrine."[33] Later, however, during Elizabeth's celebrated visit to Cambridge in 1564, Perne was selected to preach before the queen in King's College Chapel, even though Grindal warned that Perne would not be well received, "his apostasy," it was said, "being so notorious." The sermon, on obedience, proved a success, but in a subsequent theological disputation about whether scripture or tradition carried more authority, Perne, arguing on the side of tradition, not only vigorously asserted the subordination of scripture to the Church but insisted that the Church of Rome was not a whore, as his zealous opponent alleged, but *apostolica et matrix ecclesia* ("an apostolic church and our mother"). No one in authority was well pleased; Perne was thus removed from the list of both court preachers and those thought fit for a bishopric.[34] Whether or not the gossipy Nashe's tale is entirely accurate, his satirical journalism certainly has a ring of truth about it since other contemporary accounts suggest Tarlton was known to be a bitter satirist in matters of religion.

The anti-papist John Harington's *New Discourse of a Stale Subject, Called the Metamorphosis of Ajax* (1596), for instance, similarly emphasizes the

---

32 Patrick Collinson, "Perne, Andrew (1519?–1589)," in *Oxford Dictionary of National Biography* (Oxford, 2004); available online at www.oxforddnb.com/view/article/21975. All subsequent information on Perne in the paragraph that follows is from this source.
33 Ibid.
34 Ibid.

religiously charged barbs in Tarlton's clowning when recalling a famous bit involving the language of circumcision:

> What should I speake of the great league betweene God and man, made in circumcision? impressing a panefull stigma or character in God's peculiar people, though nowe most happlily taken away in the holy sacrament of baptisme. What the worde signified I have known reverent and learned have bene ignorant, and we call it a very circumcision, and uncircumcision, though the Remists, of purpose belike to varie from Geneva, will needs bring in Prepuse, which worde was after admitted into the theater with great applause by the mouth of Mayster Tarleton, the excellent comedian, when many of the beholders, that were never circumcised, had as great cause as Tarleton to complaine of their Prepuse. Nungezer, *Dictionary of Actors*, 358.

The precise significance of the joke eludes us today (though part of the point was undoubtedly a rejoinder to that famous opponent of the theatre Stephen Gosson's complaint in *The Confutation of Plays* [1582] that players were "uncircumcised philistines"[35]). Exactly why Tarlton was jesting about his foreskin, and just what any of this had to do with Calvinist Geneva or "Ramism" (the rhetorical and logical training of the puritans' intellectual hero Peter Ramist, considered in chapter 3), I confess I do not know, but what is all too clear here is that the comedy dealt with some once-familiar religious controversy that remains to be unearthed.

Setting the pattern for subsequent clowning, Tarlton's clownage was evidently even more frequently topical and satirical – often politically and, hence, religiously so – than has been sufficiently recognized. Though Peter Thomson has rightly emphasized "the delight audiences took in [his] scurrilous satire" and his "dramatic exploitation of local scandals"[36] and has further aptly claimed elsewhere that his clown persona emerges as "an adversary of radical Protestantism, anti-Catholic too,"[37] Thomson's insight has had too little effect. Yet, it is

---

35 E. K. Chambers, *The Elizabethan Stage*, 4 vols (Oxford, 1923), 4: 214.
36 Peter Thomson, "Clowns, Fools and Knaves: Stages in the Evolution of Acting," in *The Cambridge History of British Theatre*: vol. 1, *Origins to 1660*, ed. Jane Milling and Peter Thomson (Cambridge, 2004), 407–23; 411.
37 Peter Thomson, "Tarlton, Richard (d. 1588)," in *Oxford Dictionary of National Biography* (2004); available online at www.oxforddnb.com/view/article/26971.

partly due to Tarlton's daring pursuit of an insistently topical and often weighty comic line that "No other Elizabethan actor," Nungezer reported in his *Dictionary of Actors*, "has been the object of so many notices in contemporary and later writing, or has been remembered with such various and practical tokens of esteem."[38] Little wonder that players like the Shakespearean actor Will Kemp and other clowns to come, as we will see, would follow Tarlton's lead not just in appropriating his rustic/mechanical persona but in exploiting contemporary issues and scandals – especially religious ones – for topical, satirical humor, for "The grave and wise, as well as rude, / At him did take delight."[39]

Many critics have recently attempted to recover the authority of performance, but few have done justice to the clown's authority. Robert Weimann and Douglas Bruster have ably discussed the special improvisatory power of the Vice and the descendant clown in performance.[40] Furthering such understanding, I would argue that religious ideology authorized the fool/clown's license on the stage – and continued to do so long after critics assume the Renaissance stage was wholly secular. After all, the natural fool was originally "licensed" because he was theologically held to be an "innocent," not culpable for unwittingly transgressive, sinful behavior; such license amounted to a sort of special dispensation to speak or act outrageously. On another level, the Vice in the plots and performances of medieval and early Renaissance drama, hardly innocent, was given authorization to break the rules for morally edifying purposes, one reason why "the principal means for free improvisation in the interlude lay on the hands of the Vice."[41] If the stage clown tradition evolved in part out of the Tudor Vice and if Tarlton is the innovator credited with fusing the Vice and clown traditions, the related claim that Tarlton had "completely

38 Nunzeger, *Dictionary of Actors*, 355.
39 James Orchard Halliwell-Phillips, *Tarlton's jests, and News out of purgatory: with notes, and some account of the life of Tarlton* (London, 1844), xliv; citing Harl. MS. 3885, f. 19.
40 Weimann and Bruster, *Shakespeare and the Power of Performance*.
41 David Mann, *The Elizabethan Player: Contemporary Stage Presentations* (London, 1991), 22.

secularized the vice" is certainly overstated, since Tarlton's clown was famous for religio-political satire in quips and in plays like *The Seven Deadly Sins*. When Tarlton died in 1588, as Margreta de Grazia notes, "more than the loss of a clown was lamented," for as a contemporary remarked, " 'Now Tarleton's dead, the Consort lackes a Vice,' "[43] an observation which suggests that the Vice's moral/religious function was not completely absent in Tarlton's clownage.

But we also need to recognize that the religious rationales and function underlying clownish incarnations did not suddenly disappear or die off post-Tarlton. In fact, de Grazia rightly emphasizes that Tarlton's "dual role as Clown and Vice survived him into Shakespeare's time through his successor, Will Kempe, known as 'Jest monger and vice-regent generall to the Ghost of Dick Tarlton.' "[44] Whereas the critical tradition has long clung to a notion that Renaissance drama flourished because it left behind a presumably confining religious mode of "medieval" drama, religion and attendant politics actually spurred and enriched the development of "Renaissance" drama – comedy and the clown in particular. Not coincidentally, by way of comparison, the earliest full-scale, five-act Terentian comedies written in English were the Edwardian plays *Gammer Gurton's Needle* (*c.* 1551–52) and *Ralph Roister Doister* (*c.* 1552), both authored, significantly, by evangelical scholars and churchmen (and with both plays including polemical elements of mock-papist ritual). According to Bruce Smith, one reason tragedy developed more slowly than comedy was that classical tragedies "make no claims for the justice of the universe," as opposed to traditional morality plays which had assumed "certain providence."[45] It is also true that the comic – and chiefly the clown – was most readily adaptable to various religious (and other political) agendas. And, it is high time that we attended to such.

Whatever the reason for the reluctance to see religion in approaching the comic, the critical tradition's frequent secular bias, as some scholars

---

42 Robert Weimann, *Shakespeare and the Popular Tradition in the Theater: Studies in the Social Dimension of Dramatic Form and Function* (Baltimore, MD, 1987), 187.
43 Margreta de Grazia, *Hamlet without Hamlet* (Cambridge, 2007), 180.
44 Ibid.
45 Smith, *Ancient Scripts*, 202.

have come to realize, has been grossly anachronistic in its failure to appreciate the deeply "religious culture" it considered. After all, as Debora Shuger has explained,

> Religion during this period supplies the primary language of analysis. It is the cultural matrix for explorations of virtually every topic: kingship, selfhood, rationality, language, marriage, ethics, and so forth. … That is what it means to say that the English Renaissance was a religious culture, not simply a culture whose members generally were religious.[46]

As we shall see, the figure of the clown definitely embodies Shuger's sense of religion as relevant to virtually all aspects of the culture.

NEW DIRECTIONS

Ensuing chapters draw upon religious and other political and theatre history, biography, aesthetics, close reading, semiology/iconographic scholarship, sociology, archival research, textual/editorial studies, and recent examinations of audience response, as the means for re-examining supposedly long familiar comic figures and attending to their particular allusiveness. Moreover, the chapters likewise incorporate a diverse range of literary and non-literary sources (mysteries, moralities, and interludes, other canonical and non-canonical plays, educational debates, religious polemic, propaganda, and iconography; psalter illuminations, woodcuts, Revels and Records of Early English Drama accounts, diaries, letters, both early and modern performance "reviews," etc.). Aiming thereby to illustrate just how such historical remnants reveal what animates the comic in the Renaissance as well as what informs its influence, I make no pretense to covering all of the clown traditions from the periods this book addresses. Instead, I will simply deal with the import of four particular major clown traditions (two supposedly familiar ones involving notable Shakespearean actors) that have either been overlooked or not fully appreciated and then offer

---

[46] Debora Shuger, *Habits of Thought in the English Renaissance: Religion, Politics and the Dominant Culture* (Berkeley, CA, 1990), 6.

an epilogue examining the struggle to sustain a characteristically Renaissance mode of clowning from the late Jacobean through the Interregnum periods.

Serving as an apt prologue to the power of fooling prior to the close of the Renaissance, the first chapter, "Folly as Proto-Racism: Blackface in the "Natural" Fool Tradition," analyzes the contexts and ideology of racism (or "proto-racism") in a previously unnoted early blackface comic tradition that appeared by the late Middle Ages. This discussion focuses on early representations of blackness as emblematic of the so-called "natural" fool type, whose transgressiveness was unwitting because he was permanently, inherently mentally deficient. Whereas a troubling legacy of folly promoting an association between blackness and irrationality has heretofore been overshadowed by arguments interpreting blackness largely as an emblem of evil, an investigation of blackfaced natural fools in medieval illuminations and Tudor interludes yields the discovery of an even more virulent source of racist ideology in this early comic and iconographic tradition. Specifically, the chapter offers an argument about the way dark skin color was, in the late Middle Ages and sixteenth century, insidiously linked through blackface comedy to irrationality, degradation, and folly in a way that sheds light on the foundation of slavery and racism as cultural institutions and ideologies. The discussion here thus challenges pervasive critical assumptions of utter novelty in later antebellum minstrelsy as it illuminates the (il)logical ideological underpinnings of racism and the construction and dissemination of racist stereotypes in an earlier period. Evidence of a heretofore overlooked blackface comic tradition – one that became an ideological Trojan Horse – requires substantial revision of the history of racial thought and slavery from the late Middle Ages through the Renaissance and beyond. The blackface comic tradition comes out of religious contexts – psalter illuminations, devils in the mystery plays, fools in moral interludes – and such auspices for the ideology underlying the comic would hardly cease in subsequent clowning.

Indeed, turning to polemical contexts and focused primarily on the late Henrician and Edwardian regimes, Chapter 2, " 'Sports and Follies Against the Pope': Tudor Evangelical Lords of Misrule," recovers an unexpected tradition of carnivalesque evangelical comedy. Revels Accounts, Reformation polemic, and reports of foreign ambassadors and English diarists alike reveal that late Henrician and Edwardian Protestants at Cambridge and at court patronized a clownishly irreverent, iconoclastic Lord of Misrule to a degree not seen before or since. Early evangelicals, far from always standing in opposition to the comic, as is often assumed, enthusiastically employed the carnivalesque misrule that subsequent puritan evangelicals would abhor. This discussion aims to make clear how politically potent satire employing misrule was performed in Henrician and Edwardian Cambridge entertainments. Consequently, this chapter requires a rethinking of how early Protestants advanced their revolutionary cause, and it looks ahead to how such tactics incited a backlash against radical Protestants who exploited a carnivalesque, clownish stereotype.

Chapter 3, " 'Verie Devout Asses': Ignorant Puritan Clowns," investigates the construction of puritans in theatrical satire as backwardly ignorant and anti-intellectual. The puritan emerges on the professional stage in the 1590s in the context of the Marprelate and Hacket controversies, anti-academic puritan polemic, parodies of godly education, heated educational debate about Ramism, and at least one colorful Cambridge University drama puritan persona as a caricature at once overly "enthusiastic," anti-rational, anti-educational, anti-literary, stupid, arrogant, and rustic/mechanical. I conclude that, as puritan claims to the superiority of divine inspiration to traditional intellectual inquiry pitted Counter-Renaissance religious enthusiasm against Humanist reason, representations of a stereotypically rustic, ignorant puritan clown type shored up ideological boundaries, buttressing established modes of ministry, classical education, rhetoric, and logic against zealous attacks. Yet, parts played by the clown Kemp, including those resulting from actor–author collaborations with Shakespeare, complicated audience reactions to the stage puritan – and likely to actual puritans in the audience.

Shifting to "the fool" per se, the fourth chapter, "The Fool 'by Art': The All-Licensed 'Artificial' Fool in the *King Lear* Quarto," focuses on the most famous mingling of clown and king in the drama of the period, *King Lear*, Shakespeare's boldest response to "Sidneian" neoclassicism – in the Quarto, that is, where a witty, bitter Fool is shown mingling with an absolutist monarch, all of which some suspect prompted censorship of the character perhaps extant in revisions in the Folio. If the Fool was initially the most obvious example of the "all-licensed fool" in Shakespeare's drama, an examination of the two texts of *King Lear* (the 1608 Quarto and the Folio) may reveal the impact of politics on the aesthetics of the drama, and vice versa. Here the unearthed contexts for examining textual variants are criteria for making the historical distinction between natural and artificial fools, the influence of particular actors on the repertoire, and, in the Folio, aesthetic trends in the theatre reflecting the neoclassical influence of the playwright John Fletcher on the King's Men. The two texts thus reveal two very different fool types, changing aesthetics, and neoclassical attitudes toward the comic that would gain influence over the remainder of the Renaissance, and, in the later text, a commensurate retreat from the satirical mode that had characterized much Renaissance clowning. The Q-Fool reflects a satirical type quite different from that discerned in the more pathos-inflected neoclassical F text, where pointed satire is almost entirely removed.

The epilogue, "License Revoked: Ending an Era," serves as a prolegomenon for further research as it reintroduces a number of comic actors from the late Jacobean period through audacious, outlawed performances during the Commonwealth. This examination thus looks ahead to what happened next in the story of Renaissance clowning by offering a brief overview of the careers of now lesser-known clowns in the late Jacobean, Caroline, and Interregnum periods. Even with the ascendency of neoclassicism over the Stuart drama, and subsequently puritan antipathy to theatre and laughter, the satiric clown was to prove stubbornly resilient; the stage clown, particularly at the Red Bull Theatre, often remained satirically, frequently politically, engaged through the end of the Renaissance. At the Red Bull, in fact, this characteristically "Renaissance" mode of clowning was so vital and resilient that it finally took not just censorship but actual violent opposition – even assassination – to stamp it out.

Chapter 1

FOLLY AS PROTO-RACISM: BLACKFACE IN THE "NATURAL" FOOL TRADITION

O NE OF the more obscure(d) early clown traditions emerges, to begin with one extraordinary instance, in an account from the court of Elizabeth I. It can be dated to April of 1566, when signs of strain appeared in the relationship between Elizabeth I and her longtime visitor, Princess Cecilia of Sweden. Once a favorite at the English court, Cecilia had overstayed her welcome during an extended visit (through her extravagant free-loading), and had abruptly left the country to rejoin her husband. She was unwilling to accept any blame for the rift, however, and presented a retaliatory list of complaints to her brother John, newly become Swedish king, who then forwarded it to Queen Elizabeth's secretary Cecil. More than its revelation of fractured diplomatic relations, and especially since political power is not really my interest in this study, by far the most striking grievance here is Cecilia's statement that, "beinge bydden to see a comedye played, there was a blackeman brought in, ... full of leawde, spitfull, and skornfull words which she said did represent ... her husband."[1] Certainly, this reference to a comic depiction of a "blackeman," apparently "represent[ed]" by an actor in blackface, raises a number of questions, e.g., Why should Cecilia's husband have been represented as black at all? Or, at least, why would she *think* that he had been? Was blackface a mechanism for ridicule? If so, why? What would such blackness have symbolized in a

---

[1] *State Papers, Foreign, 1569–71*, No. 2149. Quoted in Ethel Seaton, *Queen Elizabeth and the Swedish Princess: Being an Account of the Visit of Princess Cecilia of Sweden to England in 1565 [1566]* (London, 1926), 21.

24

"comedye"? And, how many black people were living in England at the time? How might this knowledge shape our understanding of such comedy?) The scant critical tradition addressing the episode has focused on just one question, determining the particular work to which Cecilia referred.[2] Ironically, such a narrow scope has contributed to a continued ignoring of a much more far-reaching revelation; whatever play the insulted princess described, it was hardly the period's lone instance of blackness being associated with a comic figure.

Given that many scholars are currently re-examining the origins of racism and slavery in Western tradition,[3] the emergence of early evidence of a comic association with blackness would seem to be worth exploring. Drawing on existing work to explain the subject is hardly easy, however, given that evil, not folly, is virtually the only symbolic aspect of blackness to which medieval and Renaissance scholars have attended. Recent research has focused on Judaism, Christianity, and Islam to seek, and find, origins of racism solely in theological associations of the color black and evil,[4] overlooking other religiously inspired connections that are also available and which would become at least as significant in defining Western attitudes toward blackness. Dympna Callaghan sums up current scholarly consensus when she observes that slavery "had comparatively weak ideological foundations, relying on fairly inchoate connections between black skin and the Prince of Darkness."[5] Even though such origins are notably ambiguous since there is

---

2   In *Queen Elizabeth and the Swedish Princess*, Seaton attempted to answer this question and suggested that the play may well have been the Boys of Westminster School's Latin play, *Sapientia Solomonis*, or *The Wisdom of Solomon* (January, 1566). For an opposing argument, see Elizabeth Rogers Payne, Sapientia Solomonis: *Acted Before the Queen by the Boys of Westminster School January 17, 1565/6* (New Haven, CT, 1938), 148 n.30.

3   See particularly David Brion Davis, *Inhuman Bondage: The Rise and Fall of Slavery in the New World* (Oxford, 2006) and George M. Frederickson, *Racism: A Short History* (Princeton, NJ, 2002), especially 15–48.

4   See, for instance, David M. Goldenberg, *The Curse of Ham: Race and Slavery in Early Judaism, Christianity and Islam* (Princeton, NJ, 2003) and Stephen R. Haynes, *Noah's Curse: The Biblical Justification of American Slavery* (Oxford, 2002); see also Frederickson's chapter on "Religion and the Invention of Racism" in his *Racism: A Short History*, 15–48.

5   Dympna Callaghan, *Shakespeare Without Women: Representing Gender and Race on the Renaissance Stage* (London and New York, 2000), 93.

no biblical source, "the association of blackness with evil," Anthony Gerard Barthelemy and others have noted, "has a long history on the English stage" as "the tradition goes back at least to early medieval drama" where Lucifer and other devils "were represented by actors painted black."[7] Likewise, as Virginia Mason Vaughan has recently demonstrated in her study *Performing Blackness on English Stages, 1500–1800*, "the association between black skin and damnation [also] permeated early modern English culture."[8] Scholars have so locked on to the color symbolism of evil that they have yet to attend to an equally demeaning, buried, moralizing tradition of early blackface comedy, one that associated blackness with degradation, irrationality, prideful lack of self-knowledge, transgression, and, related to all of these, folly. With disturbing frequency, blackface served as one commonplace mark of foolishness in the religiously inspired iconography of the so-called "natural" fool – in medieval and Renaissance English parlance, a butt, laughed at because he was mentally deficient (whether ignorant, dull-witted, or mad) and often physically different as well (e.g., hunch-backed, dwarfish, lame, ugly, blackfaced).[9] To be clear, I do not mean to

---

6   According to noted historian of the Devil, Jeffrey Burton Russell, "The color black (as opposed to absence of light) is not a symbol of evil in the Old Testament or in the Apocalyptic period. ... Even where color symbolism is striking ... neither red nor black becomes symbolically fixed as evil as both would do in Christian iconography." Likewise, "nowhere does [the New Testament] describe Satan as actually black," and "Only in the later Apocryphal literature is blackness specifically assigned to the Devil." *The Devil: Perceptions of Evil from Antiquity to Primitive Christianity* (Ithaca and London, 1987), 217 n. 95, 247.

7   Anthony Barthelemy, *Black Face, Maligned Race: The Representation of Blacks in English Drama from Shakespeare to Southerne* (Baton Rouge, LA, 1987); here quoting 3–4; see also Eliot Tokson, *The Popular Image of the Black Man in English Drama, 1550–1688* (Boston, 1982); Jack D'Amico, *The Moor in the English Renaissance Drama* (Tampa, FL, 1991).

8   Virginia Mason Vaughan, *Performing Blackness on English Stages, 1500–1800* (Cambridge, 2005), 24. On the blackness of the Devil, damned souls in the medieval cycle plays, and drama inspired by such, see 19–25, 34, 39, 62, 75, 81, 82, 87, 89, 91, 120.

9   The *Oxford English Dictionary* defines the noun "natural" as "one naturally deficient in intellect; a half-witted person" (*OED* 2). Likewise, the *OED* defines the adjective "natural," when used in "natural fool," as "one who is by nature deficient in intelligence; a fool or simpleton by birth." Natural folly included connotations of two *OED* definitions of "folly" itself: "the quality or state of being

imply that *every* natural fool appeared in blackface; I simply invite focus on a surprising number that *did*.

In what follows, I want to interrogate this long-overlooked tradition, to examine some of its roots and its bitter fruit alike, and to suggest its importance not only in understanding medieval and Renaissance drama but in dismantling subsequent constructions of baffling racist stereotypes. Ultimately, I will argue here, previously ignored fool iconography forged early links in the enslaving fiction of the "Great Chain of Being," at least adumbrating, if not originating, later racist notions, since it was in part the blackface tradition which lay behind early slavers' inexplicable assumption that Africans were utterly irrational and, hence, could be treated as beastlike. Such findings also complement those of Benjamin Isaac in his magisterial study *The Invention of Racism in Classical Antiquity* (2004). Though he addresses an earlier period, Isaac similarly finds that, rather than having origins solely in nineteenth-century evolutionary scientific thought, prototypes of racism, forms of "proto-racism," were in fact already extant throughout the Greco-Roman world in racial prejudice, discrimination, stereotyping, and hatred aimed at foreign peoples, including Jews. Such proto-racism actually served as the antecedent – laying the intellectual origins leading – to modern, so-called "scientific" racism. Since Isaac unfortunately omits Africans from his study, this chapter explores often ignored connections between Africa and Britain as it considers the ways in which the religious and intellectual thought underlying the comic in early blackface traditions similarly constituted a variety of proto-racism underlying subsequent pseudo-scientific racist ideology.

That there was a moralizing, religiously inflected blackface fool tradition in sixteenth-century drama – and later – challenges the dominant critical narrative about race and race-inflected performance particularly, and most relevantly the contention of scholars of minstrelsy who

foolish or deficient in understanding; want of good sense, weakness or derangement of mind; also unwise conduct" (*OED* 1) and "madness, insanity, mania" (*OED* 4). For criticism on natural fools, see Enid Welsford, *The Fool: His Social and Literary History* (1935; rpt Gloucester, MA, 1966); Leslie Hotson, *Shakespeare's Motley* (New York, 1952); Walter Kaiser, *Praisers of Folly: Erasmus, Rabelais, Shakespeare* (Cambridge, 1963); and John Southworth, *Fools and Jesters at the English Court* (Stroud, 1998), 48–60.

maintain the utter novelty and *native* character of clown types in the American minstrel tradition.[10] This body of scholarship has encouraged the belief that any prior, pre-American comic use of blackface or black masking only accidentally resembles an antebellum tradition characterized as an "emergent social semantic" that formed what was, quite simply, an "historically new articulation of racial difference."[11] This essentially "nativist" line of criticism has thus deemed the possibility of *any* influence by previous, foreign or trans-Atlantic blackface comic traditions on the latter one as implausible. And yet, the disturbing implications that necessarily follow from such arguments are surely far more unlikely; that is, in order to assume absolute novelty in minstrelsy, the nativist argument requires that we, upon finding evidence of an early blackface fool tradition, accept the untenable conclusion that blackness would, independently and inevitably, come to be associated with laughable folly, irrationality, degradation, and ignorance in cultures separated by oceans and centuries. Yet it is far more likely that such repetitions of demeaning associations with blackness are the result of a stubborn cultural retentiveness than coincidence.

THE DESCENT INTO RACISM: THE DEVIL AS FOOL

As an illustration of the prevalent and longstanding inattention to a range of buried symbolic religious associations with blackness, consider the mystery plays, the most frequently cited instances of blackness being identified with evil in the English theatre tradition. The Towneley/ Wakefield mystery cycle's *The Creation [and the Fall of Lucifer]* (c. 1460), for example, depicts its fallen angels lamenting:

---

10 For examples, see Brander Matthews, "The Rise and Fall of Negro-Minstrelsy," *Scribner's* LVIII (1915): 754–9; 754; Russell Nye, *The Unembarrassed Muse: The Popular Arts in America* (New York, 1970), 162; James H. Dormon, "The Strange Career of Jim Crow Rice (with apologies to Professor Woodward)," *Journal of Social History* 3.2 (winter 1969–70): 109–22; 118; George F. Rehin, "Harlequin Jim Crow: Continuity and Convergence in Blackface Clowning," *Journal of Popular Culture* 9.3 (winter 1975): 682–701; 687, 696; W. T. Lhamon Jr., *Jump Jim Crow: Lost Plays, Lyrics, and Street Prose of the First Atlantic Popular Culture* (Cambridge, 2003), 3, 7, 25.
11 Eric Lott, *Love and Theft: Blackface Minstrelsy and the American Working Class* (New York, 1993), 5, 6.

Alas, alas and welewo! …
We, that were angels so fare,
and sat so hie aboue the ayere,
Now ar we waxen blak as any coyll [*coal*].[12]

While these lines seem merely to suggest, as most critics have observed, that the fallen angels are now black, the quote actually continues: "Now ar we waxen blak as any coyll / *and vgly, tatyrd as a foyll* [*fool*]" (ll. 136–7; emphasis added).[13] These fallen angels are not just black devils, then, but black *fools*, suffering degradation in part as a consequence of their folly. While steering clear of a discussion of blackness in their study of the medieval fool, Martin Stevens and James Paxson have demonstrated that, here and elsewhere, "Evil in the Wakefield plays … depends … on the demon/fool, whose conversion from the angelic … develops into a range of personifications of folly."[14] But even Paxson and Stevens seem finally to resist the implications of their own findings, insisting instead on novelty and claiming that "the Wakefield playwright … created a devil who is quite different from his counterparts in the other extant cycles," one "[u]nlike any other cycle."[15]

And yet, contrary to such notions of exceptionality, the Chester *Fall of Lucifer* features a similar focus on folly. In the Chester play,[16] Deus warns Lucifer of the requirement that he remain wise with "Loke that you tende righte wisely" (l. 71). Of course, Lucifer soon ignores the warning, foolishly speculating that if he were in the throne "the[n] shoulde I be as wise as hee" (l. 131). As he begins to plot usurping the throne, he is again warned, this time by another angel: "My counsell is that you be wise" (l. 148). But his companion Lighteborne urges him on,

---

12 *The Creation*, in *The Towneley Plays*, ed. Martin Stevens and A. C. Cawley (Oxford and New York, 1994), vol. 1, ll. 132–6, 37; emphasis added. All subsequent references will be cited parenthetically.

13 As Martin Stevens and James Paxson have shown, the word "foyll" certainly means "fool" as elsewhere in the Towneley cycle Jesus's enemies taunt him calling him "a flateryng foyll" and "fond foyll." "The Fool in the Wakefield Plays," *Studies in Iconography* 13 (1989–90): 48–79; here quoting 48.

14 Ibid., 76.

15 Ibid., 49, 76.

16 *The Chester Mystery Cycle*, ed. R. M. Lumiansky and David Mills, Early English Text Society, Supplementary Series 3 (London, 1974). Cited hereafter parenthetically.

saying, "yee may be as wise withall / as God himselfe" (ll. 160–1). After the fall, when Lightborne rebukes him, the blackened Lucifer defensively insists on their shared responsibility for their fall when he responds: "Thy witt yt was as well as myne" (l. 246). Clearly, a lack of wit and wisdom is meant to be one primary characteristic of the Chester Devil as well.

Consistent with the Wakefield and Chester plays, the York pageant of *The Fall of the Angels* (*c.* 1460s) features black devils, but ones that have even more clearly fallen into folly. Here, where the devils ultimately find themselves made "blackest," it is again God who charges them with folly as he warns the newly created angels that they shall enjoy favor only "To-whiles [they] are stable in thought,"[17] that is, so long as they remain rational and wise. As the Cherubim prudently recall God's warning that they shall have "All bliss … To-whiles we are stable in thought" (ll. 61–2) and the Seraphim devoutly proclaim "With all the wit we wield we worship thy will" (l. 73), Lucifer not only vainly preens and remarks that he is "fairer by far than my feres [companions]" (l. 53), but he also foolishly boasts that he is superior by virtue of "my wit" (l. 67) and gloats about being "deft" (l. 92) or clever – immediately before his fall and his crying out "Oh, deuce! all goes down" (l. 93). Then, having discovered his sudden blackness ("My brightness is blackest … now" [l. 101]), the prideful Lucifer, somewhat humorously, accuses Second Devil of having "smore me in smoke" (l. 117). Traditionally, the word "smore" has been glossed nonsensically as "smother,"[18] but it appears perhaps more likely that the line could read as "you *smeared* me with smoke" or soot, consistent with *The Oxford English Dictionary*'s "To smear, bedaub" (*OED* 3 as in "1530 Pals[grave] … 'where have you ben, you have all to smored your face'"), precisely because it is the devils' blackness that is at issue. More importantly, finding himself "brent" or burnt (l. 107) and "lorn" of "light" (l. 108), and being no longer stable in thought, Second Devil laments, "Out, out! I go wood [i.e., mad] for woe, my wit is all went now" (l. 105), with both madness and lost wits – and, apparently,

17 *The Creation, and the Fall of Lucifer*, in *Everyman and the Medieval Miracle Plays*, ed. A. C. Cawley (1956; rpt London, 1999), l. 101, 6 and l. 30, 4. Hereafter cited parenthetically by line numbers.
18 Ibid., 7.

blackness – being conventional attributes of "natural" folly. Finally, the devils' comically childish bickering over the cause of their new state prompts God to call these mad, black devils "[t]hose fools" (l. 129). Therefore, while it is partly true, as Vaughan believes, that "the visual code of the cycle plays was a simple binary: salvation versus damnation,"[19] that binary was far more subtle than simply good versus evil. Blackness in these mystery plays was instead associated less with evil (at least as we know it) than with folly, madness, and an absence of that divine gift, the "light" of reason. The overtly foolish Devil of the mystery play tradition contained, then, what was surely a significant development in the history of racism; here was not simply a black Devil's fall into the depths of hell but, more importantly, a depiction of his descent into the degradations of folly via blackness.

It would later be a stereotype of irrationality that was, ironically, most damning, lingering on inexplicably well after African American "Negro spirituals," churches, and temperance societies had long since belied an evil stereotype. Although the blackness of early devils was perhaps, typically, not *expressly* linked to race – even though devils *were* "often compared to Ethiopians"[20] – the irrationality associated with blackfaced devils was nonetheless to have an enduring influence on notions of blackface, and thus blackness. In particular, the specter of madness already observable especially in the York pageant haunted the blackface tradition from early to late, something evident in illustrations of the rolling-eyed, deranged-looking "Jim Crow" in the 1830s, in Crow originator T. D. Rice's farce *Bone Squash Diavolo* in which a stage direction reads "*Enter* Bone Squash, *crazy*,"[21] or in a newspaper's charges that blackface entertainer George Washington Dixon, famed for singing "Zip Coon," was "wanting in his upper story," via what Dale Cockrell has described as implications that he was "crazy and degenerate enough that he might really *be* black."[22] In one way or another, antebellum

19 Vaughan, *Performing Blackness on English Stages*, 15.
20 Meg Twycross and Sarah Carpenter, *Masks and Masking in Medieval and Early Tudor England* (Burlington, VT, 2002), 202.
21 Lhamon, *Jump Jim Crow*, 204.
22 Dale Cockrell, *Demons of Disorder: Early Blackface Minstrels and Their World* (Cambridge, 1997), 106; emphasis mine. Surprisingly, Cockrell does not develop the connection.

whites were determined to "prove" a connection between blackness and irrationality, especially when "the Negro" was left to his own devices. So it was that dubious methods and pro-slavery zeal led to an 1840 census purporting to have found a rate of insanity and idiocy eleven times greater among freed blacks than among slaves.[23]

Even long after emancipation, the longstanding symbolic association between blackface and madness or irrationality more generally was used to explain why not all of the black actors blacked up in the minstrel movie *Pitch a Boogie Woogie* (1928): "We put on blackface when we had something *crazy* to say."[24] One critic has recently celebrated such blacking up in minstrelsy, proclaiming, "I want to figure out a history of blackface that can account for that eager spirit of licensed madness" within it,[25] but this particular association of blackness with irresponsible and degenerate irrationality was anything but liberating for peoples of African descent not only because "the 'Jim Crow' that meant white male liberation on the minstrel stage later designated the 'Jim Crow' discrimination laws that successfully kept blacks in a state of de facto slavery"[26] but because it assumed mental debility. After all, as Enid Welsford put it, the natural fool's "mental deficiencies" often "deprived him both of rights and responsibilities."[27] Thus, the short-term license established through blacking up in comic, irrational contexts was, paradoxically, actually limiting over the long haul, perpetuating a stereotype of irresponsibility and irrationality that endorsed systematic slavery and the stubborn denial of meaningful freedom for African Americans until the Civil Rights Act of 1964 and the Voting Rights Act of 1965. Notably, the New York State Constitutional Convention of 1821, which denied the franchise to black New Yorkers through prohibitive property requirements, did so on the grounds that, as one convention member maintained, "The minds of

---

23 Edward Pessen, *Jacksonian America: Society, Personality, and Politics* (1969; rev. edn: Urbana and Chicago, 1985), 42.
24 W. T. Lhamon Jr., *Raising Cain: Blackface Performance from Jim Crow to Hip Hop* (Cambridge, 1998), 188. Lhamon does not address madness.
25 Ibid.
26 Brenda Dixon Gottschild, *Digging the Africanist Presence in American Performance: Dance and Other Contexts* (Westport, CT, 1996), 98.
27 Welsford, *The Fool*, 55.

32

blacks are not competent to vote." Significantly, then, it was a ratio
nally impaired, blackened Devil that first embodied the association
between blackness and mental incompetence.

To really begin to appreciate the enormous influence of the Devil's
folly on constructions of blackness we must come to recognize that the
foolish black devils of the mystery cycles are anything but anomalous, in
spite of John D. Cox's recent, provocative claim that the Devil in English
drama was noted above all for his "seriousness."[29] Peter Happé has
demonstrated, by contrast, that in Tudor moral interludes the Devil "is
essentially a comic figure"[30] whose appearance is ridiculously ugly.
Notably, he is so "evill favoured" in *All for Money* (c. 1577) that Ill Report
comments, "You neuer saw such a one behynde / As my Dad is before."[31]
Happé concludes that the range of visual characteristics of the Devil
usually "appears to have been reduced in the interludes to the large,
black-masked head."[32] In any case, while finding that the black-masked
Devil is "irredeemably foolish" and "most frequently seen as a butt …
inviting ridicule,"[33] Happé seems puzzled by his discovery. "Perhaps out
of fear," he muses, "the Devil is usually made ridiculous," for he is noted
for "simplicity."[34]

Evidently, I would argue, the cycles' and interludes' masked Devil was

28 Patrick Rael, "The Long Death of Slavery," Chapter 4 in *Slavery in New York*, ed.
    Ira Berlin and Leslie M. Harris (New York, 2005), 111–46; 140.
29 John D. Cox, *The Devil and the Sacred in English Drama, 1350–1642* (Cambridge,
    2000), throughout, but especially on 23, where Cox employs a curiously selective
    criterion for establishing the "seriousness" of theatrical devils, so that he offers as
    the one supposed exception proving his rule, the following: "Only N-Town
    includes the merest suggestion of scatological humor in the first play: when
    Lucifer encounters hell, he exclaims, 'For fere of Fyre a fart I cracke!' (*N-Town
    Play*, 24/8r)."
30 Peter Happé, "The Devil in the Interludes, 1550–1577," *Medieval English Theatre*
    11.1–2 (1989): 42–55; here quoting 43.
31 Ibid., 48–9.
32 Ibid., 51. Devils could appear either in black masks/heads or in painted black-
    face, as in the records of Coventry, where one finds numerous payments "for
    blakyng the Sollys fassys." See R. W. Ingram (ed.), *Coventry*, Records of Early
    English Drama (Toronto, 1981), 224, 230, 237, 464, 474–5; for "peynttyng of the
    demones hede," see 93; for "the devyls hede," see 59, 74, 84, 93, 111, 177 (dating
    from 1477–1554); and for "the devells facys," see 220, 278, 464, 468, 474.
33 Happé, "The Devil in the Interludes," 47, 43.
34 Ibid., 45, 47.

33

a type of natural fool whose blackness connoted not simply (or even primarily) evil, as critics assume, but folly. Such a conclusion is supported by historian of theology Jeffrey Burton Russell who notes that the medieval Devil, though sometimes clever, was also "a total fool," "the personification of … our own foolishness," "at bottom a fool who understands nothing."[35] In antiquity, theologians explained that the Devil's rational powers and intellect were impaired – "darkened by folly," as Augustine would have it – after the fall.[36] The Devil was mad as a result, a belief that informs widespread medieval and Renaissance assumptions that madness itself was due to demonic possession or punishment for sin. Witness the ironic mockery of that censorious "kind of puritan" (2.3, 140) gull Malvolio in *Twelfth Night,* as if he were mad, in terms of demonic possession: "What, man, defy the devil! Consider, he's an enemy to mankind" (3.4, 97–8); "and you speak ill of the devil, how he takes it to heart!" (ll. 100–1); "What, man, 'tis not for gravity to play at cherry-pit with Satan. Hang, him foul collier!" (ll. 115–17); "Out, hyperbolical fiend! How vexest thou this man!" (4.2, 25–6); "Fie. Thou dishonest Sathan!" (l. 31). The prevalence of the Devil's own assumed mental impairment is further reflected in Stith Thompson's inclusion of a devil in connection with the category "Absurd Ignorance" in the *Motif-Index of Folk-Literature.*[37] Moreover, the Devil, being foolish, "could be overcome by man's … laughter,"[38] and the devil-fool figure was a popular icon that carried over into Elizabethan and Jacobean devil plays, such as Greene's *Friar Bacon and Friar Bungay* (c. 1589), Haughton's *Grim the Collier of Croydon* (1600), Dekker's *The Merry Devil of Edmonton* (1602) and *If This Be Not A Good Play The Devil Is In It* (1611), and Jonson's *The Devil is an Ass* (1616), the latter title being proverbial.[39]

35 Jeffrey Burton Russell, *Lucifer, The Devil in the Middle Ages* (Ithaca, NY, and London, 1984), 60, 76.
36 Jeffrey Burton Russell, *Satan, The Early Christian* Tradition (Ithaca, NY, and London, 1981), 213.
37 See "J7730 Absurd Ignorance": "D834…. Man gets shelter in storm; devil gets wet. Devil gives man magic objects in return for information as to how he kept dry." Stith Thompson, *Motif-Index of Folk-Literature,* vol. 4: J-K, Indiana University Studies 22 (Bloomington, IN, Sept., Dec., 1934), studies nos. 105, 106, 151–2.
38 Happé, "The Devil in the Interludes," 95.
39 The stubbornness of comic associations with the Devil – and blackness – is

Just as the Devil was so often foolish, foolishness in turn could be seen as diabolical and sinful. In the morality plays, sin itself is repeatedly associated with transgressive folly. Thus, in *The Castle of Perseverance* (*c.* 1425), featuring the Devil in the guise of "Belyal the blake,"[40] Avaricia insists that the other vices/sins

> … must, what-so befall,
> Feffyn hym [Mankynd] wyth youre foly …
> For whanne Mankynd is kendly koveytous
> He is proud, wrathful, and envyous;
> Glotons, slaw, and lecherous …
> Thus every synne tyllyth in othyr
> And makyth Mankynde to ben a foole. (ll. 1030–8, 119)

Here, the Seven Deadly Sins are explicitly associated with "foly" as it is "synne" that makes Mankynde a "foole." Or, to take a later example, in *Mundus et Infans* (*c.* 1520–22), when Manhode asks Conscyence "what thyng callest thou folly?" (l. 457), Conscyence answers, "pride, wrath, and envy, / Sloth, covetise, and gluttony, – / Lechery the seventh is" (ll. 458–60), concluding, "These seven sins I call folly" (l. 461).[41] In both plays, sin and folly are treated as synonymous, just as the word "folly" itself sometimes had definite wicked connotations: "Wickedness, evil, mischief, harm" (*OED* 2.a.); "A wrong-doing, sin, crime" (*OED* 2.b.); and "Lewdness, wantonness" as in the French *folie* (*OED* 3.a.). In 1604, Shakespeare was still able to employ precisely such wanton-wicked connotations when Othello believed Desdemona had "gone to burning hell" (5.2, 127) because she "turned to folly; and she was a whore" (5.2, 130).

Before turning shortly to actual fools in moral interludes, we have also to consider the iconography established through the opening verse of Psalm 52 ("The fool said in his heart, 'There is no God' ") in the

evident in William Mountford's *The Life and Death of Doctor Faustus Made into a Farce With the Humours of Harlequin and Scaramouche* (London, 1697) in which a stage direction reads: "*Enters Several Devils, who black Harlequin and Scaramouche's Faces, and then Squirt Milk upon them*" (sig. D1ᵛ).

40 *Four Morality Plays*, ed. Peter Happé (Harmondsworth, 1979), l. 199.
41 *Three Late Medieval Morality Plays*, ed. G. A. Lester (London and New York, 1981), 132.

illuminated tradition, in which the historiated "*D*" that introduces this psalm in Latin (*Dixit insipiens in corde suo: non est Deus*) often contains "the portrait of a fool."[42] Illuminations of Psalm 52 often depict a devil or devils (i.e., in lieu of a fool), the fool with devils, the fool as diabolical, the fool possessed by the irrational Devil, or even the fool or *insipiens* as Antichrist (as in the Evesham Psalter [*c.* 1250], where Antichrist holds a fool's bladder[43]). The psalter fool's denial of God's existence was, after all, pridefully and foolishly Satanic and thus, as the archetypal *insipiens*, the Devil was on some deep level less a trickster than a natural. Thus, in the early fifteenth century Lydgate could write of Satanic disbelief: "The chief of foolis, as men in bokis redithe … Is he that nowther lovithe God ne dredithe."[44] Moreover, Psalm 52 itself continues: "Are they so ignorant, these evil men …?"[45] Equally important, in terms of emergent racial constructions, St Augustine's *Enarrationes in Psalmos* "established the central theme of Psalm 52 – the 'non est Deus' – which is the rejection of the Christian faith and the denial of Christ by individuals, infidel sects, Jews, and pagans."[46] The insipient fool is, as a result, often depicted as foreign, dark-faced, or even as black, as is the leaping and shirtless black man wearing a leopard spotted conical cap and Turkish pants in the famed ninth-century Stuttgart Psalter,[47] not coincidentally, I suggest, the work also noted for the Devil's "first clear [illustrated] appearance as black."[48] Not only is the Devil repeatedly depicted as black in the Stuttgart Psalter, and not only is the *insipiens* himself black, but when the *Dixit* verse repeats later, the letter *D* is represented,

42 D. J. Gifford, "Iconographical Notes Towards a Definition of the Medieval Fool," in *The Fool and the Trickster: Studies in Honour of Enid Welsford*, ed. Paul V. A. Williams (Cambridge, 1979), 18–35; 18. See also, again, Southworth, *Fools and Jesters*, 36–7.

43 British Library, MS. Add. 44874, fol. 75.

44 *A Selection from the Minor Poems of Dan John Lydgate*, ed. James Orchard Halliwell-Phillips (London, 1860), 164.

45 Southworth, *Fools and Jesters*, 37.

46 Ahuva Belkin, "Antichrist as the Embodiment of the *Insipiens* in Thirteenth-Century French Psalters," *Florilegium* 10 (1988–91): 65–77; here quoting 71–2.

47 See the excellent facsimile edition, *Der Stuttgarter Bilderpsalter Bibl. Fol. 23 Wurrtembergische Landesbibliothek Stuttgart* (Stuttgart, 1965), vol. 1, of 2, sig. 15ʳ. The *insipiens* is on the upper right.

48 Russell, *Lucifer*, 133. Russell makes no reference to the black *insipiens*.

atypically, with even its center blackened so that the color black alone now connotes folly. We know that such symbolism survived because dark-faced *insipientes* are apparently not altogether uncommon. Another example of an *insipiens* as "a Fool with blackened face" is Bodleian MS Liturg. 153 (see Figure 2).[50] More to the point, this particular striking early fifteenth-century illumination appears in a portable psalter that was produced in Britain and was found in the Diocese of Norwich,[51] a fact which leads one to presume that the authors of some of the works we will now examine likely saw an English one like it. In any case, by the ninth century, devil and fool alike were already on their way in the descent into the blackfaced folly that was to prove so damning in constructions of blackness that helped to rationalize slavery and racism.

THE PLAY OF WIT, THE "MARKE" OF IDLENESS, AND THE IMPOSITION OF SAMENESS

The kind of connection between blackface and "natural" folly that I am suggesting was at work in the Devil's irredeemable folly or in the *insipiens'* incorrigible foolishness appears clearly in three Tudor moral interludes, the "Wit" marriage plays. In each of these, a Vice lulls the youth or everyman figure Wit to sleep, blackens his face, and leaves him to be discovered a fool, after which Wit is restored to whiteness and set finally on a path to redemption, ascent, and union with either Science or Wisdom. In the first of these plays, John Redford's *Play of Wit and Science* (c. 1534), the Vice Idleness sings Wyt to sleep, proclaiming, "whyle he sleepeth in Idlenes lappe / *idlenes marke on hym shall I*

---

49 For illustrations of devils as black in the facsimile edition of *Der Stuttgarter Bilderpsalter*, see sigs. 10ᵛ, 16ᵛ, 38ʳ, 70ᵛ, 102ᵛ, 107ʳ, 107ᵛ, and 147ᵛ. For the blackened "*D*," see sig. 65ʳ.
50 Sandra Billington, *A Social History of the Fool* (New York, 1984), 12.
51 Kathleen L. Scott, *Later Gothic Manuscripts 1390–1490*, 2 vols, A Survey of Manuscripts Illuminated in the British Isles 6 (London, 1996), 2: 75, and Scott's "Limning and Book-producing Terms and Signs *in situ* in Late-Medieval English Manuscripts: A First Listing," in *New Science out of Old Books: Studies in Manuscripts and Early Printed Books in Honour of A. L. Doyle*, ed. Richard Beadle and A. J. Piper (Aldershot, 1995), 142–88; here citing 165 n. 29.

Figure 2. *Insipiens* with black mask from Psalm 52, early
fifteenth-century portable psalter from the Diocese of Norwich.

clappe." After marking Wyt and then dressing him in the "fooles cote" (l. 598) of her attendant, "Ingnorance" (*sic*), Idlenes observes, "so [he] beguneth to looke *lyke a noddye*" (l. 587), using one of several early English synonyms for both a fool and a black bird.[53] The Cain-like "marke" of Idleness clapped on Wyt to make him look like a noddy here undoubtedly signifies blackface, since Wyt subsequently so resembles a "naturall foole" (l. 806) that Science claims not to recognize him: "Who is this?" (l. 732), she asks. Science then contrasts Wyt's "fayer" (l. 795) portrait to his now "fowle … & vglye" (l. 796) visage – significantly for the history of racism, it is Science who shuns a blackened character, just as pseudoscience would be trotted out to condemn blackness in later centuries. Thereafter, upon examining his reflection in his "glas of reson" (l. 824), Wyt exclaims:

> … gogs sowle a foole[,] a foole by the mas
> …
> deckt by gogs bones lyke a very asse
> …
> & as for this face[, it] is abhominable
> *as black as the devyll.* (ll. 826, 828, 839–40; emphasis added)

Finally, while examining the audience's reflection in the mirror to test its accuracy ("How loke ther facis heere rownd abouwte?" [l. 833]), he comments on the contrast: "All fayre & cleere they, evry chone; / & I, by the mas, a foole alone" (ll. 834–5). Thus, Wyt concludes that he is "a foole alone" because he alone is "black as the devyll" rather than "fayre."

---

52 John Redford, *Wit and Science*, ed. Arthur Brown (Oxford, 1951), ll. 434–5; emphasis added. All subsequent citations refer to this edition and will be cited parenthetically.

53 Emphasis added. Associations between both lustful natural folly and blackness and between episodes of trickery and the blacking of a "gulled" comic butt are to be found in several prevalent synonyms for the word "fool" involving black- or black-headed birds as with the words "noddy," "jackdaw," "loon" "booby," and "gull" (particularly the common or black-headed gull or *Larus ridibundus* and the laughing gull or *Larus atricilla*, whose cry resembles human laughter). See my essay, "Blackfaced Fools, Black-Headed Birds, Fool Synonyms, and Shakespearean Allusions to Renaissance Blackface Folly," *Notes & Queries* 55 (2008): 215–19.

The damning symbolism of blackfaced folly in Redford's play is all the more unavoidable given its emphatic depiction of the "foole" Ingnorance as a mirror image of the folly-fallen Wyt, for Ingnorance is indeed a black fool from the beginning. Such mirroring is clear, after Wyt's face is blackened and Ingnorance and Wyt have exchanged coats, when Ingnorance observes, "He is I now" (l. 599), Idlenes then asks, "Is he not a foole as wel as thow?" (l. 601), to which Ingnorance responds, "Yeas" (l. 602). Following the blackening of Wyt, he and Ingnorance are virtually twins. In fact, the blackened Wyt is actually taken for "Ingnorance, or his lykenes" (l. 668). That the now-blackfaced Wyt has been transformed into the fool Ingnorance's double is apparent when, upon seeing Wyt so unwittingly disguised, even Science ostensibly mistakes her fiance for the fool, addressing him with "What sayst thow, Ingnorance[?]" (l. 737). Emphatically, then, like the York Pageant, this interlude includes a duo of blackfaced fools. Significantly, given that Wit essentially temporarily loses himself (i.e., his "wit" or very identity), after having his face blackened, the play suggests that a black face, that is, blackness alone, has the power to erase individuality, marking characters as identical – here identically *ignorant*.

Such is the very essence of stereotyping in embryo, if not fully born. Similar assumptions appear, ironically, in arguments dismissing *any* racial import in, or racialist effect through, "popular masking" in blackface. While maintaining that black-masking represented "simple disguise,"[54] merely an "impulse to conceal," since "easily available domestic materials like soot, lampblack, or charcoal" were "all matt monotone black which blanks out the features,"[55] such arguments fail to pursue the consequences of such thinking. That is, the logic of blackface as disguise "alone" refuses to acknowledge the damning assumption that blackness erases individuality, producing a stereotypical sameness, the imposed social invisibility explored in Ralph Ellison's *Invisible Man*. After all, the trope that blackness did render invisibility was actually invited in blackface traditions, whether in minstrel plays in which characters could be described archly with "The rest of the characters are

---

54 Lhamon, *Raising Cain*, 42.
55 Twycross and Carpenter, *Masks and Masking in Medieval and Early Tudor England*, 11, 316.

all so dark that they cannot be seen" or in the black-masked Harle
quin's ability to "simply point to one of the black patches on his suit and
become invisible, a trope that has become central to black literary tradition."[57]

In scenes imitating Redford's play, such as in *The Marriage of Wit and
Science* (c. 1569–70),[58] performed by the Children of Paul's under
Sebastian Westcott's mastership,[59] the connection between blackface
and folly seems clearer still, as it is assumed readily with less effort on the
author's part. In Westcott's "Wit" play, following the scene in which
"Witte" is transformed into the likeness of the black fool Ignorance,
Science and her father Reason mistake Witte for a fool and contemptuously refer to his blackness – "Thy loke is like to one that came out of
hell" (sig. E.ii.^{r}) – and, when comparing a picture of Witte alongside his
altered visage, they report: "[W]hy loke, they are no more like; / … then
blacke to white" (sig. E.ii.^{r}). Witte then looks in his glass of Reason,
remarking in dismay, "By the Masse I loke like a very foole in deede"
(sig. Eii.^{r}).

Similarly, the latest of the three Wit plays, Francis Merbury's *The
Marriage Between Wit and Wisdom* (1579),[60] includes the stage business:
"*Here, shall [W]antonis sing … him a sleepe … then let her set a fooles
bable on his hed … colling [coaling] his face.*" In the song, Wantonnes
announces her intention to

> *trick this prety doddy*
> *& make him a noddy, …*
> *& now of a scholar*
> *I will make him a colliar.* (ll. 431–8)

After Wit's face is "collied," that is, begrimed or blackened, apparently

56 Alexander Saxton, "Blackface Minstrelsy and Jacksonian Ideology," *American
Quarterly* 27.1 (March 1975): 3–28; here quoting 23.
57 See Henry Louis Gates, *Figures in Black: Words, Signs, and the "Racial" Self* (New
York and Oxford, 1987), 51.
58 *The Marriage of Wit and Science*, ed. John S. Farmer (London and Edinburgh,
1909), v. All citations refer to this edition and will be cited parenthetically.
59 Reavley Gair, *The Children of Paul's: The Story of a Theatre Company, 1553–1608*
(Cambridge, 1982), 84.
60 *The Marriage Between Wit and Wisdom*, ed. Trevor N. S. Lennam (1966; rpt
Oxford, 1971), ix.

either with coal or by one of several other methods available to render the face black[61] (but this time without benefit of Ignorance or a fool's coat), a character enters crying, "o god ... the company made the[e] a foole / that thou of late wast in" (ll. 464–6), after which appears the stage direction: "*He washeth his face and taketh off his bauble*" (l. 475). Evidently, a fool's coat and Ignorance's or some other double's assistance were no longer required to mark folly in this scene because blackface and bauble were now sufficient. It is also significant that, as we learn in Anthony Munday's *Sir Thomas More* (c. 1590), *The Marriage Between Wit and Wisdom* was an especially familiar play, indeed a byword, when it was included, along with plays such as *Dives and Lazarus* (a play about damnation) and *Lusty Juventus* (which includes a comic devil), as part of the old-fashioned repertoire of the small wandering troupe, the "Lord Cardinal's players" (3.2, 50).[62] Therefore, blacking episodes such as those in the "Wit" plays and other works with foolish black devils would likely have been seen through much of England.

FROM CHILDS' PLAY(S) TO SLAVERY

Rather than the "Wit" plays being isolated anomalies, a marked association between blackface and folly was, though hardly ubiquitous, fairly widespread in late medieval and Renaissance drama. In fact, it is also extant in a number of other plays, including, I believe, John Rastell's *The Nature of the Four Elements* (c. 1520; printed c. 1527), a work known to have influenced Redford's *Wit and Science*.[63] Here, a blacking episode probably appeared during a mysterious gap of eight missing leaves (sigs. D 1–8) in the copy since, after the missing leaves, the vices Yngnoraunce

---

61 For a discussion of such, see Richard Blunt's fascinating "Recreating Renaissance Black Make-Up," dissertation for M. Litt in Shakespeare and Renaissance Literature in Performance (Mary Baldwin College, VA, spring 2006).

62 *Sir Thomas More: a play by Anthony Munday and others; revised by Henry Chettle, Thomas Dekker, Thomas Heywood and William Shakespeare*, ed. Vittorio Gabrieli and Giorgio Melchiori (Manchester, 1990), 142–3.

63 *Three Rastell Plays:* Four Elements, Calisto and Melebea, Gentleness and Nobility, ed. Richard Axton (Cambridge, 1979), 59. Subsequent citations from this edition appear by line number.

and Sensuall Appetyte find the everyman Humanyte, now a "mad fole" (l. 1183), "clene out of [his] mynde" (l. 1202), down on the ground, while his "tayle totyth out behynde" (l. 1195) and his head is, somewhat curiously, initially concealed ("Why, what is cause thou hydest the[e] here?" [l. 1200]). Looking upon his newly transformed head, Yngnoraunce jests: "Hit were evyn great almys / To smyte his hed from his body" (ll. 1185–6). The point of the joke and the surprise appearance of the everyman's head seems to be that the transformed Humanyte now has the laughable head of a fool. Moreover, Sensuall Appetyte explains that Humanyte's now-foolish face or head is the result of a temporary disguise: "Nay God forbed ye sholde do so. / For he is but an innocent, lo, / *In maner of a fole*" (ll. 1187–9; emphasis added). As Trevor Lennam observes, "Whatever action has occurred … the lines indicate that Humanity is degraded as a fool."[64] Even though we can only conjecture here as to what happened in the missing leaves to make Humanyte degraded, ugly, and foolish, a blacking or masking episode would certainly explain the many curious details in the scene that follows the gap because blackness in contemporary plays had become an emblem of degradation, madness, folly, and ugliness alike.

More definitely, blacking occurs in a different context in boy company author John Heywood's *Johan Johan* (printed 1533), when the cuckold Johan is tricked into chafing wax at the fire to mend a leaky pail while his wife Tyb and a cuckolding priest eat up all his dinner. While working at length before the fire, Johan is blackened with smoke, as we learn when he complains that "the smoke puttyth out my eyes two. / I burne my face, and ray my clothes also" (ll. 509–10), and when he afterward repeats for emphasis, "For the smoke put out my eyes two, / I burned my face, and rayed my clothes also" (ll. 637–8). That the smoke that has blackened his clothes and face makes him a fool is evident when this poor "wodcok" (l. 488) is subsequently called an "ape" (l. 514) and a "dryvyll" (l. 655), both synonyms for fool, with the dominant coloring of both "ape" and "woodcock" invoking blackness.[65]

---

64 Trevor Lennam, *Sebastian Westcott, the Children of Paul's, and* The Marriage of Wit and Science (Toronto, 1975), 94.
65 *The Plays of John Heywood*, ed. Richard Axton and Peter Happé (Cambridge, 1991), 88 and 91.

As with the rise of the black-masked clown Harlequin in Italy, according to Dario Fo, during "a revival of slavery" when *commedia* originated,[67] the tradition of the blackfaced fool in England became especially pronounced alongside the expanding slave trade in Europe, particularly with the development of an *English* slave trade. The connection between natural folly and blackface may thus have become stronger over the course of the sixteenth century due to the expansion of the African slave trade. The Mediterranean slave trade based in Italian cities like Venice and Genoa had collapsed by the end of the fifteenth century, as Black Sea slave marketing in Tartars, Circassians, Armenians, Georgians, and Bulgarians was sealed off by the Turks after their capture of Constantinople.[68] By that time, the Portuguese had already developed a slave trade from West Africa to fill the void; in fact, in 1444, Portugal had launched the modern slave trade from the Guinea coast.[69] Over the next three decades, by one count, roughly 12,500 Africans were taken to Europe.[70] From 1450 to 1500, by another estimate, 35,000 victims were seized from Africa, via Lisbon, to be slaves in Europe, especially in Portugal, Spain, and Italy.[71] The Portuguese launched the trans atlantic slave trade around 1530. In 1537, New World traffic in African peoples was spurred on when Pope Paul II differentiated between American Indians and Africans by denying the sacraments to any colonist who enslaved the former, because they were rational and thus capable of Christianity; Africans were not so deemed.[72] The human trafficking in African peoples was thus already well under way by the time English

---

[66] Although *commedia* troupes appeared in London in 1573 and 1574, it was not until 1578, when a "Drusiano" performed in London, that a Harlequin is known to have appeared. Harlequin thus seems not to have appeared in England until well after a number of English plays featuring blackfaced fools. On *commedia* in Renaissance England, see Richard B. Zacha, "Iago and the Commedia dell'Arte," *The Arlington Quarterly* 2.2 (autumn, 1969): 98–116; 101.

[67] Dario Fo, *The Tricks of the Trade*, trans. Joe Farrell (New York, 1991), 42.

[68] David B. Davis, *The Problem of Slavery in Western Culture* (Ithaca, NY, 1966), 43.

[69] Elizabeth Donnan, *Documents Illustrative of the History of the Slave Trade to America*, vol. 1, of 4 vols (1930; rpt New York, 1965), 1.

[70] Harry Harmer, *The Longman Companion to Slavery, Emancipation and Civil Rights* (London, 2001), 3.

[71] Joseph E. Harris, *Africans and Their History*, 2nd rev. edn (1972; New York, 1998), 81.

[72] Davis, *Problem of Slavery in Western Culture*, 170.

blackface characterizations such as those in the mystery cycles (*c.* the 1460s), *The Nature of the Four Elements* (*c.* 1520), *Johan Johan* (printed 1533), *Wit and Science* (*c.* 1534), and its two derivative plays (*c.* 1569–79) appear.

Admittedly, England did not enter the slave trade in any considerable way for some time after Portugal had, but that was hardly from a lack of trying. Edward IV (1471–83) unsuccessfully asked the pope to allow English trade in Africa. And, in 1481, hearing rumors that Englishmen William Fabian and John Tintam were preparing a venture to Guinea, the Portuguese protested on the grounds of their monopoly and the expedition was stayed.[73] While there were certainly black people, both free and enslaved, in England before 1530,[74] fifteenth- and sixteenth-century English slave trading from Guinea is "underdocumented because of its surreptitious nature."[75] Still, we are able to gather that William Hawkins, father of famous slave trader and pirate John Hawkins, had begun some sort of trading on the northern Guinea coast by the 1530s, with probable ventures there in 1530, 1531, 1532, likely in 1536 on behalf of "the English African company," and, even more likely, again in 1539–40.[76] We also know that Captain Thomas Windham made an expedition to Guinea and Benin in 1553. And we learn of five Western African "Negroes" being transported to England by trader William Towrson in 1554 and "kept" there "till they could speak the language," and brought back to Africa only "to be a helpe to Englishmen" there.[77] Similarly, in 1554–55, the pirate John Lok brought back from Guinea "certain blacke slaves whereof some were tall and strong men and could wel agree with our meates and drinkes. The cold

73 Kim F. Hall, *Things of Darkness: Economies of Race and Gender in Early Modern England* (Ithaca, NY, 1995), 19 n. 24.
74 See Paul Edwards, "The Early African Presence in the British Isles," in *Essays on the History of Blacks in Britain: From Roman Times to the Mid-Twentieth Century*, ed. Jagdish S. Gundara and Ian Duffield (Aldershot, 1992), 9–29; Sue Niebrzydowski, "The Sultana and Her Sisters: Black Women in the British Isles Before 1530," *Women's History Review* 10.2 (2001): 187–210.
75 Hall, *Things of Darkness*, 21.
76 Donnan, *Documents Illustrative of the History of the Slave Trade to America*, 1: 8.
77 Winthrop D. Jordan, *White Over Black: American Attitudes Toward the Negro, 1550–1812* (Chapel Hill, NC, 1968), 6.

and moyst aire doth somewhat offend them." Such efforts reflect a determination to expand on some ongoing trade.

Whereas the Catholic Queen Mary had largely respected the papal bulls granting an African monopoly to Portugal, Queen Elizabeth "surreptitiously supported" the slave trade: "Of necessity, Elizabeth's reign was characterized by official reticence and actual aggression toward the African trade."[79] Indeed, when in 1561 English ventures, backed by four royal vessels, were determined to establish a fort and trading base on the Guinea coast, which they finally did under John Lok's leadership in 1562, the Queen's profits amounted to £1,000. By 1562–63, "being amongst other particulars assured that Negros were very good merchandise ... and that the store of Negros might easily bee had upon the coast of Guinea," John Hawkins "resolved with himselfe to make triall thereof."[80] On this expedition, the pirate Hawkins put an end to the Portuguese monopoly, as we learn from his boast to have "got into his possession, partly by the sword, and partly by other meanes, to the number of 300 Negroes at the least, besides other merchandises."[81] Whereas Queen Elizabeth had officially opposed slavery, stating, "If any African were carried away without his free consent it would be detestable and call down the vengeance of Heaven upon the undertaking," in 1564 she was investing again, this time in Hawkins' second expedition to Guinea.[82] The crown remained active in slave trading interests; when a 1588 patent granted exclusive English trade on the coast of Guinea to merchants of London and Devonshire in order to ward off foreign interference with English trafficking, the English slave trade was well under way. In 1619 in Jamestown we learn of "20. and odd Negroes, w[hi]ch the Governor ... bought ... at the best and easyest rate."[83] Between 1576

[78] James Walvin, *The Black Presence: A Documentary History of the Negro in England, 1555–1860* (London, 1971), 61, 212 n.1.
[79] Hall, *Things of Darkness*, 19.
[80] Donnan, *Documents Illustrative of the History of the Slave Trade to America*, 1: 45.
[81] Walvin, *Black Presence*, 50.
[82] Harmer, *Longman Companion to Slavery, Emancipation and Civil Rights*, 6.
[83] Engel Sluiter, "New Light on the '20. and Odd Negroes' Arriving in Virginia, August 1619," *William and Mary Quarterly*, 3rd ser., 54 (1997): 396–8; John K. Thornton, "The African Experience of the '20. and Odd Negroes' Arriving in Virginia in 1619," *William and Mary Quarterly*, 3rd ser., 55 (July 1998): 421–34.

and 1675, some 425,000 Africans were transported to British North America.[84]

By the heyday of Shakespeare's career, there were also "probably several thousand black people in London, forming a significant minority of the population."[85] By 1589, the connection between Africans and slavery was so well established that Richard Hakluyt was calling five Africans brought into England "black slaves."[86] By 1596, referring to "divers Blackamoores brought into these realms," Queen Elizabeth asserted in a letter to the Mayor of London that "there are already here to[o] manie."[87] By 1597 the Privy Council was attempting to *export* "slaves" to Portugal and Spain,[88] and, by 1599 and 1601, the slave trade had been substantial enough that Queen Elizabeth now issued proclamations actually decrying "the great numbers of Negroes and blackamoors which … are carried into this realm" and encouraging "their masters" to assist her attempts "to have *those kind of people* sent out of the lande."[89] As a result, Elizabeth even licensed sea captain Caspar van Senden to deport slaves and prompted those "possessed of any such blackamoors" to relinquish them upon the captain's demand,[90] while speaking of their condition of "servitude."[91] Although the English did not begin their rise to eventual dominance of the slave trade until the 1655 seizure of Jamaica from Spain,[92] we know that plays featuring blackface nonetheless proliferated alongside such inhumane trafficking.

84 Harmer, *Longman Companion to Slavery, Emancipation and Civil Rights*, 13–14.
85 For parish records at St Botolph's, Aldgate, and All Hallow's, Barking, see Michael Wood, *Shakespeare* (New York, 2003), 251–2, and Marika Sherwood, "Black People in Tudor England," *History Today* (Oct. 2003).
86 Jordan, *White Over Black*, 60.
87 See Peter Fryer, *Staying Power: The History of Black People in Britain* (London, 1984), 4–12.
88 *Tudor Royal Proclamations*, ed. P. L. Hughes and J. F. Larkin, 3 vols (New Haven, CT, 1964–69), 3: 221 n.
89 Ibid., 3: 221–2; Errol Hill, *Shakespeare in Sable: A History of Black Actors* (Amherst, MA, 1984), 8; Walvin, *Black Presence*, 64.
90 Virginia Mason Vaughan, Othello: *A Contextual History* (Cambridge, 1994), 58; emphasis added.
91 Wood, *Shakespeare*, 251.
92 Harmer, *Longman Companion to Slavery, Emancipation and Civil Rights*, 10–11.

WHAT "THE FOOL SAID IN HIS HEART": TOWARDS AN INCORRIGIBLE STEREOTYPE

There is at least one play from the period that seems to promote the slave trade. Certainly, the understandings of folly we have seen in the "Wit" plays are further exploited to different effects in William Wager's moral interlude *The Longer Thou Livest the More Fool Thou Art* (*c.* 1560–8). Here, the natural fool is Moros, whose name is derived from the ancient Dorian minic fool, *moros* (μωρός). Interestingly, whereas the "Wit" figures have their faces blackened only to be redeemed, Moros is permanently blackened. He resembles Ingorance, but in a more fallen way. Moros is an *insipiens* who is black, since he calls to mind not only a "monster" (l. 1693) and "a devil of hell" (l. 1698) at a time when devils were typically represented as black on stage but is, simultaneously, immediately recognizable as a fool by his face alone – "Have you seen a more foolish face? / I must laugh to see how he doth look" (ll. 699–700) – and since he has "*a foolish countenance*" (*s.d.* following l. 70). This fool already seems damned well before being piggy-backed off to hell, for God is angry that "such fools in their hearts do say, / That there is no God, neither heaven, nor hell" (ll. 1783–4). In fact, Moros "hath said there is no God in his heart" (l. 1767), exactly echoing the opening verse of Psalm 52, which featured natural fool iconography in the illuminated tradition. When Wager refers to Moros as an "insipient" (e.g., ll. 844, 1125), then, he overtly links him to the iconography of the God-denying *insipiens* of Psalm 52.

Like the fifteenth-century psalter fool from Norwich in Bodleian MS Liturg. 153,[93] Moros' emblematic blackness marks him as a foolish *insipiens*, but the meaning of blackness has nonetheless changed somewhat; for the "staunch Calvinist" Wager,[94] it also marked Moros as inherently reprobate and degenerate from birth. Here we must recognize that Calvin, referring to Jeremiah's question at 13:23 ("Can the Ethiopian change his skin? Or the leopard his spots?"), likened what he referred to in *Commentaries on the Book of the Prophet Jeremiah* as the

---

[93] See Figure 2 above on page 38.
[94] David Bevington, *Tudor Drama and Politics* (Cambridge, MA, 1968), 132.

"Blackness … inherent in the skin of the Ethiopians" to being "enslaved," "corrupted," and lacking in "discernment," that is, to being out of one's "right mind":

> Blackness is inherent in the skin of the Ethiopians, as it is well known. Were they to wash themselves a hundred times daily, they could not put off their blackness. … We now then see what the prophet means – that the Jews were so corrupted by long habit that they could not repent, for the devil had so *enslaved* them that they were *not in their right mind; they no longer had any discernment,* and *could not discriminate between good and evil.*[95]

For Calvin, Carolyn Prager shows, blackness thus connoted "the fixed nature of the sinful state" and stood "for the accrued stain of sin which has become as permanent as an 'incurable' disease"[96] – and, I would add, a state of sin that affects chiefly the "mind" and "discernment." In keeping with this Calvinist view, the black fool Moros has an "evil nature … past cure" so that, we are told, "nothing can [his] crookedness rectify" (ll. 46–8); he "can not convert" (l. 1805).

Nor, it would seem, can he learn, contrary to the belief in Humanist amelioration through discipline initially held, mistakenly, by at least one of the Virtue-characters in the play who treat Moros as if he is redeemable. In particular, the Calvinist character of Piety initially differs with the Humanist figure of Discipline, who takes a while to come around to his colleague's view. When Piety tells Discipline, "Let us lose no more labor about this fool, / For the more he is taught the worse he is" (ll. 397–8), Wager alludes obliquely to another bigoted proverb, "To wash an Ethiope is a labor in vain," which *Biblioteca Eliota* (1545) defined as follows: "Thou washest a Mooren, or Moore, A proverb applied to him that … teacheth a naturall foole wisdome." The play's emphasis on Moros's inability to learn thus draws upon traditions of iconography, theology, and proverb alike connecting blackness and inherent, incorrigible "folly," in varying senses. Remarkably, it was just such assumptions about blackness that slavers like John Barbot, writing in *A*

95 Carolyn Prager, " 'If I Be Devil': English Renaissance Response to the Proverbial and Ecumenical Ethiopian," *Journal of Medieval and Renaissance Studies,* 17.2 (fall 1987): 257–79; here quoting 262 (emphasis added).
96 Ibid., 261–2.

Description of the Coasts of North and South Guinea (1732), subsequently held in justifying slavery: "it must be owned, [Africans] are very hard to be brought to a true notion of the Christian religion … being *naturally* very stupid and sensual" – *not evil* – "and so apt to continue till their end."[97] Similarly, when Wager emphasizes that Moros is reprobate in terms of his inability to learn due to his "nature" (e.g., ll. 44, 46), he puns on "natural" fool, so that Moros "*naturally* play[s] the part" (l. 60; emphasis added) of "such as had lever to folly and idleness fall" (l. 53). Moros is so "naturally" a fool that, we are told before he first appears, he is "[r]epresented" as the very "image of such persons" (ll. 51, 50). Unfortunately, part of that damning "image" of folly was apparently blackness.

Equally disturbing, in terms of the formation of racist stereotypes, the reprobate Moros is attended by the vices Ignorance, Idleness, Wrath, and, eventually, Confusion, the latter being the humiliating "portion of fools" who "abideth with them forever" (ll. 1817–18) as a shameful "companion" (l. 1814) and as "the reward of such … foolish ass[es]" (l. 1813). Confusion enters "*with an ill-favored visure and all things beside ill-favored*" (*s.d.* 1806) as a perpetual sign of Moros's "shame and confusion" (l. 1807). Consistent with Renaissance symbolism, Confusion, like the foolish and wicked Moros himself, would probably have been black, since the conventionally black Satan in Ulpian Fulwell's *Like Will to Like* is similarly described as having an "ill face" (l. 96) and since "ill-favored" was regularly deemed the opposite of "fair."[98] God's Judgment then commands: "Confusion spoil him of his array; / Give him his fool's coat for him due" (ll. 1819–20). The irony here is that Moros, mocked for his looks by the Vices fooling him throughout the play, becomes a double to the fool Confusion, but, being vain and lacking self-knowledge, he is unable to recognize his mirror image, preferring to be carried off straight to the Devil, another double, rather than to be seen with such an "ill-favored knave" (l. 1851).

---

97 Harris, *Africans and Their History*, 7; italics added.
98 Stephen Booth notes that the meaning of blackness was "established by its contrast to fair: … ugly (Shakespeare and his contemporaries regularly use black as if it were a simple antonym for 'beautiful' …)." *Shakespeare's Sonnets*, edited with analytic commentary (New Haven, CT, and London, 1977), 434; here commenting on Sonnet 127.

Worse still, in terms of subsequent racial stereotyping, God's Judg
ment curses Moros's descendants (almost as if he were the biblical Cain
or Ham) in a manner that disparages all those of his supposed "nature,"
here, all who are black: "Thy wicked household shall be dispersed, / Thy
children shall be rooted out to the fourth degree / Like as the mouth of
God hath rehearsed" (ll. 1792–4). In the end, Moros's story seemingly
serves as a propagandistic myth of origin endorsing pro-slavery views
about Africans that were already current in Wager's day; Moros is incorrigible but he must be subjected to harsh discipline and education. Such
an argument, as we shall see, anticipates the racist chop-logic of the
eighteenth- and nineteenth-century philosopher Georg Wilhelm
Friedrich Hegel, who assumed Africans "capable of no development or
culture" whatsoever, but paradoxically deemed slavery a necessary
"phase of *education*."[99]

LINKS IN A CHAIN: TRANSMIGRATION,
TRANSCODIFICATION,
AND RATIONALIZATION OF BLACKFACED FOLLY

But were the assumptions that rationalized the slave trade and those
associated with the blackface tradition linked at all in the early modern
mindset? And if so, how? While a direct connection in the historical
record is difficult to prove, looking back, there is no lack of suggestive
evidence of such a link. Consistent echoes of the characters Wit and
Ingnorance surface particularly in English traditions of travel and
pseudoscientific literature. Notably, the "Second Voyage of John
Hawkins, 1564–65" from Hakluyt's famed *Principall Navigations,
Voiages and Discoveries of the English Nation* (London, 1589) includes a
reference to West Africans Hawkins encountered as simply "the ignorant people" who "knewe not" about guns and so were shot; here, their
pain is described in comic terms: "[They] used a marveilous crying in
their flight with leaping and turning their tayles, that it was strange to
see, and gave us great pleasure to behold them."[100] Similarly, an account

---

99 Gates, *Figures in Black*, 18–20.
100 Donnan, *Documents Illustrative of the History of the Slave Trade to America*, 1:
      48.

of voyages to the West African coast *c.* 1562–63 (omitted from the 1598 edition of Hakluyt's *Principall Navigations*) described inhabitants

> Whose likenesse seem'd men to be,
>   but all as blacke as coles.
> Their Captaine comes to me
>   as naked as my naile,
> *Not having witte* or honestie
>   to cover once his tale.[101]

Here, too, as in the Wit plays (one of which, the latest, was still familiar as late as the 1590s), the connection between blackness and assumed ignorance and lack of wit is clear enough, as it is in Peter Heylyn's claims in his *Little Description of the Great World* (1631) that the sub-Saharan African utterly lacked "the use of Reason which is peculiar unto man; [he is] of little Wit."[102] Of course, Leo Africanus's *History and Description of Africa* (1526; English translation *c.* 1600) had also represented "Negroes" as gulls "being utterly destitute of the use of reason, of dexteritie of wit,"[103] and Leo had been surprised when one African with whom he was "acquainted" was not irrational: "[H]e is blacke in colour but most beautifull in minde and contions [conscience]."[104] As Leo's remark suggests, even when commentators remarked on supposed black immorality (here an assumed lack of conscience), they regularly did so with respect to purported lack of rational powers. For John Boemus in *A Fardle of Facions* (1555), then, Africans "carry the shape of men, but live like beast[s]: they be very barbarous … *neither do the[y] discerne any difference betwixt good and bad.*"[105] Though later commentators might sometimes debate about whether such supposed witlessness was "natural" or "ingrained" through the circumstances of "savagery" or slavery, the presumption of defective reason was

---

101 Jordan, *White Over Black*, 5; emphasis added. Jordan makes no connection to the blackface fool tradition in his work, but the evidence he cites supports its existence.
102 Gates, *Figures in Black*, 15.
103 Jordan, *White Over Black*, 34.
104 Eldred Jones, *Othello's Countrymen: The African in English Renaissance Drama* (London, 1965), 23.
105 Here citing the 1611 edition: Johann Boemus, *The Manner, Lawes, and Customes of All Nations* (London, 1611), 49.

consistently pronounced in the history of early modern European encounters with Africans.[106] And indeed, the connection between Africans and terms of natural folly appeared in the subsequent rhetoric of slavers, as in Barbot's previously noted observation: "it must be owned, they are very hard to be brought to a true notion of the Christian religion ... being *naturally* very stupid and sensual, and so apt to continue till their end."[107] So also for slavers in the American South, "a white skin was the distinguishing badge of mind and intellect,"[108] so that blackness was once again the emblematic opposite.

If, as Pulitzer Prize-winning historian of slavery David Brion Davis has theorized, impositions of "bestialization" were central to the history of slavery since slaveholding societies often compared slaves to domesticated animals,[109] it was irrationality that was once again at issue in slavery and blackface traditions alike. Here it is perhaps useful to mention that well before the African slave trade, western European serfs were commonly portrayed as actually blackened by sun or soil and as naturally stupid or spiritually simple.[110] Such a detail may suggest that the blackface tradition laid the fertile ground for a kind of proto-racism. Centuries later, the leap from an emblematic imposition of foolish reasoning to an assumed beastlike irrationality was, unhappily, evidently no great one. Once Africans were viewed as irrational, partly it seems via a blackface tradition that goes back at least as far as the ninth-century Stuttgart Psalter's *insipiens*, they could be forced into the most bestial servitude. Such is the case in Richard Ligon's view, following his stay in Barbadoes in the 1640s, that its residents were "as neer beasts" or in Henry Whistler's account a few years later in which he describes African slaves as "apes whou [the planters] command as they pleas."[111]

106 Jordan, *White Over Black*, 26.
107 Harris, *Africans and Their History*, 7.
108 Davis, *Inhuman Bondage*, 189.
109 David Brion Davis, "At the Heart of Slavery," in idem, *In the Image of God: Religion, Moral Values, and Our Heritage of Slavery* (New Haven, CT, 2001), 123–36; *Problem of Slavery in Western Culture*, 14; *Inhuman Bondage*, 2–3, 32.
110 Paul Freedman, *Images of the Medieval Peasant* (Stanford, CA, 1999), 133–73, 300–3.
111 Philip D. Morgan, "British Encounters with Africans and African-Americans, circa 1600–1780," in *Strangers Within the Realm: Cultural Margins of the First*

In the same manner, as Winthrop D. Jordan observed, the assertion of African irrationality and witlessness was made by way of direct or implied appeals to a pseudoscientific "Chain of Being" in which Africans were represented as being less than human, that is, one step up from apes in a supposed ascent toward the white man.[112] Thus, Edward Topsell, author of *The Historie of Four-Footed Beastes* (London, 1607), asserted that Africans "are Libidinous as Apes that attempt women" and are actually "deemed fools" because they have "thicke lippes, the upper hanging over the neather, ... like the lips of Asses or Apes."[113] Likewise, "Pigmeys ... are not men, because they *have no use of Reason*, ... and although they speak, yet is their language imperfect; ... and their imitation of man, do plainly *prove them rather to be Apes then Men*."[114]

Topsell's reasoning here meets one standard definition of "racism" as "a rationalized pseudoscientific theory positing the innate and permanent inferiority of nonwhites" – a definition its author, George M. Frederickson, believed applied to racial prejudice only after the early decades of the nineteenth century.[115] Instead, here already we glimpse the "simian imperialism" that Anne McClintock has postulated as a significant link between "scientific" and popular racism,[116] that is, another type of proto-racism. Although Jordan is thus certainly correct in noting early modern Europeans' frequent association of apes with Africans, he is admittedly less clear about *why* they might make such a leap in logic in the first place: "The inner logic of this association ... rather tenuously ... connected apes with blackness."[117]

One missing term in Jordan's argument here (and an assumption often either implicit or explicit in early modern rationalizing) is

British Empire, ed. Bernard Bailyn and Philip D. Morgan (Chapel Hill, NC, 1991), 174.

112 Jordan, *White Over Black*, xii, xx, 65, 219.

113 Edward Topsell, *The Historie of Four-Footed Beastes* (London, 1678), 3.

114 Ibid., 3; emphasis added.

115 George M. Frederickson, *The Black Image in the White Mind: The Debate on Afro-American Character and Destiny, 1817–1914* (New York, 1971), xi. Frederickson generally assumes that racism has no long history, as in his punning title, *Racism: A Short History*.

116 Anne McClintock, "Soft-Soaping Empire: Commodity Racism and Imperial Advertising," in *Travelers' Tales: Narratives of Home and Displacement*, ed. George Robertson et al. (New York, 1994), 131–54; 139.

117 Jordan, *White Over Black*, 30.

suggested by Topsell's references to apes "hav[ing] no use of Reason" and being "deemed foolish," since both "Asses and Apes" were associated with the irrational natural fool type, who we have seen was often represented as black in the period. In fact, it is fools or "divers[e] Jesters" and "laughter" that Topsell has very much in mind at the outset of his discussion of apes. For example, he tells his readers that the Greeks termed them "*Gelotopoios*, made for laughter," and he cites the authority of "*Anacharsis the Philosopher*," who remarked that "men do but feign merriments, whereas Apes are *naturally* made for that purpose."[118] Interestingly enough, fools such as Henry VIII's fool Will Somer in the king's 1545 family portrait in Hampton Court Palace and dwarfs such as Henrietta Maria's "*hypopituitaristic* or proportionate dwarf" Geoffrey in Anthony Van Dyck's 1633 portrait[119] in the National Gallery of Art in Washington, DC are often depicted with monkeys, since court fools traditionally "were put in charge of pet apes."[120] This same juxtaposition is at work in Daniel Mytens' portrait of Charles I and Henrietta Maria, where the sitters preside over a scene featuring a black groom scantily clad in a leopard skin (suggestive of the leopard and Ethiope of Jeremiah that are unable to change their nature) and holding a horse's bridle, the fool-dwarf Geoffrey Hudson holding a dog by a leash, and, on the viewer's lower right, a monkey astride the back of a dog.[121] As Kim F. Hall remarks, especially in evoking "a connection between apes and blacks," "these figures represent a … marginal humanity."[122] Clearly, such representations suggest hierarchical tableaux of a Chain of Being in terms not just of scale but proportions of reason.

In such a context we are able to see that Topsell's logic, however grossly faulty, was not a wholly idiosyncratic leap (i.e., from African to Ape), but rather a chain of prevalent and once closely related, demeaning symbolic associations between African/Blackness, the Blackfaced Natural Fool, and the Ape-as-Natural-Fool by way of the natural fools' conventional association with both blackness and apes. That is to say, in

---

118 Topsell, *Historie of Four-Footed Beastes*, 2; emphasis added.
119 See Southworth, *Fools and Jesters*, 75, 121, 153.
120 H. W. Janson, *Apes and Ape Lore in the Middle Ages and the Renaissance* (London, 1952), 211.
121 Hall, *Things of Darkness*, 237, Fig. 19.
122 Hall, *Things of Darkness*, 236.

the iconography of the blackface tradition, the early Chain of Being that reflected the logic of a "simian imperialism" was not merely Rational Man over Irrational Man over Ape but rather the following Chain of Being: Rational/*White* Man over Irrational Man/ *Blackfaced* Natural Fool/*African* over Foolish *Black* Ape. Clearly, such a rationalized assumption of reason as the exclusive, natural inheritance of "whites," as against purportedly innately, permanently irrational and beastlike "blacks," who were deemed natural or "born" fools, prefigured and prepared the way for nineteenth-century "scientific" racist discourse on the "nature" of different races that may be traced in part to the natural fool tradition.

After all, the spirit or essence of the folk tradition of blackface experienced many transmigrations into more respected or refined forms of discourse – whether natural history, philosophy, linguistics, pseudo-science, pseudo-biblical theories, or, as we will see, even modern psychology. In particular, the mixing of an emblem or sign from folk tradition (here, blackface) and scientific discourse (as in Topsell on nature) is an instance of the dynamic of "transcodification," mentioned by Vaughan, by which the codes of one type of discourse transfer to another. Vaughan speculates that such transference of blackface as "a simple sign … to other sorts of discourse systems" may have been "widespread,"[123] and, though the sign was in reality not always so simple, my own findings demonstrate that transference in fact occurred between early blackface and emergent racist discourse. For instance, early nineteenth-century articulations of racist scientific theories such as "polygenesis" – the theory of the separate creation of races as distinct species, according to which, to cite an example from 1830, there was a "vast preeminence of the Caucasian in intellect" as a "gift of *nature*" – introduced some (yet surprisingly little) new terminology, but no fundamentally new ideas.[124] That is, the pseudoscientific pose of reason in the nineteenth century was not really essentially different than that of "proto-racist" Renaissance science.

It was no mere coincidence therefore that early dramatists were

---

123 Vaughan, *Performing Blackness on English Stages*, 23.
124 Frederickson, *The Black Image in the White Mind*, 73; emphasis added. See also William R. Stanton, *The Leopard's Spots: Scientific Attitudes Toward Race in America, 1815–1859* (Chicago, 1960).

staging personifications of "Science" shunning a character in blackface as a fool in the "Wit" plays; such drama was not merely inadvertently foreshadowing future developments, since Renaissance science was *already* being appropriated to slur blackness as an innate mark of congenital folly. Nineteenth-century scientific poseurs re-enacting the foolish logic and spirit of the blackfaced fool tradition and the stereo-types it had long promoted may have become more sophisticated – or, rather, even more sophistic – in their treatment of "nature," but when they based their irrational assumptions on appeals to nature, the ideas were not new; if the form of discourse seems different, the old code of blackness connoting natural folly was one and the same. Here was the essence of blackface transmigrated into a higher form, or perhaps merely dressed-up in the latest scientific garb, but the old, "tatyrd" medieval-Renaissance fashion of the natural fool shows through all the same.

Before biased and unwitting nineteenth-century evolutionary scientists, eighteenth-century thinkers had already attempted to rationalize the codes of blackface folly by applying the philosophical veneer so admired in their day upon what was still finally the dubious old moralizing logic underlying a time-worn blackface mask. Henry Louis Gates has demonstrated, for instance, that philosophers such as Hume, Kant, and Hegel, in turn, each conflated a black complexion and diminished intellectual capacity. For example, in "Of National Characters" (1748), "suspect[ing] the negroes … to be naturally inferior," and asserting that "There never was a civilized nation of any other complexion than white," Hume dismissed "talk of one negroe as a man of parts and learning," believing that he must "be admired for very slender accomplishments, like a parrot who speaks a few words plainly." Writing in *Observations on the Feeling of the Beautiful and Sublime* (1764), Kant similarly asserted, "so fundamental is the difference between [the black and white] races of man, and it appears to be as great in regard to mental capacities as in color" and, more bluntly, "blacks are lower in their mental capacities than all other races." Kant can thus dismiss a black man's comments through chop-logic: "[I]n short, this fellow was quite black from head to foot, a clear proof that what he said was stupid." Subsequently, Hegel, likewise assuming Africans "capable of no development or culture" whatsoever, deemed slavery a necessary "phase of *education* – a mode of becoming participant in a higher" civilization (the very argument enacted through the dramas of the naturally incorrigible Ingnorance and Moros).[126] In each instance, eighteenth-century philosophers found a black complexion less theologically (i.e., in terms of evil) than intellectually damning. And yet, assumptions derived from the no less moralizing blackfaced fool tradition were still being exploited in attempts to legitimize slavery.

Not "evil" broadly but specifically transgression, Linda Woodbridge notes, pertained to blackness especially in the Renaissance when blackface was "a hallmark of popular rites."[127] A link between blackface and associations with often inversive, festive folly appears, for instance, in corn riots, which, Natalie Zemon Davis demonstrates, were led by women or men dressed as women, who, Woodbridge argues, often wore blackface.[128] C. R. Baskervill cites John Aubrey's *Remains* for the game "Cap Justice," in which, Baskervill explains, "the judge who presides has his face blackened by those who plead before him."[129] Similarly, Barry Reay recounts an early modern tradition in Middleton in Lancashire on Easter Tuesday in which " 'some unlucky fellow who had got himself so far intoxicated as not to be able to take care of himself,' " was elected mock-mayor, had his face "daubed with soot and grease," was dressed in every possible " 'article of adornment and deformity,' " and was paraded through town on a chair.[130] Of course, blackface was also often assumed by participants in Carnival. In his section, "Von fassnacht narren" ("Of Carnival Fools"), Sebastian Brant spoke contemptuously in his *Ship of Fools* (1495, second edition) of those maskers who blacked themselves

---

125   Gates, *Figures in Black*, 18–20.

126   For Ingnorance as unteachable, see the episode in *The Play of Wit and Science* in which he is depicted in a sort of language "lesson" (l. 452), parroting the vice Idleness, who "play[s] the schoolemystres" (l. 450), attempting unsuccessfully to teach him to say his own name.

127   Linda Woodbridge, *The Scythe of Saturn: Shakespeare and Magical Thinking* (Urbana, 1994), 21.

128   Natalie Zemon Davis, "Women on Top," in idem, *Society and Culture in Early Modern France* (1965; reprint, Stanford, CA, 1978), 179, 156; Woodbridge, *The Scythe of Saturn*, 21.

129   C. R. Baskervill, *The Elizabethan Jig and Related Song Drama* (Chicago, 1929), 315.

130   Barry Reay, *Popular Cultures in England 1550–1750* (London, 1998), 134.

and ran amok, just as Englishman Alexander Barclay remarks in his free translation *Shyp of Folys*: "The one ... paynteth his visage with fume in such case ... / And other some besyde theyr vayne habyte / Defyle theyr faces."[131]

I would suggest that blackface in these customs, in conjunction with popular rites featuring comic butts in blackface, invoked the tradition of the natural fool, whose transgression was both licensed and mocked. After all, "[s]ince he does not comprehend the conventions of society," Walter Kaiser observes, "the natural fool is invariably irreverent of those conventions, not out of any motives of iconoclasm but simply because he does not know any better."[132] As Enid Welsford put it, his "mental deficiencies" can often have the effect of "put[ting] him in ... [a] position of virtual outlawry";[133] by his very nature the natural fool "stand[s] outside the law" and tends "to turn the world upside down."[134] A black face became a sign of one marked as both transgressor and butt and thus as a scapegoat, a whipping boy, an *insipiens*, a fool – and also a slave. Here again the license authorized by blackface, which modern scholars have occasionally invoked as liberating, was symbolically and stereotypically limiting.

If since at least the fifteenth century the blackface tradition had the effect of rationalizing slavery, by the nineteenth century it was especially underwriting the myth of the happy but incorrigible plantation slave. Notably, in the 1850s, Thomas R. R. Cobb's influential defense of slavery, *An Inquiry into the Law of Negro Slavery*, rested partly upon the idea that black peoples were "mirthful by nature." Years earlier, writing of southern slaves, John Pendleton Kennedy was likewise "quite sure" in his *Swallow Barn* (1832) that "never could they become a happier people than I find them here."[135] The black man was, of course, believed innately happy because he was assumed to be simply a natural. In fact, as Joseph Boskin argues, his humor was depicted as similar to that of "the

---

131 Twycross and Carpenter, *Masks and Maskingin Medieval and Early Tudor England*, 76, 85.
132 Kaiser, *Praisers of Folly*, 7.
133 Welsford, *The Fool*, 55.
134 Kaiser, *Praisers of Folly*, 129, 284.
135 Joseph Boskin, *Sambo: The Rise and Demise of an American Jester* (New York, 1986), 54, 97.

fool." Washington Irving thus found the "negroes" he described in *Knickerbocker's History of New York* (1809) as "famous for their risible powers," while English comedian John Bernard, following a visit to America between 1797 and 1811, termed "the negroes the greatest humorists of the union" because of their "profound simplicity," their "*natural* drollery," which was "*Nature's* spontaneous product in full bloom."[136] Boskin demonstrates further that "once the conception of the black male as the fool became the primary focus of white imagery, it assumed a centripetal energy of its own, as stereotypes often do."[137] A key in such stereotyping was the figure of Sambo: "slow-witted, loosely shuffling, buttock-scratching, benignly optimistic, superstitiously frightened, childishly lazy, irresponsibly carefree, … sexually animated. His physical characteristics added to the jester's appearance: toothy-grinned, … slack-jawed, round-eyed."[138] But this description seems as apt for the age-old natural fool as for the more recent blackface minstrelsy of the nineteenth and early twentieth centuries, for Sambo is but the latest name for the natural fool in blackface. Reduced under such a stereotype to the level of a smiling, dehumanized buffoon, any black male could be deemed impervious to pain and incapable of sorrow, so that real guilt or culpability on the part of slaveholders – as opposed to the maudlin sentimentality and disabling pathos sometimes attached to the natural fool tradition and plantation myth alike – was not only unnecessary but inconceivable. That is, through such a Sambo stereo-type, black men were constructed as childishly incapable of caring for themselves, assisting the condescending paternalism and "degraded man-child" stereotype that was "an ideological imperative of all systems of slavery,"[139] but especially of the American South.

Of course, as with other natural fool traditions, the specific planta-tion stereotype of the irrepressibly childlike Sambo found its origins in ridicule and shame. His name, for instance, in addition to owing a debt to the pejorative Spanish *zambo*, also apparently derives from West

136 Ibid., 54–5, 66, 61; emphasis mine.
137 Ibid., 63.
138 Joseph Boskin, "The Life and Death of Sambo: Overview of an Historical Hang-Up," *Journal of Popular Culture* 4.3 (winter 1971), 647–57; 649.
139 Orlando Patterson, *Slavery and Social Death: A Comparative Study* (Cambridge, MA, 1982), 96, 299–333.

African cultures, particularly the Mende and Vai communities, among whom *sambo* or *sam bo* meant "to disgrace"; the name, as applied to African slaves, appears at least as early as 1692–93, when the ship *Margarett* included as recorded cargo: "2 Negroes Sambo and Jack."[140] But the origins of Sambo before that, Boskin observes, have always been obscure: "There is no precise date, but Sambo was apparently conceived in the minds of Western Europeans in their early interactions with Africans in the fifteenth and early sixteenth centuries and was born during the early period of the slave trade."[141] Elsewhere, Boskin speculates: "In all probability, the American Sambo was conceived in Europe, particularly in England, and drew his first breath with initial contact with West Africans during the slave-trading years. Sambo was a concept long before assuming a specific identity."[142] But we are presently able to move beyond Boskin's apt conjecture, since we know now that at least one of the "concepts" he posits was that of the natural fool and that the enduring type that came to be known finally as Sambo took some of his earliest breaths on the stage under names like Tutuvillus, Ingnorance, Moros, and Harlequin, the latter of whom was already an international icon of popular culture by the late sixteenth century. Subsequently, under the name Sambo, a word of disgrace, the blackfaced fool became "a multipublic figure by the eighteenth century," and he achieved fame that lasted through the early twentieth century.[143] Yet, we must now admit as much for the blackfaced fool generally, for "Sambo" was simply one of the most enduring names given to an old fool-type.

CONCLUSIONS

Blackface in the performance tradition was not a simple sign associated with evil alone, since other buried religiously inflected associations between blackface and folly had, as we have seen, numerous reinforcing connections, some subtle, others not. More important, though long-ignored, associations between blackness and folly would prove to

140 Boskin, *Sambo*, 35.
141 Ibid., 43.
142 Ibid., 7.
143 Ibid., 12, 10.

be more damning than the association with "evil" in the construction of stereotypes that were used to justify racial domination and to rationalize slavery. Whether used to mark the *insipiens*, a foolish devil, Johan Johan, Humanyte, a gulled Wit, Ingnorance, the lewd "blackeman" that offended Cecilia, Moros, a participant in any of several European popular rites, Grime the Collier, Harlequin, or Sambo, blackface masks were emblematic of the natural fool, a gull who was laughed at, scapegoated, and abused while being constructed as mentally deficient, transgressive, and essentially "other." Although popular cultures are undoubtedly subject to discontinuities and inventions, the long-ignored early blackface tradition, like much fool custom generally, was especially stubborn and resilient. The iconography of blackface as an emblem of folly is the result of the influence and conflation of many old popular traditions, each of which, no doubt, originally had different potential symbolic terms that were distilled over time as emblematic of folly. Whatever its origins, myriad transmigrations, and unconscious transcodifications, the palimpsest that was the blackfaced natural fool tradition had devastating consequences as its codes lay behind and beneath dehumanizing racist theories articulated more fully, but often only in slightly different idiom (ranging from religious to philosophical and scientific discourses), in later centuries. Because such depictions originated some of the racist fantasies staged by blackface minstrels and contributed to otherwise inexplicable racist theories of African inferiority, forging early links in the enslaving fiction of the "Great Chain of Being," the widespread, yet previously overlooked natural fool iconography of blackness warrants examination. In the end, one thing we will find is that racism was – and is – not only folly but often the stuff of actual fools' play as well. Just as we have seen in this initial examination of early blackface that associations with folly taken from religious contexts – e.g., the *insipiens*, the devil, and the once-related senses of sin and folly – transmigrated through many aspects of Western culture, so we will see in the next chapter that religion in Renaissance England similarly inflected later clown traditions, especially those related to misrule.

Chapter 2

"SPORTS AND FOLLIES AGAINST THE POPE": TUDOR EVANGELICAL LORDS OF MISRULE

B EFORE WE can re-examine the early Lord of Misrule in the context of comic history, a little perspective is necessary. Consider the following illustration, undoubtedly the most arresting Tudor likeness in the National Portrait Gallery, London, William Scrots's anamorphosis (NPG1299). As if modeled after a funhouse mirror reflection, this colorful oil on panel painting depicts within a stretched oblong, framed within a thin horizontal rectangle, the profile of a grotesque figure with red hair and a head far wider than it is tall; measuring 63 x 16¾ inches, the portrait itself is, the Gallery website reports, its "squattest" ("nearly 4 times wider than it is high"). Its short-lived sitter's nose juts out, Pinocchio-like, under a low bump of overhanging brow, as the chin recedes cartoonishly under a marked overbite. The subject seems to prefigure the whimsical grotesques of Inigo Jones's antimasques decades later rather than to depict, as it does, the heir apparent of Henry VIII. Such is underrated Flemish master Scrots's *tour de force* portrait of a nine-year-old Prince Edward in 1546, a year before his accession. As the gallery's website explains, "[Edward] is shown in distorted perspective (anamorphosis)." When viewed from the right, however, i.e., from a small cut-out in that side of the frame, he can be "seen in correct perspective."[1] This delightful anamorphic image, coupled with the Gallery's dry commentary, provides an ironic but apt metaphor for the critical tradition

---

[1] See the National Portrait Gallery website at
www.npg.org.uk/live/search/portrait.asp?search=sa&sText=scrot&LinkID=
mp07539&rNo=0&role=art and http://195.172.6, 37/live/unusual.asp.

addressing Edward's reign and its theatrical spectacle: only when viewed from a one-sided point of view – in hindsight, from the anachronistic vantage point of an English and Anglo-American tradition inflected by subsequent Protestantism – can the boy king, his often riotous court spectacle, and mid-Tudor evangelicals in general be made to resemble the "correct" portrait of the Protestant sobriety, indeed the dour puritanism, ascribed to them.

The anachronistic imposition of that stereotype from the later era has, in fact, produced a distorted critical perspective, a curious, reverse historical anamorphosis that insists upon upholding an illusory proportionality where it did not exist. Particularly in terms of the eruption of misrule registered under Henry and Edward, the one-sided view of proto-puritan sobriety ascribed to Edward's reign distorts grotesque realities, while the humorous funhouse image of Scrots's spectacular oil painting captures much truth. Indeed, given the misrule that would so mark Edwardian court spectacle and collegiate revels alike, Scrots's anamorphosis affords a useful emblem of the surprisingly carnivalesque character and disproportionate impact of a foreshortened reign whose monarch was crowned, fittingly, during the Shrovetide season.

More pertinent to the study of clowns and the comic is the broader historical distortion of continuity conventionally imposed in analyses of Renaissance misrule. Rather than being characterized by continuous popular customs or a sustained onslaught by Protestants against said misrule, carnivalesque traditions in the wake of Tudor Reformations were instead marked by significant discontinuities, as contexts, motivations, and meanings changed. Above all, Edwardian misrule did not continue or extend traditional rites, such as the defunct Boy Bishop or long-absent court Lord of Misrule, but revived and expanded the zealous revels initiated by evangelicals in the 1530s. Not surprisingly, late Henrician and Marian traditionalists moved to check such charged misrule, just as puritans later opposed carnivalesque rites like the Morris dance when they were turned against them. Opposition to misrule was rarely an ideological absolute but instead was usually contingent upon the ideology underlying enactments of misrule.

"SPORTS AND FOLLIES AGAINST THE POPE": CROMWELLIAN-INSPIRED APPROPRIATIONS OF MISRULE

As Patrick Collinson has observed, "The first [English] generation of Protestant publicists and propagandists … made polemical and creative use of cultural vehicles which their spiritual children and grandchildren later repudiated."[2] Evangelizing arrogations of unexpected cultural vehicles are nowhere more apparent than in developments in that festive mode characterized by license, parody, and inversion known in England under the category of misrule. In marked contrast to the stereotypical Protestant seriousness that would emerge later in the Renaissance, early evangelicals enthusiastically employed – in service of propaganda – the carnivalesque misrule their spiritual descendants would come to abhor. Diarmaid MacCulloch claims early Tudor evangelical propaganda was characterized by a "gleeful destructiveness" in "utilizing public ridicule against traditional devotion" while employing a "savagely symbolic overturning of the past."[3] So it was that contemporary Thomas More could compare William Tyndale to a clownish "abbote of mysrule in a Christemas game."[4]

Insight into the motives behind evangelical topsy-turvydom is provided by what amounts to a strategy statement left to us by Thomas Cromwell's secretary, Richard Morison, entitled "A Discourse Touching the Reformation of the Lawes of England" (c. 1534–35). Since carnivalesque processions and plays are "daily by all meanes … inculked and driven into the peoples heddes" to prop up "the bysshop of Rome," Morison reasons, reformers must fight back with the same weapons, while eradicating Catholic traditions: "Howmoche better is it that [their] plaies shulde be forbodden and deleted and others dyvysed to set forthe … lyvely before the peoples eies the abhomynation and

---

2 Patrick Collinson, *From Iconoclasm to Iconophobia: The Cultural Impact of the Second English Reformation* (Reading, 1986), 8.
3 Diarmaid MacCulloch, *The Boy King: Edward VI and the Protestant Reformation* (Berkeley, CA, 2002), 71, 74.
4 St Thomas More, *The Confutation of Tyndale's Answer*, ed. L. A. Schuster et al., in *The Complete Works of St Thomas More* (New Haven, CT, 1973), 8: 42.

wickednes of the bisshop of Rome, monkes, ffreers, … and suche like." To make reformation appeal to "the commen people," for whom "thynges sooner enter by the eies, then by the eares," some things "are to be born withal, thowghe som thing in them … be misliked"; Morison thus advocates that the English "ought [to] … go in procession" as a festive "memoryall of the distruction of the bishop of Rome out of this Realm."[6] In short, Morison's plan promoted the appropriation of the carnivalesque as a means of inculcating Reformation. Gritting teeth bared in laughter, evangelicals exploited the very cultural vehicles some already seem to have "misliked" in order to instill antipathy toward Catholicism. This polemical arrogation would radically reshape the meaning of, and the very reasons for, Renaissance misrule.

After all, Morison's strategy was put into practice with a vengeance through what Sydney Anglo calls an "extensive campaign of Reformation propaganda, organized by the government." Two exemplary highlights of this campaign were the jeering February 1538 public sermon in London exposing the puppet-like Boxley Rood (with its mechanisms for moving Jesus's eyes, mouth, and limbs), which ended with the throwing down of the once-miraculous image for "rude people and boyes" to gleefully dismember, and a raucous June 1539 royal triumph on the Thames during which "at last the Pope and his cardinalles were overcome, and all his men cast over the borde into the Thames." As such official propaganda touched off what Anglo characterized as "a veritable fever of iconoclasm [that] seized the country,"[7] it also helped to spur expressions of the "anticlericalism" Christopher Haigh identifies as a "result rather than a cause of the Reformation."[8] Notably, in 1538 at the Cornish parish of St Stephen's, Launceston, "riotous and misruled persons" harassed their chaplain, while in 1540 "misruled and wild persons" in Pawlett, Somerset, prevented their vicar from offering

5 Sydney Anglo, "An Early Tudor Programme for Plays and Other Demonstrations Against the Pope," *Journal of the Warburg and Courtauld Institutes* 20 (1957): 177–8.
6 Ibid., 178.
7 Sydney Anglo, *Spectacle, Pageantry, and Early Tudor Policy* (1969; rpt Oxford, 1997), 272–3, 270, respectively.
8 Christopher Haigh, "Anticlericalism and the English Reformation," in *The English Reformation Revised*, ed. Christopher Haigh (1987; Cambridge, 2000), 56–74; 58.

communion as they "stood at the chancel door" and on another occasion dragged him out and "cast him over the churchyard wall."[9] In July 1539, the French ambassador Marillac, reporting from London, protested the frequent occurrence of "sports and follies against the Pope." There was, it seemed to the Frenchman, "not a village feast nor pastime anywhere in which there [was] not something inserted in derision of the Holy Father."[10] "Misruled persons," then, were among the vanguard of the Reformation.

In this context of successful promotion of polemical misrule, a royal proclamation altering feast days, dated July 12, 1541, documents an effort to disrupt innovative misrule in that, while *reinstituting* the lately abrogated Catholic feasts of St Mary Magdalene and others, it also *banned* inversionary rites touching upon religion:

> And whereas heretofore diverse and many superstitious and childysshe observations have been usid, and yet to this day are observed and kept in many and sundry partes of this realm as upon sainte Nicolas, ... the holye Innocentes, and such like; children be strangelye decked and apparelid to counterfaite priestes, bysshopps ...; and boyes doo singe masse and preache in the pulpit, ... the kyng's majestie therefore ... commaundeth that from henceforth all such superstitions be loste and clyerlye extinguished throughowte ... his realms.[11]

Most assume that this section of the proclamation simply reflects a Protestant ban on the ceremonies of the Boy Bishop associated with the Catholic feasts of St Nicholas (December 6) and of Holy Innocents (December 28). If so, why did Protestants also reinstate other Catholic feasts? And why did they ban customs that would seem to allow the iconoclastic mockery recently proposed by Morison that had become so politically notable as to be lamented by the ambassador Marillac? And, why was there such a marked concern about "childysshe" misrule engaged in by "children" or "boyes"? For that matter, why would a ban

9 Ethan Shagan, *Popular Politics and the English Reformation* (Cambridge, 2003), 136–7, 131.
10 James Gairdner and R. H. Brodie (eds), *Letters and Papers, Foreign and Domestic, Henry VIII* (London, 1894), vol. XIV, part 1, 558.
11 *Tudor Royal Proclamations*, no. 203, 33 Henry VIII (1541), 1: 301–2.

on *Catholic* misrule be considered necessary at this time? Ultimately, historical context and accounts of boyish misrule at the colleges not only demonstrate that a crackdown on so-called papist festivities was unnecessary as of 1541, but also that church traditionalists now in power, notably Stephen Gardiner and Edmund Bonner, appear to have been reversing course and reining in iconoclastic excesses in misrule that Cromwell had unleashed before his fall.

At Cambridge, especially, misrule reflected the innovative and iconoclastic propaganda promoted by radical evangelical reformers. Indeed, the Boy Bishop's last appearance in the college records of Cambridge was at King's College in 1534–35,[12] at a time when evangelicals had dampened enthusiasm for the tradition and well before the 1541 ban. By 1530, the tradition of a Boy Bishop at King's, where entries "*pro tunica ordinanda pro Episcopo*" had appeared on "die *sancti Nicholai*" semi-regularly from 1450–51 through 1529–30 (yearly since 1527) had already broken down,[13] as first Erasmian- and Lutheran- and then Cromwellian-inspired iconoclasm flourished. Waning enthusiasm for the custom suggests that traditional inversionary rites faded as former participants witnessed their character being converted by Reformation appropriation. Following 1530–31,[14] theatrical accounts, now entered by evangelicals in English rather than Latin, are dominated by iconoclasm at Christ's (founded in 1439 and refounded under its current name in 1505), and, after 1534–35,[15] St John's (founded 1511).

It should further be noted that most surviving evidence not drawn from "sixteenth-century partisan propaganda" points to a traditional Boy Bishop ceremony strikingly different in character than Reformation-era misrule.[16] Whereas an inventory for the Boy Bishop from King's College, Cambridge, in 1505–6 included such carefully preserved items as "a gowne of skarlett with a whode for the same furred with white," "a miter of white damaske with … perles and vj other stones," "ffyne knytt

---

12 Alan H. Nelson (ed.), *Cambridge*, Records of Early English Drama, 2 vols (Toronto, 1989), 2: 731 (hereafter cited as REED).

13 Ibid., 1: 32–100.

14 Ibid., 1: 102 ff.

15 Ibid., 1: 109 ff.

16 Richard L. de Molen, "The Boy-Bishop Festival in Tudor England," *Moreana* 45 (February 1975): 17–28; 18.

gloves," "a noche of gold havyng a precius stone in the myddes and iij grete perles aboute [it]," and "Rynges of gold for the bisshop,"[17] accounts for the post-Reformation Lord of Misrule, we shall see, would include instead "olde ... vestmente[s]"[18] representing proverbial "Romish rags." Like the inventory at King's, other pre-Reformation records of *Ornamentis Episcopi Puerorum* consist of "precious" vestments elaborately decorated, including: "i white cope, ... with ... orferes [i.e., borders of] redde sylkes, with does of gold," "i vesture, redde, with lyons of silver, with brydds [birds] of gold," "i myter, well garneshed with perle and precious stones," "iiij rynges of silver and gilt, with four redde precious stones," "i pontifical with silver and gilt, with a blew stone in hytt," "a hode of skarlett, lyned with blue sylk."[19] Westminster Abbey inventories contained items of such extraordinary beauty and detail as

> The vj myter of Seynt Nycholas bysshoppe, the grounde therof of whyte sylk, garnysshed complete with floures, gret and small, of sylver and gylte, and stones ..., with the scripture, *Ora pro nobis Sancte Nicholai*, embroidered theron in perll, the sydes sylver and gylt, and the toppys sylver and gylt, and enamelyd with ij labelles of the same, and garnysshed in lyk maner, and with viij long bells of sylver and gylt.[20]

Consistent with such ornate, ceremonious vestments that more likely inspired reverence than riot, other evidence unearthed by Richard de Molen reveals that the Boy Bishop seems to have been less about "catharsis and burlesque" than spiritual, Pauline-inspired inversion.[21] Later anti-papist misrule, featuring burlesques of Catholic ritual (and of the Boy Bishop himself), was of a very different stripe than the traditional Boy Bishop ceremony; its licensed, jeering iconoclasm attacked ritual, hierarchy, and devotion in ways radically different than pre-Reformation Pauline inversion of authority.

17 REED, 1: 79–81.
18 Ibid., 1: 123, 127.
19 John Gough Nichols (ed.), *Two Sermons Preached by the Boy Bishop at St Paul's ... with an Introduction ... by Edward F. Rimbault* (Westminster, 1875), xxiv–xxv.
20 Ibid., xxvi.
21 de Molen, "The Boy-Bishop Festival in Tudor England," 18.

Given the Boy Bishop ceremony's status as "religious ceremony, per se,"[22] and the absence of such rites at Cambridge after 1535, it is all the more significant that at stoutly evangelical Christ's College, Cambridge, the earliest payments to "the Lorde in Chrystynmes" – the favored Cambridge name for the Lord of Misrule presiding over pastimes during the Christmas season – "for players garmentes" are recorded as of 1539,[23] that is, at the peak of an iconoclastic Reformation campaign featuring an "orgy of destruction and dissolution" of relics and monasteries between 1536 and April of 1540.[24] Such college revels were spurred on by Cromwell's campaign, and payments appear in Cambridge accounts from 1536–37, 1537–38, and 1539–40 for "mimis domini Cromwell" and "lorde Crumwelles players," who left an increase in anti-papist revels in their wake.[25]

At St John's College, evidence of iconoclastic and innovative playing includes the contents of costume chests traceable from 1540.[26] After Cromwell and Cambridge reformer Robert Barnes were martyred later in that year, the "St John's College Register of Inventories" of 1540–41 and 1541–42 defiantly catalogues "Plaiares Garmentes Lienge in the chest," including a number of vestments used for performances, such as "Item xxviij[ti] stoles," "Item ij grene vestimentes," "Item a yellow olde silke cope," "Item a olde white vestmente," "Item ij white aulter clothes with rede crosses," and "an owld cope now turned yn to a cote garded with stoles"[27] (guarded long coats being the wear of fools), while noting "[v]estmentes," remarkably, in connection to "ye comedies."[28] As the anti-papist plays Morison had envisaged were set forth "before the peoples eies," such playing struck the eyewitness John Christopherson, who received his BA from St John's, Cambridge, in 1540–41, and his MA in 1543, as impious:

22 Ibid., 17.
23 REED, 1: 117. 1539 coincides with the presence of evangelical Nicholas Grimald, who took zealous revels with him to Oxford with *Christus Rediuiuus* (Cologne, 1543). F. S. Boas, *University Drama in the Tudor Age* (Oxford, 1914), 26.
24 Roger Lockyer, *Tudor and Stuart Britain, 1471–1714* (1964; New York, 1993), 61.
25 REED, 1: 112, 114, 119.
26 Ibid., 1: 111.
27 Ibid., 1: 123, 127.
28 Ibid., 1: 122.

At [that] tyme ... y̆ devil, for y̆ better furtherauce of heresy, piked out ... people, that shuld ... set forward his purpose, as wel as false preachers dyd in the pulpet: that is to say, ... players ... to set forth openly before mens eyes the wicked blasphemye, that they had co[n]trived for the defacing of all rites, ceremonies, and all the whole order, used in the administration of the blessed Sacramentes.[29]

At Christopherson's own St John's, in defiance of the 1541 ban on "counterfaite" churchmen, a Lord of Christmas (i.e., Lord of Misrule) and his attendant seasonal revels were promoted in the statutes of 1544–45, whereas neither the prior statutes (1516, 1524, 1530) nor the subsequent ones (1560) mention a Lord at all.[30] Accounts reflect payments of "xx s" for "playinge the lorde" or "playng the lord in Chrystynmas" as early as 1545–46.[31] Cromwell's anti-papist brand of misrule was not to be deterred among the "boyes" at college, whatever proclamations might say.

Indeed, at Christ's College, even more definitive evidence of evangelical theatrical misrule surfaces in the sensational scandal recorded in the 1544–45 letters exchanged between Stephen Gardiner, the traditionalist bishop of Winchester (1531–51 and 1553–55) named Chancellor of Cambridge to replace Cromwell during the Henrician regime's religious retrenchment,[32] and Protestant Matthew Parker, who was vice-chancellor at Cambridge and, along with the martyred Thomas Bilney and Robert Barnes, one of a group of Cambridge Reformers promoting the Reformation in England.[33] The letters were prompted by Gardiner's discovery of the performance of an "intolerable" play called *Pammachius*, "late played in chrystys college," that was aptly deemed provocation to "Innouation and disorder."[34]

29 Boas, *University Drama*, 43, 44.
30 G. C. Moore Smith, *College Plays Performed in the University of Cambridge* (Cambridge, 1923), 18.
31 REED, 1: 143.
32 C. D. C. Armstrong, "Gardiner, Stephen (*c.* 1495/8–1555)," in *Oxford Dictionary of National Biography* (Oxford, 2004); available online at www.oxforddnb.com/view/article/10364.
33 D. J. Crankshaw and A. Gillespie, "Parker, Matthew (1504–1575)," in *Oxford Dictionary of National Biography* (Oxford, 2004); available online at www.oxforddnb.com/view/article/21327.
34 REED, 1: 133.

The decidedly polemical *Pammachius*, authored by German Reformation propagandist Thomas Kirchmeyer, was first published in 1538 and republished at Wittenberg in 1542 in a collection of the author's plays dedicated to the reformer Archbishop Cranmer. As a piece of polemical satire against papal ceremony and abuses, both real and imaginary, Kirchmeyer's ribald play achieved considerable fame throughout Europe among extremist reformers. *Pammachius* tells the sensational story of a fictional pope who determines to worship Satan rather than Christ. With Satan's help, this imaginary pope takes his place as Antichrist, deposes Caesar, and institutes blasphemous ceremonies until God allows the apostle Paul and Truth to return to earth to expose Pammachius's abuses. The satire ends with the result undetermined,[35] in an urgent call to action that reverberated in the halls at Christ's for decades after the 1544 performance.

In letters unfolding the details of the production, it becomes clear that the play proceeded with the full support of resident Protestant authorities. For instance, the college paid "wellnigh xx nobles allowed bi the master" to bring it off. Although Parker insisted that the master had omitted "all such matter wherby offense might Iustly haue risen," the traditionalist Gardiner would learn that the play "reproved Lent fastinges[,] al ceremonies[,] and albeit the words of sacrament and masse wer not named[,] yet the rest of the matier wryten in ... the reproofe of them was expressed." Far from restraining "wylde wanton libertie," Cambridge authorities promoted a play that would "presumptuously mok and skorne the direction of their prince in matier of religion." Parker responded that the "entent" was merely "to plucke downe ye popes vsurped power," followed by the somewhat feeble assurance that he had discovered "by Inquistion not aboue two that wer offended." Gardiner, by contrast, found "thinges [to] be very far out of ordre both openly in the vniuersitie and seuerally in the colleges" – a measure of how widespread evangelical misrule may have become at Cambridge – and the Privy Council instructed Parker that "no suche matter eyther in playe or in ernest [should] be ... medled with" and that in the future

35 On *Pammachius*, see James Bass Mullinger, *The University of Cambridge: From the Royal Injunctions of 1535 to the Accession of Charles the First* (Cambridge, 1884), 73–4.

Cambridge heads must take "speciall ... care as if any misordre be among the yowugth ye refourme it."[36] It is unclear, however, whether ensuing payments at Christ's for "souing ye pleyers gere and sowynges the albes [clerical vestments]" in 1546–47[37] reflect quite the kind of "refourme" the Council had in mind.

The 1541 proclamation banning religiously inspired misrule cannot be taken as unambiguous evidence of a sustained Reformation "onslaught on many kinds of inversionary laughter" – implicitly Catholic – "which had hitherto flourished largely unchecked,"[38] since, ironically, most of the evidence points to the conclusion that it was instead restraining the radical misrule Cromwellian-era evangelicals had initiated and unleashed. Indeed the 1541 ban merely extended Henry's administrative efforts to reverse course. In 1539, the conservative Six Articles had reaffirmed most Catholic doctrine, and, in 1540, Cromwell had been executed. The 1541 proclamation against "children ... strangelye ... apparelid to counterfaite priestes[,] bysshopps," and "boyes ... sing[ing] masse"[39] was part of a traditionalist crackdown by the Privy Council on heretical "misordre ... among the yowugth."[40]

Subsequent injunctions further clarify that it was the Protestant "Innouation and disorder" opposed by Gardiner that were undoubtedly the target of the Privy Council bans. In April 1542, for instance, London's staunch traditionalist bishop, Edmund Bonner, ordered the clergy not to "permit or suffer any manner of common plays, games, or interludes, to be played, set forth, or declared" in mockery of "the blessed sacrament ... or any other sacrament ministered." By January 1543, Parliament, too, was trying to restrain iconoclastic misrule, drawing up an act that attacked the recent slew of polemical "printed bokes printed balades *playes* rymes songes and other fantasies" advocating Reformation and appealing "*speciallye [to] the youthe*."[41]

The motives behind such official sanctions against boyish evangelical

---

36 All previous quotes in this paragraph are from REED, 1: 133–40.
37 Ibid., 1: 144.
38 Keith Thomas, "The Place of Laughter in Tudor and Stuart England," *Times Literary Supplement* 21 (January 1977): 77–81; 79.
39 *Tudor Royal Proclamations*, 1: 301–2.
40 REED, 1: 140.
41 Anglo, *Spectacle*, 271; emphases added.

misrule appear all the more clearly against the backdrop of Susan Brigden's findings in her classic essay, "Youth and the English Reformation," according to which Henrician traditionalists viewed Protestantism as "a conspiracy in which 'lewde laddys' took concerted action to spread their heresy." When proclamations banning religious misrule were issued, traditionalists did in fact have cause to worry about "lewde laddys" or "foolish boys." Early attacks upon the mass were frequently undertaken by youths, so that the young were "among the first Protestant martyrs for their sacramentarianism," and when assaults upon the clergy became widespread throughout England in the 1540s "it was usually young people who were the aggressors." If Brigden is correct in observing that iconoclasm – and I would specify iconoclastic *misrule* – was among the "new ... pastimes" ushered in by the Reformation, then it is surely no coincidence that "it was the young," to whom misrule was most likely to appeal, "who were the statue smashers."[42]

"WHAN YE CHRISTENMAS LORDES CAME": FROM EDWARD'S COURT TO INNS OF COURT AND CAMBRIDGE

Despite late Henrician efforts to repress it, evangelical misrule expanded during the zealous reign of Edward VI (1547–53), when royally sponsored entertainments at court were dominated by anti-papist revels. Such revels were initially organized by Sir Thomas Cawarden, Master of Revels and a "committed evangelical"[43] who "collaborated in devising and producing propaganda under Somerset['s Protectorship]."[44] Revels Accounts indicate that the first season of Edwardian entertainment, at Shrovetide, 1547–48, included an anti-papist play in which Edward himself performed as a priest[45] and which required "Cardynalles hates

---

[42] Susan Brigden, "Youth and the English Reformation," in *The Impact of the English Reformation 1500–1640*, ed. Peter Marshall (London, 1997), 55, 65, 67, 72, respectively.

[43] William B. Robison, "Cawarden, Sir Thomas (*c.* 1514–1559)," in *Oxford Dictionary of National Biography* (Oxford, 2004); available online at www.oxforddnb.com/view/article/37270.

[44] Streitberger, *Court Revels*, 195.

[45] Albert Feuillerat (ed.), *Documents Relating to the Revels at Court in the Time of King Edward VI and Queen Mary* (Louvain, 1914), 20, 22, 194, 255–8.

for players" and "ffyne golde for the making of Crownes & Crosses for the poope in playe." The 1550–51 season likewise involved papist "me[i]ters for plaiers."[46] But it is especially entertainments performed by the crown favorite George Ferrers, "promoted to the royal household," appropriately enough, "by Cromwell in 1539"[47] and later appointed as the Lord of Misrule for the last two years of Edward's reign, that best reveal the incredible scale – and zeal – of Edwardian misrule.

Ferrers's innovative antics as the Lord of Misrule can only be appreciated fully if considered in contrast to the reigns of other Christmas Lords. As Anglo observed, "royal Lords of Misrule, though of annual appointment, had never played a major part in court festivals" prior to Ferrers,[48] and the Lord of Misrule himself appears not to have been so prominent in any court before Edward's. Thus, E. K. Chambers noted that, although household accounts under Henry VII mention "a Lord or Abbot of Misrule for nearly every Christmas in the reign" and under Henry VIII "annually … with one exception, until 1520," "Little information can be gleaned as to the functions of the Lord of Misrule in the first two Tudor reigns."[49] As for that little which is definitely known, W. R. Streitberger finds that a William Ringley was named as either Abbot or Lord of Misrule in 1491–92, 1492–93, 1495–96, 1500–1, and 1501–2,[50] just as a William Wynnsbury was named in records as Abbot of Misrule in 1508–9 and Lord of Misrule in 1509–10, 1512–13, 1513–14, and 1514–15 and was perhaps the unnamed Lord in 1510–11 and 1511–12.[51] Of those entertainments, Streitberger speculates that "given the amounts of … imprests, payments, and rewards (which on occasion mention 'revels')," at least Wynnsbury's entertainments between 1508 and 1515 were "probably elaborate," since their cost points to the lavish "participatory revels" which Henry VIII "preferred to plays."[52]

---

[46] Ibid., 5–6, 26, 49, respectively.
[47] Streitberger, *Court Revels*, 194.
[48] Anglo, *Spectacle*, 309.
[49] E. K. Chambers, *The Medieval Stage*, 2 vols (Oxford, 1903), 1: 403–4.
[50] Streitberger, *Court Revels*, 429.
[51] Ibid., 89. Other unnamed Abbots or Lords of Misrule are also recorded in 1489–90, 1502–3, 1504–5, 1505–6, 1506–7, 1507–8, and 1534–5 (429).
[52] Ibid.

Although evidence unearthed by the REED project may some day alter the picture, it is worth noting that the Lord of Misrule himself, the English embodiment of the character "Carnival," seemingly never became so important a figure in England as in mainland Europe, just as Shrovetide never developed in England quite as it did elsewhere.[53] In the same way, the tradition of the Feast of Fools, so important on the continent, did not long remain in England: "the few notices of it are all previous to the end of the fourteenth century."[54]

Clearly, previous analysis of English misrule insisting that Edwardian favorite Ferrers's "reign" points to a "continuum" with prior traditions (even though his is "the first [Lord of Misrule] … whose reign can be enjoyed in any detail") is mistaken, all the more so when claiming continuity with revels at the inns of court (Ferrers had studied law at Lincoln's Inn after receiving his BA from Cambridge in 1531).[55] Rather, an innovative Edwardian expansion in misrule is especially noteworthy at the inns where, prior to Edward, drama and Lords of Misrule had not been prevalent: few records of revels involving dramatic entertainment exist at all at any inns before the 1550s.[56] At Gray's Inn, for instance, the Lord of Misrule first appeared after Edward's accession.[57] Accounts of the first appearance of a Lord of Misrule at Gray's Inn, in 1550, actually reveal haphazard innovation in ordering that "*thenceforth* there should

---

[53] See Chris Humphrey, *The Politics of Carnival: Festive Misrule in Medieval England* (Manchester, 2001), 65, 68; C. Davidson, "Carnival, Lent, and Early English Drama," *Research Opportunities in Renaissance Drama* 36 (1997): 123–4.

[54] Chambers, *The Medieval Stage*, 1: 321–2.

[55] Marie Axton, *The Queen's Two Bodies: Drama and the Elizabethan Succession* (London, 1977), 8. In his study, William Ball cites only masques from the Jacobean period and a Restoration mock court. *Lincoln's Inn: Its History and Tradition* (London, 1947), 51.

[56] W. C. Richardson, *A History of the Inns of Court* (Baton Rouge, LA, [1975]), 211. Prior festivity focused on eating and holding courts. F. A. Inderwick, *A Calendar of the Inner Temple Records*, vol. 1: *1505–1603* (London, 1896), 57. Iconoclastic misrule did appear in 1526 at a Gray's Inn performance by John Rowe featuring Morris dances. The chronicler Hall wrote that such was "highly praised of all menne, sauyng … Cardinall [Wolsey]," who was "sore displeased" (Anglo, *Spectacle*, 238–9). Some participants were jailed and the lead, "known Protestant activist" Simon Fish, fled to the continent. Paul White, "Theatre and Religious Culture," in *A New History of Early English Drama*, ed. John D. Cox and David Scott Kastan (New York, 1997), 138.

[57] Chambers, *The Medieval Stage*, 1: 417.

be no comedies called Interludes in this House out of Term times, but when the Feast of the Nativity ... is solemnly observed" and in proclaiming that "when there shall be any such Comedies, then all the Society at that time in the Commons, [shall] bear the charge of the Apparel."[58] Like Cambridge statutes, such orders point to an attempt to perpetuate *recently instituted* innovations (here, comedies).

Edwardian efforts to establish a continuous tradition of misrule revels failed, however, as subsequent instances were abortive and sporadic. Indeed, at Gray's Inn, where the "Lord" or "Prince" came to be known by the title "Purpoole" (after the area in which the inn was situated), the first known Purpoole did not reign until 1587.[59] At the Inner Temple, the first dramatic revels to draw notice, also occurring subsequent to Ferrers's absurd Edwardian misrule at court, were the stately Christmas revels of 1561–62. These extraordinary revels occurred during the reign of Lord Robert Dudley (Elizabeth's staunchly Protestant earl of Leicester) as Christmas Lord, when the first known five-act tragedy in English, *Gorboduc*, was performed.[60] As F. A. Inderwick concluded, "Excepting the special entertainment for Lord Robert Dudley in 1561, the revels were not apparently so fully kept up from 1555 till the end of Elizabeth's reign."[61]

Just as it had at the inns, iconoclastic misrule at Cambridge expanded dramatically under Edward. Whereas only the vaguest sense of the tradition of Tudor Cambridge Lords prevailed in theatre histories, more can now be gleaned from Cambridge accounts compiled in Alan H. Nelson's Records of Early English Drama (REED) volumes. These records reveal that the eruption of misrule in the late 1540s is not merely an accident of recordkeeping, but that Cambridge Lords of Misrule and their theatrical revels were actively promoted by the militant Edwardian administration at the colleges, just as they had been promoted by Henrician era reformers. At St John's College, for instance, after misrule was vigorously restrained by Henry's administration in 1545, payments to a Lord of Misrule reappear in 1547–48, 1548–49, and 1549–50, and a costume

---

58 Reginald J. Fletcher (ed.), *The Pension Book of Gray's Inn: 1569–[1800]* (London, 1901–1910), Appendix II, 1: 496; emphasis added.
59 Richardson, *History of the Inns of Court*, 227.
60 Ibid., 221.
61 Inderwick, *Calendar of the Inner Temple Records*, 1: 490.

inventory appears in 1548. Receiving overt court approval, such misrule was prompted by the appearance at Cambridge of "the Kynges players" and "my lorde Protectors players" in 1547–48.[63]

An indication that evangelical St John's particularly established precedents promoting iconoclastic misrule may be found in the history of its disciple, Trinity. John Dee boasted that after he was "out of St Iohn's Colledge" and then "chosen Fellow of Trinity Colledge" (founded 1546–47), it was "by my advise, & by my endeavours" that there was a "Christmas Magistrate, first named … emperor" there, *c.* 1547. Although actual payments to the "lord in Christynmas" were not recorded until 1552–53, other Trinity accounts show "An Inuetory off all vestymentes coppes & altar clothis" (1547–48), including entries for no fewer than fourteen "cop*pes* and alt*ar* clothis" that were "*brokin att plais for players garments*"; that is, Catholic vestments converted into, or used as, theatrical costumes.[64] G. C. Moore Smith found as well Christmas-Shrovetide charges at Trinity in 1549–50 "for puddings," "for Cheese," and "for good aile [for] M[r] Atkingesons players" and his "play," and, in 1550–51, "for ii Loynes & a breste of mutton for M[r] Atkynsons players" again. In the latter year, accounts show an unprecedented boom in theatrical activity, totaling six performances of "play[s]" or by "players,"[65] likely overseen by the Trinity "emperor" acting, as did other Christmas Lords, as a master of pastimes.

Like St John's and its imitator Trinity, other Cambridge colleges experienced Edwardian inspiration for misrule and revels. For example, the first record of a mock Christmas king at King's College appears in 1547–48.[66] Novel costume chests are recorded not just at St John's in connection with the 1547–48 revels but at Queens' College (founded under its current name in 1448) in 1547–48[67] and at King's College in 1552–53,[68] a year in which we also find 4*s.* were paid at King's "for

62 REED, 1: 152, 159, 165.
63 Ibid., 1: 154.
64 Ibid., 1: 155, 183, 152–3, respectively; emphasis added.
65 Moore Smith, *College Plays*, 44, 53.
66 REED, 2: 731.
67 Moore Smith, *College Plays*, 31.
68 Alan H. Nelson, *Early Cambridge Theatres: College, University, and Town Stages, 1464–1720* (Cambridge, 1994), 111.

makynge thunder against the plays" and that Catholic vestments there, too, were "transposyd into players garmentes."[70] Queens' College, characterized by its marked "sympathy with the Reformers,"[71] definitely followed the Edwardian pattern of revels innovation in recording payments for items such as marmalade, cakes, wine and fruit in 1546–47, 1547–48, and 1548–49 when the Christmas king of the college ruled ("*quando rex collegii regalis*").[72] In the last season, polemical, anti-papist tenor in misrule is reflected in the title of one of the plays: *Hypocrisis*, a "*tragoedia.*" More enigmatic perhaps, though consistent with misrule of some kind, is the 1551–52 riotous fenestra-clasm indicated in payments of 8*s*. 4*d*. for repairs to forty panes of glass from the western windows of one hall after a play ("*pro reparatione* 40 *pedum vitri in occidentali fenestra aulae post lusus*").[73] During the same period that three of Queens' College's altars were overthrown and the painted images on the walls were whitewashed,[74] a stage was built between the years 1546–47 and 1548–49,[75] a heavens was erected for plays ("*erectione coeli in lusu*") for the riotous season of 1551–52, and an inventory of players garments was completed in 1552–53.[76] Finally, the same evangelical Nicholas Robinson,[77] who would later praise what "a wonderful thing" Nicholas Udall's lost iconoclastic Henrician comedy *Ezechias* was when it was revived during Elizabeth's 1564 Cambridge visit,[78] is associated under Edward with a "commoedia" for which he had "taken downe

69 Moore Smith, *College Plays*, 29.
70 Nelson, *Early Cambridge Theatres*, 64.
71 Mullinger, *University of Cambridge*, 45.
72 REED, 1: 146, 150, 157.
73 Moore Smith, *College Plays*, 52, 45, respectively.
74 V. H. H. Green, *Religion at Oxford and Cambridge* (London, 1964), 94.
75 Alan H. Nelson, "Early Staging in Cambridge," in *A New History of Early English Drama*, eds John D. Cox and David Scott Kastan (New York, 1997), 59–67; 59. The Queens' College stage, constructed some thirty years before the Theatre in Shoreditch, could be erected and dismantled annually, and lasted some ninety years, according to a 1638 inventory (59).
76 Moore Smith, *College Plays*, 29; Nelson, *Early Cambridge Theatres*, 113, 183–4.
77 Robinson opposed "the dreggs of [popish] superstition" and "the closing up of God's word … in an unknown tongue" (i.e., Latin) and even boasted a "reputation … as a severe persecutor of Catholics." J. Gwynfor Jones, "Robinson, Nicholas (*c.* 1530–1585)," in *Oxford Dictionary of National Biography* (Oxford, 2004); available online at www.oxforddnb.com/view/article/23860.
78 REED, 2: 1137–8.

... ij kassokes of sylke" in 1552 at Queens' College. Here was theatrical innovation indeed, as Cambridge witnessed an unprecedented flurry of iconoclastic revels and misrule, with the most activity centered in Protestant seedbeds.

In addition to burgeoning drama, misrule processions also emerged at the university. John Mere's diary yields evidence of such a practice in two Marian era entries from 1556–57. One of these tells us: "On sonday ... ye lorde of christes college *came Christmas lyke* thither *with a drum* before hym &c." Although here there is only an ambiguous reference to a full-scale procession, a drum and the coming "Christmas lyke" would almost surely have encouraged such a following. The second entry clearly reflects some sort of procession: "One Tuesday candlemas day ... Item ye Christmas lorde at trinite college was had from ye churche to ye hall with drum[,] bylles &c which [was] ... liked not." In this case, a journey from the church to the college hall proceeded "with drum," weapons, and the tantalizing "&c." The only other accounts of Lords that "came" to the university, evidently in procession, are from zealous Christ's, one in 1539–40, in the wake of Cromwellian iconoclasm, and the other an Edwardian reference from 1552–53.[80] If we are not told *how* these Lords came, more detailed information and more promising evidence of processions and their often iconoclastic character appear in the "St John's College Register of Inventories" in 1548–49.

Building on the aforementioned statutes of 1544–45, the 1548–49 entry includes a "decree of the Master and the xij Seniors" that the "Plaiers Apparell" listed "be preserved & kept from yere to yere of him, which shalbe Lord In Christmas, And so the said Lord to deliuer the same apparel bi Indenture to his next Lorrd successor."[81] The record reflects both the prior misrule established in 1544–45 and a still some-what novel determination to preserve a tradition "kept from yere to yere," in perpetuity, by statute. Among items listed here are some that we might expect from any generic Lord (e.g., several "fooles coote[s]" in various states of repair, "ii Crownes one Imperial & ye oyer regal," "iij scepters," "a fooles dagger of wodd," and "A silk gold cap with a cockes

79 Ibid., 1: 182.
80 Ibid., 1: 62, 200, 174 and 2.736, respectively.
81 Ibid., 1: 159–60.

hed in ye crown"), but also others hinting at more pointed anti-papist intent: "A miter," "A long pest of silk & gold lined with blew bokeram" (likely a Catholic priest's stole), "iij shildes ... two with [superstitious] red draggones," "ii [other] draggones," "ii black develles cootes with hornes," two "steple capp[s] [perhaps bishops' hats]," one being "couered with painted clothe" and the other in two of the fool's traditional colors "painted blew & grene," and "ii past[e] hates."[82] The several pairs listed here suggest their use in mock religious processions, going two by two, for "religious procession ... [was] featured in evangelical propaganda."[83]

Given that Edwardian Cambridge probably witnessed an anti-papist tradition of misrule processions by 1548–49, it is interesting to note that at St John's, ultimately one of "the colleges with the strongest puritan element,"[84] the "Master" appears three times in the "Register of Inventories" as an authorizing official for the aim of establishing and perpetuating its recent tradition. The identity of the 1548–49 Lord of Misrule is noteworthy, for he would later be of some importance: "Item to Mr leaver for playng ye lord yn chrystynmas." This "Mr leaver" is the same one into whose "Custodie" the apparel in the coffers is "committed": "to the Custodie of Mr Thomas Lever" until this "said Lord [is] to deliuer ... [them] to his next Lord successor."[85] Not coincidentally, this Thomas Lever, having been thoroughly indoctrinated via such anti-papist misrule, would later declare himself to be one of the "godly preachers which have utterly forsaken Antichrist *and all his Romish rags*."[86] Lever indeed "quickly became the leader of the more advanced evangelical party" at the university,[87] a prominent leader of the puritan party, a thorn in the side of the Elizabethan church, and a

82 Ibid., 1: 161–2.
83 R. W. Scribner, *For the Sake of the Simple Folk: Popular Propaganda for the German Reformation* (Cambridge, 1981), 96. Scribner does not refer to Cambridge accounts here.
84 Patrick Collinson, *The Elizabethan Puritan Movement* (1967; Oxford, 1990), 127–8.
85 REED, 1: 159.
86 Collinson, *Elizabethan Puritan Movement*, 48; emphasis added.
87 Ben Lowe, "Lever, Thomas (1521–1577)," in *Oxford Dictionary of National Biography* (Oxford, 2004); available online at www.oxforddnb.com/view/articlc/16535.

colleague of noted puritans such as Miles Coverdale, Anthony Gilby, John Foxe, Robert Crowley, Hugh Latimer, John Gough, John Field, and Thomas Cartwright. After Lever was made Master of St John's by royal mandate in 1551, he mentored Thomas Cartwright, who originally came up in 1547.[88] Cartwright's zealous sermons and lectures would eventually "thrust the university into turmoil" and "much divided" it, according to John Strype, "into two factions," being "the younger sort ... much for innovations" who "were followers of Cartwright's principles" versus "the graver sort" who "laboured to restrain" them.[89] Though Cartwright's fiery Elizabethan sermons might initially seem far removed from the misrule of his Edwardian youth, his appeal to "the younger sort" as well as his "radically anti-authoritarian" program were, in spirit, surprisingly resonant.[90] In any case, far from opposing misrule as would later puritan fellows,[91] in 1548, the Master of St John's, later exiled under Mary, promoted it.

When we turn to Christ's College, there too we find striking Edwardian enthusiasm for misrule. After a hiatus following innovation in the misrule of 1539–40, there are extant records of costume chests in 1550–51,[92] of visits by parish Lords of "trinitie parish" and "saint andrewes" who performed "shewes" in 1552–53,[93] and of payments to "ye carpenter for ... setting ... vp ... ye houses and other things" in connection with "S. Stephenson['s] play" in 1551–52.[94] This play was likely the clever mock-Terentian comedy *Gammer Gurton's Needle*,

<hr />

88 Collinson, *Elizabethan Puritan Movement*, 48–9, 51, 72, 74, 90, 92, 112.
89 Ibid., 123, 122.
90 Ibid., 124. During the 1564 royal visit to Cambridge in which Elizabeth deigned not to see all of the revival of Udall's iconoclastic *Ezechias* ("[a]fter enough had been seen"), the Queen first refused and then, being "so importuned ... that at last she consented," was unwittingly subjected to evangelical misrule: "The actors came in dressed as some imprisoned bishops. First came the bishop of London carrying a lamb in his hands as if he were eating it as he walked along, and then ... one ... in the figure of a dog with the Host in his mouth.... [T]he queen was so angry that she at once entered her chamber using strong language, and the men who held the torches ... left them in the dark, and so ended the ... scandalous representation." REED, 2: 1138, 1142–3.
91 Ibid., 1: 321.
92 Nelson, *Early Cambridge Theatres*, 111.
93 REED, 1: 177, 178.
94 Ibid., 1: 173; Moore Smith, *College Plays*, 28.

which features iconoclastic, carnivalesque mock-rituals involving conjuring, superstitious oaths, kneeling, candles, arse-kissing, and more of the most notorious scatology of the era in 1.5, 2.1, 2.2, and 5.2.[95] Account entries reflect the fact that "Christ's College was Edwardian (and later positively puritan), in its sympathies. In fact, the Master, Richard Wilkes, was ejected in 1553 and there was rapid turnover in personnel in the years immediately following," including the absence of William Stevenson, apparent author of *Gammer Gurton's Needle*, as, like Lever, a Marian exile until 1559.[96]

Also indicative of the evangelical character of Cambridge revels is the influence there of Martin Bucer, a friend of Cambridge Vice-Chancellor Matthew Parker. The Strasbourg reformer and mentor to Calvin was Regius Professor at Cambridge from 1549 to his death in 1551. While there, he advocated the use of drama in order to promote godliness. In *De Regno Christi* (*The Reign of Christ*; 1551), Bucer calls for playwrights "schooled in the knowledge of Christ's kingdom" to write plays for "schoolboys" in such a way as "to create and increase ... the horror of impiety and of the sowing and fostering of every kind of evil" – "both in the vernacular and in Latin and Greek," "in either kind of poetry, [whether] comic or tragic," with comedy defined as dealing with the "actions and fortunes ... of everyday, ordinary people."[97] Comedy in and of itself was not seen as inherently objectionable to early evangelicals; it was desirable so long as it was didactic and even (from a modern perspective) decidedly propagandist. Far from being morosely suspicious of laughter, the early evangelical movement and its membership were united and defined by jeering laughter at purported papist impiety. When he dedicated this work that promotes drama (including invective vernacular comedy) to Edward, Bucer was, quite literally, preaching to the converted.

---

95 See my "Reformation Satire, Scatology, and Iconoclastic Aesthetics in *Gammer Gurton's Needle*," *The Blackwell Companion to Tudor Literature and Culture, 1485–1603*, ed. Kent Cartwright (forthcoming, 2009).

96 C. W. Whitworth (ed.), *Three Sixteenth-Century Comedies* (New York, 1984), xxv.

97 Glynne Wickham, *Early English Stages 1300 to 1600*, 3 vols (New York, 1963), 2: part 1, Appendix C, "An Extract from *De Honestis Ludis* of Martin Bucer, 1551," 329–31.

Not coincidentally, then, apart from the initial eruption of misrule in the wake of Cromwell's propaganda, the bulk of the Tudor Cambridge records of Christmas Lords appear at Protestant centers during the Edwardian period. A 1549 order of the Edwardian visitors forbidding the appointment of Lords of Misrule at Cambridge[98] appears to have been political cover, given that it was not enforced. Neither were the 1547 statutes forbidding offensive joking about the Eucharist since the otherwise apparently illicit satirical dialogue *Jon Bon and Mast Person*, of 1548, by Luke Shepherd was actually favored at court where "the Courtiers wore it in their pockets."[99] Shepherd's satire, which openly invited mockery of the Catholic Eucharistic Host, begins, in fact, with an appropriated Catholic woodcut of a Corpus Christi procession (Figure 3) above the text:

> Alasse poore fooles, so sore ye be lade …
> For ye beare a great God, which ye yourselfes made
> Make of it what ye wyl, it is a wafer cake
> And between two Irons printed it is and bake
> And loke where Idolatrye is, Christe wyl not be there
> Wherfore ley downe your burden, an Idole ye do beare
> Alasse poore Fooles.[100]

Shepherd's satire, with its arrogation of imagery of religious procession, following the precedent of Cromwell-inspired collegiate iconoclasm and being favored at the zealous court of Edward, foreshadows the iconoclastic humor to come, on a larger scale, from the Lord of Misrule as embodied by the semi-professional clown Ferrers.

98 Boas, *University Drama*, 9.
99 John Strype, *Ecclesiastical Memorials, Relating Chiefly to Religion … Under King Henry VIII, King Edward VI, and Queen Mary*, vol. 2 (Oxford, 1822), 116.
100 Luke Shepherd, *Jon Bon and Mast Person*, in *An Edition of Luke Shepherd's Satires*, ed. Janice Devereux (Tempe, 2001), 50.

ℂ John Bon and
Mast person

☞ Alaſſe poore fooles, ſo ſore ye be lade
No maruel it is, thoughe your ſhoulders ake
For ye beare a great God, which ye yourſelfes made
Make of it what ye wyl, it is a wafar cake
And betwen two Irons printed it is and bake
And loke where Idolatrye is, Chriſte wyl not be there
Wherfore ley down your burden, an Idole ye do beare
☞ Alaſſe poore
Fooles

Figure 3. Woodcut of Corpus Christi procession, appropriated in anti-papist polemic, mirroring evangelical misrule. Luke Shepherd, *Jon Bon and Mast Person* (1548). By permission of the Huntington Library.

85

"THE HOBBY-HORSE IS FORGOT":
UNINTENDED CONSEQUENCES OF FERRERS'S MISRULE

Much insight into the evangelical character of George Ferrers's misrule can be gleaned from exceptionally detailed Edwardian era Revels Accounts and reports of the colorful reactions of contemporary chroniclers, diplomats, and diarists. Revealing the potential import of Ferrers's revels is the fact that his entertainments were the most costly of Edward's reign. Whereas the revels for the combined Christmas-Shrovetide season of 1550–51 cost a total of £31 4s. 4d., and whereas Edwardian revels cost as little as £19 3s. 2d. for the season of 1548–49, by contrast, the Christmas season entertainments of 1551–52, Ferrers's first as Lord of Misrule, cost a considerable £509 0s. 9½ d.[101] These extraordinary productions aroused considerable discomfort in the less forward contemporaries at court. Imperial ambassador Jehan Schyfve, noting that "one of the King's lesser gentlemen was created Lord of Misrule, which had not been done for fifteen or sixteen years"[102] (the last in fact being recorded in 1534–35),[103] reports in a letter dated January 18 of Ferrers's first season that "Not a few Englishman were highly scandalized" and that the Catholic "French and Venetian ambassadors, who were at Court at the time, showed clearly enough that the spectacle was repugnant to them."[104] The trouble appears to have resided in their anarchic evangelism.

Little of the sobriety that would mark later zealous Protestants could be found in Ferrers's revelry. Among the entertainments offered by Ferrers in 1551–52, for example, was a "dronken Maske."[105] Special directions for costuming Misrule's fool, played by one of the King's Players, John Smith, were also provided in the Revels Accounts: "one vices dagger & a ladle with a bable pendante … delivered to the Lorde of misrules foole … & other weapons for the lorde of Mysrule & his

---

[101] Feuillerat, *Documents Relating to the Revels*, 49, 55, 35, 40, 76.
[102] Royall Tyler (ed.), *Calendar of Letters, Despatches, and State Papers. Relating to the Negotiations Between England and Spain*, vol. 10 (London, 1914), 444.
[103] Streitberger, *Court Revels* 143, 429.
[104] Tyler, *Calendar of Letters*, 10: 444.
[105] Anglo, *Spectacle*, 306–7.

fooles." But the highlight, as described by diarist Henry Machyn, was Ferrers's arrival at Tower Wharf and the subsequent procession as the Lord of Misrule on January 4 in London where, in an iconoclastic public entertainment, there "was mad[e] a grett skaffold in Chepe hard by the crosse" – later confirmed as "at the crosse in Chepe."[107] This site, "right at the heart of the city," Margaret Aston notes, was "London's leading monument" and featured a "wealth of religious imagery" and "prob-lematical iconography," including a standing figure of the Virgin Mary and Christ Child and, at the very top, a cross; it was at this Catholic monument, which zealous reformers would come to call "that gorgeous Idoll,"[108] where "my lord dranke." Here the Lord of Misrule came in procession with "a gret company all in yellow and gren," colors tradi-tionally associated with misrule, but also, following the Lord himself, a hooded retinue of "[h]alff a hundred in red and wyht,"[109] colors associ-ated with "papistry." Despite recent assertions that "the political import of [Ferrers's] revels"[110] remains undetermined, the anti-papist signifi-cance suggested here may be even more confidently located elsewhere.

Catholic practices at which Ferrers's misrule took aim included religious processions. As the ambassador Schyfve records in reference to Ferrers's first season, in addition to "several witty and harmless pranks, he played other quite outrageous ones, for example, a religious proces-sion of priests and bishops." His Lord of Misrule even offered a crude burlesque of the ritual blessing of the eucharistic monstrance: "They paraded through the Court, and carried, under an infamous tabernacle, a representation of the holy sacrament in its monstrance, which they wetted and perfumed in most strange fashion, with great ridicule."[111] Despite its vague resemblance to the long-defunct Boy Bishop ceremony, which featured a solemn blessing of the altar,[112] as the "highly scandalised" reactions of contemporaries who found "the

106 Feuillerat, *Documents Relating to the Revels*, 73.
107 John Gough Nichols (ed.), *The Diary of Henry Machyn, Citizen and Merchant-Taylor of London, From AD 1550 to AD 1563* (London, 1848), 13–14.
108 Margaret Aston, *The King's Bedpost: Reformation and Iconography in a Tudor Group Portrait* (Cambridge, 1993), 108, 110, 111.
109 Nichols, *Diary of Henry Machyn*, 13–14.
110 Axton, *Queen's Two Bodies*, 9.
111 Tyler, *Calendar of Letters*, 10: 444.
112 On such, see Nichols, *Two Sermons Preached by the Boy Bishop*, vii–x.

spectacle … repugnant" reveal, Ferrers was offering post-Reformation propagandistic revisions of a pre-Reformation custom.

Hints of anti-papist import are even indicated in Machyn's description of the 1551–52 season procession being led by "furst a standard of yellow and grene sylke with Sant Gorge."[113] This saint appeared in the wake of a recent Edwardian assault on St George as a figure of Catholic legend. By the January 1550–51 season, Edward had already purged papist vestiges from the Order of St George, which he renamed the Order of the Garter, and whose observances he moved from the feast of the saint, near summer, to the fall.[114] The new statutes read:

> First, it is agreed that, whereas this ordre was called the ordre of saint George, whereby th'onour due to God was gevin to a creature, it shal no more be so called, nor yet saint George reputed as patron therof, but it shall be called th'ordre of the gartier, or defence of the trueth.[115]

In misrule the following year, which, Ferrers warned a rival, "was not of our device but of the Counseills appoyntement,"[116] St George in turn became the patron of disorder and popish superstition.

In Revels Accounts of the subsequent season, 1552–53, anti-papal Apocalyptic symbolism recorded in Ferrers's own detailed instructions reflects the Lord of Misrule's role in evangelical propaganda presenting a comic pope as Antichrist, the inversion of godliness. Notably, the Revels Accounts indicate that for the Lord's coat of arms Ferrers would require: "[T]he serpente *with sevin heddes* … is the chief beast of myne armes. / and the wholie bushe is the devise of my Crest / my worde is *semper ferians* … always feasting or *keeping holie daie*." Both the Apocalyptic beast associated with Rome and the mockery of keeping holy days underscore an anti-papist theme, as does the inclusion among his attendants of "a divine … Iuglers / tumblers / fooles / *friers and suche other*." Here, fools and friars are all of a piece. Indeed, at least one fool was clothed as a popish Vice, this time with "a vices coote" for King's Men clown "Iohn Smith of *white and redde damaske figured with goulde*

113 Nichols, *Diary of Henry Machyn*, 13.
114 John Gough Nichols (ed.), *Literary Remains of King Edward the Sixth*, vol. 2 (London, 1857), 529.
115 Ibid., 521.
116 Feuillerat, *Documents Relating to the Revels*, 59–60.

churche worke," that is, a Roman Catholic clerical vestment.   The pro
fessional clown Smith, appearing as a Vice in a clerical gown, portrayed
one of the "Iuglers," since "juggler" was a term regularly applied in
evangelical polemic to Catholic mass-priests.[118] Reformers ranging
from Wycliffe (who had called priests "the divels iugglers")[119] to late
Henrician and Edwardian Archbishop Thomas Cranmer (whose
"favourite word for transubstantiation was 'juggling'")[120] employed
such cant in order to indicate trickery and illusion in the Catholic mass.
Given the symbolism of the Romish beast, the clown Smith's priestly
garb, and the use of evangelical cant, the target of the iconoclastic jesting
was apparently the Catholic mass, another instance of Edwardian satire
that "above all else … attacked and derided the Catholic Mass."[121]

Ferrers's evangelical propaganda represented Catholicism as not only
carnivalesque but wicked, since, in addition to adopting the Apocalyptic
beast as his emblem, the Lord of Misrule appears seated upon "a
dragons head and dragons mowthe of plate and stoppes to burne like
fier."[122] Here the dragon carrying Misrule himself recalled what
Morison had formerly called "that wicked dragon the bishop of
Rome."[123] King Edward's revels thus aggressively combined carnivalesque symbolism – one Edwardian entertainment featured upside
down men in "legges and half bodies with leggpeces lyke armes and
handes … for a maske of tumblers to goe vpon theyr handes"[124] – and
iconoclastic iconography to provoke a visceral mixture of debasing
scorn and horror aimed at Catholicism.

To further anti-papist hostility, Ferrers's 1551–52 entertainment in
London culminated in his arrival at the scaffold at Cheapside Cross,
required "stockes," "a pyllary," "a payer of manacles," "Ieylers," and,
most ominously, a "*hedding block,*" all of which were "boghte for the

---

117 Ibid., 89–90, 97; emphases added.
118 Marie Axton (ed.), *Three Tudor Classical Interludes* (Cambridge, 1982), 19–20.
119 Paul Whitfield White, *Theatre and Reformation: Protestantism, Patronage, and Playing in Tudor England* (Cambridge, 1993), 126.
120 Axton, *Three Tudor Classical Interludes*, 20.
121 Janice Devereux (ed.), *An Edition of Luke Shepherd's Satires* (Tempe, AZ, 2001), xi, xx.
122 Feuillerat, *Documents Relating to the Revels*, 107–8.
123 Anglo, "Early Tudor Programme," 178.
124 Anglo, *Spectacle*, 316–17.

lorde of misrule and occupied abowte hym." Ferrers evidently staged a popish Misrule's elaborate mock-execution before a massive audience, according to Machyn, on "a gret brod skaffold" at the cross-idol in Cheapside where "there was a hoghed of wyne [at] the skaffold, and ther my lord dranke." Misrule entered London the following year accompanied not just by friars and fools, but by "[h]ys gayllers ..., stokes, and [h]ys axe, gyffes, and boltes, sum fast by the leges and sum by the nekes."[126] In employing such theatrics on a scaffold stage, Ferrers became a semi-professional stage clown, jeering against now-criminalized Catholicism.

A final striking instance of evangelicals using humorous carni-valesque cultural vehicles as propaganda may be found in the promi-nence of the Morris dance and its characteristic hobby horse in Ferrers's entertainments. Attacks on the iconic hobby horse would contribute to its eventual scarcity so that puritan hatred of it and the Morris became a byword in later Renaissance England, remembered in the proverbial phrase, "the hobby-horse is forgot."[127] In *Bartholomew Fair* (1614), for instance, Jonson's Zeal-of-the-Land Busy, looking upon a puppet stall, would rail: "Thy hobby-horse is an idol, a very idol, a fierce and rank idol" (3.652–3).[128] And Busy would then cast down the puppet stall (and, for good measure, the gingerbread stall as well) in a fit of inspired zeal against idols. Likewise, in a comic set-piece, Fletcher's puritan cobbler clown Hope-on-High Bomby, in the tragicomedy *Women Pleased* (1619–23), would cast off his hobby horse and rant against it in a set-piece in 4.1 as if it were the Apocalyptic Romish beast:

> The beast is an unseemly and a lewd beast,
> And got at Rome by the pope's coach-horses; ...
> I do defy thee, and thy foot-cloth too;
> And tell thee to thy face, this profane riding,
> (I feel it in my conscience, and I dare speak it,)
> This unedified ambling hath brought a scourge upon us;
> This hobby-horse sincerity we liv'd in,

---

[125] Feuillerat, *Documents Relating to the Revels*, 72; emphasis mine.
[126] Nichols, *Diary of Henry Machyn*, 14, 28–9.
[127] François Laroque, *Shakespeare's Festive World: Elizabethan Seasonal Entertain-ment and the Professional Stage*, trans. Janet Lloyd (Cambridge, 1993), 124.
[128] Ben Jonson, *Bartholomew Fair*, ed. G. R. Hibbard (New York, 1997).

War and the sword of slaughter: I renounce it,
And put the beast off thus, the beast polluted ... [*Throws off the hobby-horse*][129]

This later stereotypical antipathy, and the otherwise curious belief that the hobby horse was a popish image, makes it all the more striking that the anti-papist Edwardian revels during Ferrers's reign as Lord of Misrule focused disproportionately on the hobby horse. The revels of 1551–52 included a mock combat featuring several "hoby horses."[130] The entertainment calling for "as many ... as ye may spare,"[131] was, in the end, supplied with *thirteen* hobby horses, including a grotesque one "with 3 heads" for the Lord of Misrule, bought from a carver for a comic joust.[132] The entertainments of 1552–53 would require still more – "xxvj Hobby horses."[133] On both occasions, Machyn's diary confirms the conspicuousness of "morse danse dansyng" (1551–52), the "mores dansse," "ys mores dansse," and "ys morse dansse danssyng" (1552–53)[134] that would become an abomination or enormity to full-fledged puritans.

It is significant, then, that Morison had made special mention of using Morris dance "playes of Robyn hoode [and] mayde Marian," which featured "rebawdry"[135] for propaganda. At Edward's court, anti-papist festivity incorporated the Morris with some twenty-six hobby horses or a monstrous three-headed one alongside foolish priests, monks, friars, jugglers, tumblers, fools, religious processions, and the mass. Such imagery effectively realized Bucer's vision of employing spectacle to create antipathy toward purported Catholic impiety and promoted precisely the iconoclastic impulses later exhibited by the puritan clowns Busy and Bomby.

Just how evangelicals finally made this transition to utter antipathy

---

129 *The Works of Beaumont and Fletcher*, ed. Alexander Dyce (London, 1844), 7: 62–3; no lineation.
130 Anglo, *Spectacle*, 306–7.
131 Feuillerat, *Documents Relating to the Revels*, 59.
132 Chambers, *The Medieval Stage*, 1: 406.
133 Feuillerat, *Documents Relating to the Revels*, 91.
134 Nichols, *Diary of Henry Machyn*, 13, 28–9.
135 Anglo, "Early Tudor Programme," 179; on Maid Marian in the Morris, see Laroque, *Shakespeare's Festive World*, 122–8; and on Robin Hood, see 122–3.

toward misrule is, of course, a question requiring more research. It seems likely, however, that an intermediate step before absolute aversion was gradually transferred to festivity and laughter was simply ambivalence. Real evangelicals no less than fictional ones once used the comic and festivity purposefully before they came to prohibit it.

"LIKED NOT": MARIAN DISRUPTION OF EVANGELICAL MISRULE

Many traditionalists under Mary experienced their own aversion to the new brand of misrule. All signs indicate that misrule actually met stout opposition from the Marian administration, not just a lack of official enthusiasm. The cause here went beyond a wish to control popular hatred for the match to Phillip II, who, when he "came ryding thorugh London" in January 1554, was greeted by "boyes [who] peleted at [him] with snowballes."[136] Rather, the crackdown seemed to recognize that misrule, over the decades that the Reformation had established a strong footing in England, had come to be less about the temporary inversion of accepted hierarchy than the iconoclastic tearing down of "popery." Because evangelical propaganda and polemic had promoted the idea that Catholicism *was* folly, Marian authorities labored to disassociate irreverence and religion by censoring evangelical misrule. From the traditionalists' perspective, misrule was now necessarily associated above all with heresy. Mary's first proclamation forbade religious satire, singling out "playing" in any way "touching the high points and mysteries of Christian religion."[137] In 1554, as Parliament re-enacted medieval statutes against heresy, the visitation articles of Bishop Bonner (soon to be known as "Bloody Bonner") pursued printers and book-sellers associated with "slanderous books, ballads or plays, contrary to Christian religion" or any lay people who "jangled ... or played the fool" during mass or otherwise mocked the priests.[138]

---

136 Brigden, "Youth and the English Reformation," 61.
137 *Tudor Royal Proclamations*, no. 390, I Mary I (1553), 2: 6. Excluded from the ban was the more sober Boy Bishop, restored with other Catholic practices in a sweeping proclamation (no. 407, I Mary I [1554], 2: 37).
138 Eamon Duffy, *The Stripping of the Altars: Traditional Religion in England 1400–1580* (New Haven, CT, 1992), 544.

Given overwhelming evidence of expanding misrule during Edward's brief reign, the dearth of misrule in Marian accounts offers a stark contrast, particularly at Cambridge. At Trinity, payments to Lords of Misrule occur only in 1553–54 and 1554–55.[139] The latter entry for a pro-Marian "shew ... played cawled *Anglia deformata* [*and Anglia Restituta*]" constituted a brief Marian rebuttal to the disempowered evangelicals, after which, although some plays are still recorded, official enthusiasm for redirecting misrule diminished. Instead, at King's College, one "Carleton" was paid to convert ecclesiastical vestments formerly "transposyd into players garmentes" for anti-papist misrule under Edward back into vestments ("*Item sol. Carleton sacriste pro labore in conuertendis tunicis hystrionum in vestimenta ecclesie*").[140] Other Marian instances of Cambridge misrule met a hostile response, as Mere's 1556–57 diary recounts: "Item ye Christmas lorde at trinite college was had from ye churche to ye hall with drum[,] bylles &c *which the visitors liked not.*"[141] On this occasion, there must have been a procession from the church to a Cambridge hall, with weapons ("bylles" being long shafts with blades at the end). This time, however, the Marian "visitors" or inspectors who disliked the Lord's setting out from the church apparently detected iconoclasm in a mock-procession.

Unsupportive Marian attitudes toward misrule appear at Oxford as well. At Christ Church, where a Christmas Lord reigned, Frederick Boas noted, "as early as the reconstitution of the College in 1546," there seems to have been a tighter budget for misrule under Mary: "[T]here shall be *no more allowed* yearly towards the charges of the pastime in Christmas ... but for two Comedies 20*s* a piece and for two tragedies 20*s* a piece ... towards the Lords other charges also 13*s*. 4*d*. yearly to be allowed *and no more*." That Mary's administration did not favor collegiate misrule we may further determine from the fact that Trinity, Oxford, founded under Mary in 1556, never had a Lord of Misrule at all.[142]

As for London misrule, after a gap of four years following Edward's

---

139 REED, 1: 186, 187, 190.
140 Nelson, *Early Cambridge Theatres*, 64; Moore Smith, *College Plays*, 31.
141 REED, 1: 200; emphasis added.
142 All quotes and information in this paragraph are from Boas, *University Drama*, 7–8; emphasis added.

death, in 1557, within days of "Gospellers" trying to publicly perform a mock mass suggesting that "the communion was play," after which the ringleaders were burned for "herese," Machyn records a Lord of Misrule now defiantly riding through the city. This time, he set out from the now-Catholic Westminster Abbey with "m[a]ny disgyssyd in whytt." On this occasion, far from being licensed or welcomed, Misrule himself "was browth [brought] in-to the contur in the Pultre; and dyver[se] of ys men lay all nyght ther."[143] Contrary to the patronage misrule had experienced under Edward, under Mary, the Lord's company was treated to a night in jail.

At court, evidence likewise confirms, misrule was frowned upon during the reign of Edward's successors. Chambers notes, for example, that "neither Mary nor Elizabeth seems to have revived the appointment of a Lord of Misrule at court."[144] While Anglo attributed the lack of royally patronized misrule under Mary wholly to a dreary court characterized by hated Spaniards and a "psychosomatically pregnant" Queen, "sick in mind and body,"[145] the context of prior evangelical appropriation of misrule against Catholics, combined with the Marian crackdown on heresy and religious satire throughout England, now points to a more purposeful constraint of misrule.

SIGNS OF AN AFTERLIFE:
LITERARY VESTIGES OF EVANGELICAL MISRULE

Reformation propagandists initially took on with zeal and relish, R. W. Scribner demonstrates, the challenge to "desacrilise the numinous and withdraw it from the realm of religious veneration." Their goal was "the upturning of respect to contempt. … Awe … inverted to crude familiarity, dignity to indignity, religious respect to blasphemous contempt." The logic of misrule was ideally suited to such an agenda. As evidence of the Reformation's appropriation of carnivalesque humor during the first wave of propaganda (originating in Germany), Scribner observes in particular the marked focus on the inversion of cleric and layman in

---

143 All quotes in this paragraph are from Nichols, *Diary of Henry Machyn*, 160–2.
144 Chambers, *The Medieval Stage*, 1: 407.
145 Anglo, *Spectacle*, 339.

terms that aptly describe radical English Reformation propaganda as well; such populist "social inversion is found," he explains, "running throughout evangelical propaganda, where the common man, the evangelical peasant or the poor stand for the supporters of Christ and the Gospel, while the clergy stand for its opponents."[146]

English Protestant propaganda indeed often depicts rustic laymen inverting the authority of ignorant priests, with the former pointing out or laughing at the error of the latter; such were the dynamics of Shepherd's iconoclastic *Jon Bon and Mast Person* (1548), in which an illiterate but wily rustic – one who "wyl go to ploughe an[d] carte" (l. 7) – bests his traditionalist, pedantic parson in a theological discussion of transubstantiation and the Feast of Corpus Christi.[147] The carnivalesque ploughman Jon is marked as uneducated from the outset through clownish malapropisms as he humorously fails to recognize "What saynt is copsi cursty" (l. 11), whom he also refers to ridiculously as "cropsy cursty" (l. 31). The overbearing Parson condescendingly derides Jon as a "folishe felowe" (l. 33), a "mad man" (l. 38), "a dawe" or fool (l. 38), and as one guilty of "playne heresye" (l. 52) when the rustic expresses his doubts that a man could be transformed into bread or be carried in procession "in so smal a glasse" or case (l. 18) or when he surmises that the Parson makes "Christe an elfe" (l. 36), for the eucharistic host "is but a cake" (l. 46). Here, quite simply, Shepherd makes a mockery of transubstantiation. And so, after trapping the Parson in several bumbling logical inconsistencies, the shrewd and practical Jon dismisses him:

> … masse me no more massinges. The right way wil I walke
> For thoughe I have no learning yet I knowe chese from chalke
> And yche can perceive your juggling as crafty as ye walke.
> But leue your deuilish masse & ye communion to you take,
> And then will Christ be wt you euen for his promisse sake.
>
> (ll. 151–5)

With his iconoclastic suspicion of ceremony and ritual, his irreverent and carnivalesque upturning of hierarchy and tradition, his rejection of

---

146 Scribner, *For the Sake of the Simple Folk*, 83, 165, 168, respectively.
147 *Jon Bon and Mast Person* in Devereux, *An Edition*, 50–7; hereafter cited by line number.

the supposedly "devilish masse," and his abhorrence (in what would become recognizable puritan cant) of all "abhominable matter" (l. 89), Jon Bon clearly represents a devout Protestant.

When such early evangelical polemical tactics were furtively revived under Elizabeth, the times had changed and so the results were much different. At this point, carnival itself came to be linked stereotypically, however surprising it may now seem, to full-fledged *puritans*, especially after they used a carnivalesque clown's persona to subvert the Church hierarchy in the propagandistic Martin Marprelate Tracts. These sensational pamphlets touched off what Christopher Hill has called "the biggest scandal of Elizabeth I's reign."[148] Beyond its scandalous nature, one of the remarkable features of the Martinists' brand of puritan invective was the revival of what we can now recognize as earlier evangelicals' carnivalesque tactics. Like his evangelical forefathers, Martin understood that "[t]he most part of men could not be gotten to read any thing" either about Presbyterian theology or anything critical of the episcopacy: "I bethought mee therefore of a way whereby men might be drawne to do both." Employing such a rationale, in true Rabelaisian style, the puritan Martinists used carnivalesque humor to invite laughter at the bishop's "redde nose" and his "boosing mates" playing the fool in church.[149]

In response to the Marprelate Tracts' characterization of the bishops and clergy as "so many lewd liuers / as theeues / murtherers / adulterers / [and] drunkards,"[150] in 1589, Archbishop Whitgift and, especially, soon-to-be Bishop Bancroft, who advised the commissioning of the anti-Martinist satires, began an equally savage but more widespread propaganda campaign against puritanism that included "at least twenty-one books and pamphlets published by the anti-Martinists in the years 1589–90."[151] As a result of these counterattacks against

---

148 Christopher Hill, *Writing and Revolution in 17th Century England,* vol. 1, of *The Collected Essays of Christopher Hill* (Amherst, MA, 1985), 75.
149 Marprelate, *Hay any worke for Cooper?* (1589), in *The Marprelate Tracts,* 14, 33. All subsequent Marprelate tract citations refer to this facsimile edition.
150 Marprelate, *Epistle,* 33.
151 Lockyer, *Tudor and Stuart Britain,* 164; Leland Carlson, *Martin Marprelate, Gentleman: Master Job Throckmorton laid open in his colors* (San Marino, CA, 1981), 72.

Martin's subversion, even many puritans like Josias Nichols actually blamed that "foolish jester" Martin, "how justly God knoweth," for inciting antagonism against the godly brethren. After the Marprelate subversion, Nichols bemoaned, "Then did our troubles increase, and the pursuit was hardly followed against us."[152] Other Elizabethan puritans responded ineffectually to the vast propaganda campaign by claiming that "We are no ... disordered persons," but the years following the Marprelate controversy witnessed a marked increase in puritan bashing.[153] Decades later, Richard Baxter would recall, painfully,

> I cannot forget, that in my youth ... the place of the dancing assembly was not an hundred yards from our door, and we could not on the Lord's Day either read a chapter, or pray, or sing a psalm, or catechise, or instruct a servant, but with the noise of the pipe and tabor, and the shoutings in the street continually in our ears and even among a tractable people, *we were the common scorn of all the rabble* in the streets, and called *Puritans, Precisians* and *hypocrites*.[154]

That sober puritans like Baxter, who clearly disdained the raucous festivity of what sounds to be Morris dancing, could be subject to "common scorn," numbered among "hypocrites," or characterized as "disordered persons," demonstrates how effective Elizabethan anti-puritan polemic was in defining a carnivalesque stereotype of the puritan.

Such a stereotype was perhaps partly inevitable, however, given that Martin's carnivalesque line of attack was humorously appealing precisely "because it was subversive of degree, hierarchy and indeed the great chain of being itself."[155] Not surprisingly, the anti-Martinists' humorous counterattacks threatened that the puritan opposition to hierarchy would yield an anarchic world turned upside-down; the author of *Mar-Martine* warned, "Merrie Martin sets the world at odds" (l. 16), while even puritan-sympathizer Gabriel Harvey claimed that he feared "an Universal Topsy-turvey" or "Upsy-downe." By mirroring the

---

152 Josias Nichols, *The Plea of the Innocent* (Middleburg, 1602), 32–3.
153 Collinson, *Elizabethan Puritan Movement*, 137, 400.
154 L. A. Grovett, *The Kings Book of Sports* (London, 1890), 6; emphasis added.
155 Hill, *Writing and Revolution*, 77.

logic of carnival, anti-Martinists, such as Pasquill, Mar-Martin, Cutbert Curryknave, and Marphoreus (Thomas Nashe, John Lyly, Robert Greene, Anthony Munday, and others), were able to exaggerate other carnivalesque characteristics of the Marprelate Tracts to construct the puritans as ridiculous hypocrites who embodied clownish misrule. For example, one of Nashe's pamphlets refers to a stage portrayal of the supposedly sober puritan leaders taking part in the oft-mentioned, riotous *May-game of Martinisme*:

> *Penry* the welchman is the foregallant of the Morrice, with the treble belles … *Martin* himselfe is the Mayd-Marian, trimlie drest uppe in a caste-Gowne, and a Kercher of Dame Lawsons, his face handsomlie muffled with a Diaper-napkin to cover his beard, and a great Nosegay in his hande … *Wiggenton* daunces round about him in a Cotten-coate [i.e., a fool's long coat] to court him with a Leatherne pudding, and a wooden Ladle.[156]

As they were depicted as the cast of the Morris dance, featuring a fool wooing a cross-dressed man, the puritans were made to embody the misrule of May Day.

Through such unlikely portrayals of the puritans as simultaneously hypocritical grotesques and censorious, the anti-Martinists bolstered the norm of episcopal hierarchy as they attempted to discredit and silence the vociferous puritan minority. It was the reformers' widely recognized embrace of misrule that made them seem hypocritical in opposing it as practiced by others. By "imitating … that merry man Rablays" as well, orthodox writers were able to portray the puritans as gluttonous, licentious "Hipocrites and belli-gods."[157] On stage, for instance, an anti-Martinist play showed a lecherous Martin hypo-critically trying to rape *Divinity* and "ministering a vomit" to kill her. When it was rumored that Martin had died, one author claimed that he "had no other refuge but to run into a hole and die as he lived, belching," since his grotesque nature had become a byword. In anti-Martinist tracts, Martin "copulates, vomits, drinks, gorges himself, and gives birth," so that he became "the Bahktinian grotesque body par

---

156 Thomas Nashe, *The Returne of the Renowned Cavaliero Pasquill of England*, in *Works*, ed. R. B. McKerrow, 5 vols (London, 1904), 1: 83.
157 Nashe, *An Almond for a Parrat* (1589), sig. F2v.

excellence." The puritan Martin, in short, often appeared as a veri table Lord of Misrule.

Most important to the development of puritan stage clowns is the fact that both sides of the controversy, according to Chambers, refer to the stages' involvement in the Marprelate "war" in some twelve tracts. Particular tracts allude to anti-Martinist comedies appearing on the public stages, as when Pasquill (likely Thomas Nashe) refers in *A Countercuffe given to Martin Junior* to "the Anatomie latelie taken of [Martin] … by launcing and worming him at *London* vpon the common Stage."[159] Apparently, playwrights produced a number of comedies at Martin's expense since John Lyly complained that if only "these comedies might be allowed to be played that are penned, … [Martin] would be deciphered." The evidence also clearly indicates that a substantial number of "comedies" had already been staged. Martin-sympathizer Gabriel Harvey, for instance, complained of those "that have the stage … and can furnish-out Vices, and Devils at their pleasure" to mock Martin. Another pamphlet, *Martins Months Minde*, claimed that Martin "took it very grievously, to be *made a May game upon the stage*," specifying the actual stage of "The Theatre."[160] Allusions to *The May-game of Martinisme*, "mentioned separately in three anti-Martinist pamphlets,"[161] moreover, suggest that anti-Martinist May-games actually took the stage. Ironically, given puritans' hostility to such carnivalesque festivity, and in particular, their later outrage at the *Book of Sports* (1617–18), which they called the "morris book," puritans were made to embody the very May Day Morris dance – on both page and stage – that had become an abomination to them.

By 1589, the Privy Council decreed that "there hathe growne some inconvenience by common playes and interludes in & about the cyttie of London, in [that] the players take upon [them] to handle in their plaies

---

158 Kristen Poole, *Radical Religion from Shakespeare to Milton: Figures of Nonconformity in Early Modern England* (Cambridge, 2000), 59.
159 Chambers, *Elizabethan Stage*, 4: 229–33; Nashe, *Works*, 1: 59.
160 Chambers, *Elizabethan Stage*, 4: 233; Nashe, *The Complete Works of Thomas Nashe*, ed. Alexander B. Grossart, 6 vols (London, 1883–84), 1: 175; emphasis added.
161 Charles Nicholl, *A Cup of News: The Life of Thomas Nashe* (London, 1984), 68, 288–9 n. 27.

certen matters of Divinitie and State, unfit to be suffered."   In response, Sir Edmund Tilney, Master of the Revels, ordered the theatres to stop producing anti-Martinist satire that year and closed the theatres temporarily. Whether or not the puritans were ever actually allowed to do so, Tilney at least *planned* to permit the stages' enemy, the Lord Mayor, a puritan himself, to authorize representatives thereafter to censor "such parts or matters as they shall find unfit and indecent to be handled in plays, both for Divinity and State."[163] Such a degree of censorship certainly did not occur before Martin himself and the anti-Martinists had presented depictions of puritan clowns that reinforced increasingly prevalent stereotypes both in the numerous books and pamphlets and on the public stages. Earlier, in *Theses Martinae* (1589), "Martin Junior" had complained bitterly that the stage players, "in the action of dealing against Maister Martin, haue gotten them many thousand eie witnesses, of their wittelesse and pittifull conceites" (sig. D2ᵛ). In any case, evidence suggests that censorship of anti-puritan sentiments was short-lived, limited, or infrequent, since we shall see that several stage clowns in the 1590s continued to be associated with a clownish, carnivalesque puritan stereotype.

On several counts, then, anachronistic notions of Protestants as sober and Catholics as riotous distort the evidence. In truth, Tudor evangelicals and traditionalists could, and often did, alternately reject or embrace misrule depending upon who had the upper hand or who had become most associated with stereotypes of misrule. When misrule was appropriated to demean "papistry" as Morison and Cromwell had planned, Henrician and Marian traditionalists subsequently moved to censor it. Similarly, although it is probable that an increasing ambivalence toward laughter coincided with the evangelical equation of "papist" impiety with laughter, it also appears that carnivalesque laughter began to seem really sinful to puritans only after it had been turned against them. Though the influence of reformist misrule lingered on in London apprentices' otherwise incongruous Renaissance custom

162 Quoted in notes to *Pappe with an hatchet* in John Lyly, *Puritan Discipline Tracts* (London, 1844), 49.
163 Chambers, *Elizabethan Stage*, 1: 295.

of pulling down brothels on Shrovetide,   what is certain is that Cambridge puritans did not make a break with misrule until September 1588 (the very autumn the Martin Marprelate controversy began), when St John's evangelicals requested "That noe lord of misrule ... be vsed in ye Colledge," because "there is nothing sought herein but disgrace, disfaming, and abuse."[165] Defaming abuse had previously been precisely the point, but the targets of invective misrule had changed.

The carnivalesque puritan Martin Marprelate attempted to turn back the clock by using the polemical misrule of a previous era. Though Marprelate Tracts would be revived during the Civil War era, following the anti-puritan satirical backlash Martin incited, the associations evangelicals had with impiety would increasingly expand as both antipathy toward Catholicism and resentment of mockery at the puritans' expense could extend to laughter itself, thereby demonizing it too. At least, William Prynne would later find laughter at theatre "altogether inconsistent with the gravity, modesty and sobriety of a Christian," a group of puritans in 1655 would soberly resolve never to joke, and Fifth Monarchists would debate whether all laughter was sinful.[166] Certainly, then, it is an irony of history that early evangelicals had once promoted misrule and theatre with the same zeal with which their spiritual descendants came to oppose them. As the next chapter reveals, the clown in the Elizabethan period turned against the puritans with a vengeance too.

---

164 John Stow, *Survey of London*, ed. C. L. Kingsford, 2 vols (Oxford, 1908), 1: 255–6.
165 REED, 1: 321.
166 Thomas, "Place of Laughter in Tudor and Stuart England," 81.

Chapter 3

"VERIE DEVOUT ASSES":
IGNORANT PURITAN CLOWNS

A NOTHER notable clown type in the era, one that emerges on the professional stage by the 1590s, was the stupid or ignorant puritan, a religious zealot typed by his rusticity, misspeaking, and inane logic. Such clownish figures as Stupido of the Cambridge University play *The Pilgrimage to Parnassus* (*c.* 1597–98) and the zealous Constable in *Blurt, Master Constable* (1601–2) have much in common with the type as it appears in various religious polemics of the era, such as the controversial Marprelate Tracts (1588–89), and in the similarly scandalous Hackett controversy. But a full appreciation of the ways in which the comic was turned against puritans through clowning resulting in the creation of a Renaissance puritan stereotype requires an understanding of the degree to which a sort of put-down stereotyping played a prominent, though heretofore not fully appreciated, role in defining doctrinal and ideological religious boundaries in post-Reformation England, an era in which discrediting opposing religious views was often achieved by associating one's opponents with laughable ignorance.

What is most familiar to students of the era was the fact that many Renaissance puritans promoted a learned self-image in opposition to Catholics and even to fellow (though more moderate) English Protestants, whom puritans deemed, by comparison, as intellectually and culturally deficient. Thus, in the late 1590s a yeoman from Yorkshire reviled his parish parson by proclaiming, "Parson thou art an ass … I never saw such an ass as thou art," just as a man in Buckinghamshire in the 1630s mocked a parson in his village as "tinkerly," that is, low class and unrefined. Most famously, many Renaissance "puritans," presenting their own doctrine as rational religion, insisted on associating Catholicism with ignorant, crudely magical superstition. Mocking the ritual of gospel reading during Rogation, for instance, radical Elizabethan reformer Henry Barrow called it "charming the fields,"[3] while in *Michael Wodde's Dialogue* (1554), one character jested: "As for your Latine Gospels read to the corne, I am sure the corne understandeth as much as you, and therefore hath as much profit by them as ye have, that is to sai, none at al."[4] Increasingly, as they pushed for further, more extreme reformation, puritans promoted themselves as more learned than their opponents through an avowed insistence upon a learned (but ultimately above all) *preaching* ministry. They consequently decried the supposed ignorance of "bare reading" or "dumb" (i.e., non-preaching)[5] ministers and arrogantly derided their moderate opponents as "ignorant and atheistical dolts."[6]

Mainstream English Protestants, employing what Grace Tiffany characterizes as an "'I'm rubber, you're glue' style of argument,"[7] responded to puritan self-aggrandizement by mocking so-called puritans as "godly coxcomb[s],"[8] labeling them "silly, ignorant and downe-righte English

1   Borthwick Institute, York, High Commission Cause Papers, 1597/12; Buckinghamshire Record Office, D/A/V4, fo. 53^v.
2   My use of the term "puritan" throughout echoes that of English historian Peter Lake: "The term 'puritan' is used to refer to a broader span of opinion [than the presbyterian platform alone], encompassing those advanced Protestants who regarded themselves as 'the godly' ... It is therefore used as a term of ... relative religious zeal rather than as a clear-cut party label." *Anglicans and Puritans? Presbyterianism and English Conformist Thought from Whitgift to Hooker* (London, 1988), 7; Peter Lake, "Defining Puritanism – Again?" in *Puritanism*, ed. F. Bremer (Boston, 1993), 3–29.
3   Keith Thomas, *Religion and the Decline of Magic: Studies in Popular Beliefs in Sixteenth and Seventeenth Century England* (1971; rpt New York, 1997), 64.
4   John Brand, *Popular Antiquities of Great Britain: Chiefly Illustrating the Origin of Our Vulgar and Provincial Customs, Ceremonies, and Superstitions* (1848–49; rpt New York, 1970), 203.
5   Collinson, *Elizabethan Puritan Movement*, 390, 42.
6   Marprelate, *Epistle*, 33; all subsequent Marprelate tract references are from *The Marprelate Tracts*.
7   Grace Tiffany, "Puritanism in Comic History: Exposing Royalty in the Henry Plays," *Shakespeare Studies* 26 (1998): 256–87; 269. Tiffany addresses accusations of "sophistical argument" (260).
8   *Some Annals of the Borough of Devizes*, ed. B. H. Cunnington (Devizes, 1925–26),

puritans" and "lewd [i.e., ignorant] brethren that seem and would be thought to have authority, and have none."[10] Oliver Ormerud, for instance, could write in *The Picture of a Puritaine* (1605), "they are full of pride, thinking themselves ... to have knowledge when they are ignorant" (sig. C1ʳ–C2ᵛ). Worse still, the bishops claimed, puritans planned to displace "wise, learned and discreet men, and commit the whole government of the Church to master pastor and his ignorant neighbors."[11] In short, in the Renaissance, stereotypical puritan ignorance – like censoriousness and hypocrisy – became so familiar a line of attack that Robert Bolton could complain that being termed "puritans" effectively "deprived [those so named] *ipso facto* ... of learning and good religion."[12]

Similar accusations appear frequently in Renaissance English drama. In the anonymous play, *The Puritan* (1606), for example, puritans are "proud Cocks-combes" (sig. B3ʳ) and "pure-starch'd foole[s]" (sig. C1ᵛ), just as in Ben Jonson's *Bartholomew Fair* (1614) they are not merely hypocritically gluttonous but characterized by their "arrogant and invincible dullness" (1.4, 142) as "a herd of ... proud ignorants" (5.2, 39). In the play *The Pilgrimage to Parnassus*,[13] characters mock the puritan "stricte Stupido" for his stupidity, speaking "Of stricte Stupido that puling puritane, / A moving piece of clay, a speaking ass, / A walking image and a senseless stone" (ll. 410–12) and

> that plodding puritan ...
> ... that earthcreeping dolt,

vol. 1, pt. 1, 59–64; quoted in David Underdown, *Revel, Riot and Rebellion: Popular Politics and Culture in England 1603–1660* (1985; rpt Oxford and New York, 1987), 51.

9   Peter Studley, *Looking-Glasse of Schisme* (London, 1634), 160.

10   Inner Temple Library, MS. Petyt 538/47, 526–7.

11   Christopher Hill, *Society and Puritanism in Pre-Revolutionary England* (1958; rpt New York, 1997), 199.

12   Robert Bolton, *Mr Bolton's Last & Learned Worke ... Together with the Life and Death of the Author, Published by E[dward] B[agshaw]* (London, 1632), in "Life," sig. B3ʳ⁻ᵛ.

13   *The Pilgrimage to Parnassus with the Two Parts of the Return from Parnassus. Three Comedies performed in St John's College (1597–1601)*, ed. Rev. W. D. Macray (London, 1886).

Who, for he cannot reach unto the artes,
Makes showe as though he would neglect the artes"

(ll. 417–20).

Whereas there is no enactment of the puritan's "stricte" severity, the emphasis solely on stupidity in the characterization reveals the degree to which ignorance had become a stereotypically puritan trait. Though Renaissance puritan stage clowns are hardly altogether unknown,[14] what is less familiar, to literary scholars at least, and what I hope to demonstrate here, is that, even granting the typical dynamics of put-down humor or familiar "I'm rubber, you're glue" argument outlined above, it is not immediately apparent how stupidity *alone* came to be sufficient to characterize a recognizable stage puritan in light of puritans' presentation of themselves as the learned party. Why was it that, by contrast, "contemporary critics … accuse[d] puritans of ignorance and a desire to destroy England's educational institutions"?[15] To seek answers to such questions we may begin by examining specific clues provided by Stupido himself.

MR MARTIN'S COURSE AND
THE ECCLESIASTICAL COBBLER TYPOLOGY

One notable feature of Stupido's idiocy in the first of three *Parnassus* plays is its explicit association with the clownish persona of the pseudonymous Martin Marprelate, the subversive puritan gadfly who, we have seen, skewered Church authorities in the scandalously humorous Marprelate Tracts (1588–89). "[S]ell all these books, and b[u]y a good *Martin*," Stupido arrogantly counsels, "and twoo or three hundreth of chatechismes of Jeneva's printe, and I warrant you will have learning enoughe. *Mr Martin* and other good men tooke this course" (ll. 352–6).

---

14 On the "carnivalesque puritan" type with respect to Falstaff and Martin Marprelate, see especially Kristen Poole, "Saints Alive! Falstaff, Martin Marprelate, and the Staging of Puritanism," *Shakespeare Quarterly* 46.1 (spring 1995): 47–75 and Tiffany, "Puritanism in Comic History." See also J. Dover Wilson, *The Fortunes of Falstaff* (New York, 1944).
15 John Morgan, *Godly Learning: Puritan Attitudes towards Reason, Learning and Education, 1560–1640* (London and New York, 1986), 14.

On one hand, Stupido's remark reflects the puritans' pride in their promotion of Bible reading, even as it acknowledges the limited learning that an emphasis on reading only particular editions of the Bible and very few interpretations would afford. The remark – and the *Parnassus* author – identifies Marprelate as an exemplar justifying ignorance since Stupido proposes following Mr Martin's "course."

And the clowning Martin was indeed a target, and therefore a font, of anti-puritan stereotyping. In 1589, in response to the Marprelate Tracts, the bishops commissioned and engaged in a widespread propaganda campaign against puritanism, and both sides of the controversy refer to the involvement of the stage in the Marprelate "war." Playwrights were so prolific in penning comedies at Martin's expense that the author of *Pappe with an Hatchet* (1589; attributed to John Lyly) could refer to him as virtually a "stage plaier" himself;[16] indeed, the author of *Martins Months Minde* claimed that "everie stage Plaier made a jest of him" so that Martin "took it very grievously, to be made a May game upon the stage,"[17] and "Martin Junior" complained that the stage players, "in the action of dealing against Maister Martin, haue gotten them many thousande eie witnesses, of their wittelesse … conceites."[18] Stage attacks suggesting Martin's own witlessness had rankled the puritans.

If the notoriety of Martinist satire (which, as noted in Chapter 2, Christopher Hill calls "the biggest scandal of Elizabeth I's reign")[19] might seem to point to its effectiveness, it also provoked a backlash of *anti*-puritan stereotyping. In their propaganda, following the example we saw employed in Shepherd's *Jon Bon* (1547), the Martinists sometimes assumed a low-class, ignorant persona, for, as contemporaries recognized, they had, in order to popularize their religious reforms, resurrected and appropriated the popular persona and idiom of the lower-class rustic, mechanical, or artisan stage clown employed by Dick Tarlton, the most famous comic actor of his day, "who died in early

---

16 John Lyly, *Pappe with an hatchet. Alias, a figge for my God sonne* (1589), in *The Complete Works of John Lyly: Now for the First Time Collected … with Life, Bibliography, Essays, Notes, and Index*, ed. R. Warwick Bond, 3 vols (Oxford, 1902), 3: 388–413; 408.
17 Chambers, *Elizabethan Stage*, 4: 230.
18 Marprelate, *Martin Iuniors Epilogve* (1589), sig. D3ᵛ.
19 Hill, *Writing and Revolution*, 75.

September 1588, a matter of weeks before the first tract appeared."
Martin himself invoked the recent example of Tarlton in claiming: "I
thinke Simonie be the bishops lacky. Tarleton tooke him not long since
in Don John of Londons cellor."[21] Because of Tarlton's own apparent
satire against corrupt bishops, Martin felt enough of an affinity with him
to urge others to pray for Tarlton's soul because he was an "honest
fellow" who had made "dean Johns [Bishop John Whitgift's] ears ...
longer," like an ass's.[22] And yet, any momentary effectiveness in popu-
larizing the puritans' cause achieved through the tactic of appropriating
Tarlton's stage personality was offset by the rebuttal it incited when the
puritans all but invited their opponents to compare Marprelate repeatedly to the stage clown. In *A Whip for an Ape*, for instance, the
anti-puritan Lyly observed that "Now *Tarlton's* dead ... For knave and
foole thou [Martin] maist beare pricke and price" (ll. 53–4), and in
Mar-Martin Lyly similarly noted: "These tinkers termes, and barbers
jestes first *Tarleton* on the stage, / Then *Martin* in his bookes of lies hath
put in every page" (sig. A4^v). These comparisons may even suggest some
hostility to the deceased Tarlton as a precedent for Martin's
anti-episcopal slanders, but the chief point here is that the resemblance
between the object and style of Martin's and Tarlton's satirical clowning
was apparent enough to contemporaries.

It was partly because the Martinists had occasionally (however
inconsistently) employed "the language of the street, the slang of the
craftsmen, and the dialect of the uneducated" to appeal to the common
people[23] that the anti-Martinists like Lyly incessantly mocked Martin as
"but a cobler by occupation."[24] They expanded the attack to characterize all puritans who would be portrayed as clown-like "ecclesiastical

20 Patrick Collinson, "Ben Jonson's *Bartholomew Fair*: The Theatre Constructs
    Puritanism," in *The Theatrical City: Culture, Theatre and Politics in London,
    1576–1649*, ed. David L. Smith, Richard Strier, and David Bevington
    (Cambridge, 1995), 157–69; 166.
21 Marprelate, *Epistle*, 19.
22 Marprelate, *Hay any worke for Cooper?* (1589), 46.
23 Donna B. Hamilton, *Shakespeare and the Politics of Protestant England*
    (Lexington, 1992), 76.
24 Lyly, *Pappe with an hatchet*, in *Works of John Lyly*, 3: 408.

cobler[s]," "godly Cobler[s]," and ignorant, "base mechanicall" preachers,[27] an influential "type often used in anti-Martinist material."[28] Thus, Nashe derides the puritans' "dunsticall Sermons," specifying, "Such Sermons I meane as our sectaries preach in ditches, and … when they leape from the Coblers stal to their pulpits."[29] Such anti-Martinist literature inspired derivative anti-puritan attacks which likewise mocked the brethren as cobblers and "mechanicks." The satirist John Taylor, in particular, would later make much of this tactic, skewering the "impudent rabble of ignorant Mechanicks, who have dared to presume to preach" (A4ᵛ) in *A Cluster of Coxcombes* (1642), while in *A Brown Dozen of Drunkards* (1648), a work whose subtitle refers to the "Zeale-drunk staggering Times," Taylor depicts a puritan as "a poor, silly, simple, vulgar, Mechanick Ideot" (sig. C4ʳ). And, in *A Swarme of Sectaries, and Schismatiques: Wherein is discovered the strange preaching (or prating) of such as are by their trades Coblers, Tinkers, Pedlers, Weavers, Sow-gelders, and Chimney-Sweepers* (1641), the title page of which features a woodcut of the cobbler Samuel Howe preaching from a barrel or tub in a tavern (Figure 4), Taylor derides the "Calveskin doctrin" (sig. B2ʳ) of that "most famous preaching Cobler Samuel Howe," that "zealous Cobler" or "learned Cobler" (sig. B2ʳ), in order to demonstrate that "A Cobler to a Pulpit should not mount, / Nor can an Asse cast up a true account" (sig. A3ᵛ). Taylor also plays on the cobbling pun to "mend bad Soales" (sig. B2ᵛ), just as he does in *A Tale in a Tub, or a Tub Lecture As it was delivered by Mi-Heele Mend-soale* (1641), featuring ignorant puritanical rambling by a cobbler preacher.

Undoubtedly, the puritan Martin's clownish preaching persona had invited such "scoff[ing] at the artisan-provincial base of the

25 Thomas Nashe, *An Almond for a Parrat* (London, 1590), in *Works of Thomas Nashe*, ed. R. B. McKerrow, 5 vols (London, 1904–11), 3: 344; subsequent citations are from this edition.
26 Lyly, *Mar-Martin* (London, 1589), in *Works of John Lyly*, 3: 426, ll. 97 and 98.
27 Nashe, *Christs Teares Over Iervsalem* (London, 1594), in *Works of Thomas Nashe*, 2: 62.
28 Joseph Black, "The Rhetoric of Reaction: The Martin Marprelate Tracts (1588–89), Anti-Martinism and the Uses of Print in Early Modern England," *Sixteenth Century Journal* 28.3 (fall 1997): 707–25; 719.
29 Nashe, *Pierce Penilesse* (London, 1592), in *Works of Thomas Nashe*, 1: 192.

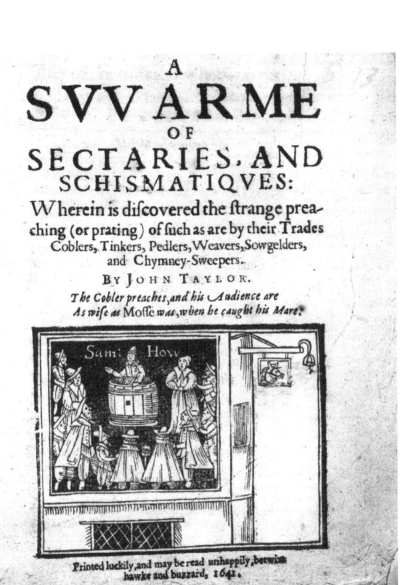

Figure 4. Title page, John Taylor, *A Swarme of Sectaries and Schismatiques* (1641), employing the ignorant cobbler stereotype of the puritan. By permission of the Huntington Library.

movement." There were actual "mechanic preachers" proselytizing throughout London and towns like Norwich,[31] but it was the Martinist authors themselves whose puritan persona had most embodied such a "tinkerly" stereotype, for as Neil Rhodes has argued, it was "Martin Marprelate and his subsequent opponents [who had] amalgamated" the roles of "clown and preacher," as they, together, fleshed out the persona of "Martin, the clowning preacher."[32] The result, I would argue, was that puritans were stereotyped for decades thereafter, as Nashe describes them, as "better beseeming a priuie then a pulpit, a misterming Clowne in a Comedy, then a chosen man in the Ministrie."[33] Martin himself, imitating the "happy unhappy answers" of Tarlton,[34] was the principal model for such a clown since the persona had in fact, like Jon Bon before him, frequently employed "misterming" or malapropisms such as "itsample" for *example*, "outcept" for *except*, "argling" for *arguing*, "ingram" for *ignorant*, and "ingramnesse" for *ignorance*. And indeed, Martin emphasized the ignorance of his own clownish persona so that, just as the ploughman Jon Bon bested the pedantic Master Parson, Martin boasted that even being "Such a simple ingram man as [he was],"[35] he would be able to prove the bishops' lack of true authority, though he pleaded: "You must then beare with my ingramnesse. I am plaine."[36] Though humorous, the lowly persona that Martin sometimes adopted to heighten the popular appeal of his carnivalesque besting of bishops exacerbated anxieties about his radical challenge to the established church.

After all, such use of misterming, "mechanical" idiom and an ignorant persona evoked the specter of lower-class radicalism, thereby inviting the association of Martin with the incessant "fear-mongering over Anabaptist tendencies" once purportedly prevalent among

30 Nicholl, *A Cup of News*, 77.
31 J. W. Martin, "Christopher Vitel: An Elizabethan Mechanic Preacher," *Sixteenth Century Journal* 10 (May 1979): 15–22.
32 Neil Rhodes, *Elizabethan Grotesque* (London, 1980), 158, 4. Rhodes argues in terms of satirical journalism not the stage clown.
33 Nashe, *The Anatomie of Absurditie* (London, 1589), in *Works of Thomas Nashe*, 1: 27.
34 Nungezer, *Dictionary of Actors*, 347.
35 Marprelate, *Epistle*, 16.
36 Marprelate, *The Epitome* (1588), 2.

puritans generally.   Martin was, of course, well aware of how nearly he sometimes resembled the commoner leaders of the Anabaptists, those radical, apocalyptic enthusiasts who had rebelled against the existing social order in Switzerland, Germany, and the Netherlands. Whereas he had enjoined the bishops to "never slander the cause of reformation or the furtherers thereof in terming the cause by the name of Anabaptistrie,"[38] Martin himself had also self-consciously incited fears of just such lower-class radicalism by threatening that "The people are altogether discontented," so that denying further reforms will "breed Anabaptistrie," which in turn, he warned, "will alienate the ... subjects from their lawfull governour."[39]

Martin's threats of radicalism reflect a desperate strategy with inherent risks: although most modern scholars would not conceive of such terms as Anabaptist and puritan as interchangeable, they were once all too often conflated post-Marprelate. In *Basilikon Doron*, James I claimed that the Anabaptists and the Familists were most deserving of the name of puritan, "because they thinke them selues onely pure."[40] Earlier, during the 1590s, Nashe wrote of the puritans in *An Almond for a Parrat*, "let the worlde knowe you heereafter by the nam[e] of Anabaptists."[41] Elsewhere, further conflating denominations, Archbishop Parker warned that the Presbyterian's "fond faction" aimed at establishing an Anabaptist "Munzer's commonwealth," claiming: "[I]f ... it will fall out to a popularity, ... it will be the overthrow of all."[42] Likewise, Archbishop Whitgift could report in the wake of Marprelate that Presbyterian (i.e., "puritan") writings contained "the very steps and degrees to anabaptism."[43] Even more overtly, Richard Cosin's *Conspiracie for Pretended Reformation: viz. Presbyteriall Discipline* (1592) asserted, from the title page on, the precise "resemblance ... vnto the like," i.e., between puritans and Anabaptists, "happened heretofore

---

37 Black, "Rhetoric of Reaction," 719.
38 Marprelate, *Epistle*, 39.
39 Ibid., 52.
40 James I, *The True Law of Free Monarchies and Basilikon Doron of James VI*, ed. Daniel Fischlin and Mark Fortier (Toronto, 1996), 94.
41 Nashe, *Almond for a Parrat*, in *Works of Thomas Nashe*, 3: 352.
42 Matthew Parker, *Correspondence of Matthew Parker*, eds John Bruce and Thomas Thomason Perowne (Cambridge, 1853), 437.
43 Collinson, *Elizabethan Puritan Movement*, 137.

in Germanie." Matthew Sutcliffe, too, warned of the dangers of puritanism by referring to the Anabaptists' recent rebellions in Munster, Amsterdam, and Strasbourg: "The precedents of the Anabaptists, doe teach us what an unbridled thing the people is, where they take the sword to worke reformation with."[44] Such fears must have seemed real enough, if, as D. G. Allan would have it, the often clown-like leaders of sixteenth-century English popular risings were "combinations as it were, of biblical saviours and lords of misrule."[45] It was not just the case that such associations with puritanism fed anxieties about Anabaptist revolt, as they also suggested anti-intellectualism and a promotion of irrationality – two other features of the puritan clown type.

Renaissance puritan claims to intellectual superiority thus took a severe blow after a sensational incident that puritan Josias Nichols called "one of three most greevous accidentes" which did "verie much darke the righteousnesse of our cause"[46] (the first two being the Marprelate scandal and the Brownists' separation from the Church). The third "accident" occurred when the puritan leader Thomas Cartwright and eight puritan ministers were on trial, on July 16, 1591, and two deluded puritans "got them vp into an emptie cart" in Cheapside and, "out of that choise pulpit,"[47] proclaimed that they were prophets and witnesses with news from Heaven. Their good news was that the supposedly gifted and divinely inspired William Hacket, actually merely an ignorant, "wholy vnlettred" (sig. C2^r), simple-minded lunatic, was the Messiah and ruler of Europe and that the Queen had abdicated the throne. Hacket had "[given] out to diuers that hee was a *Prophet* of Gods vengeaunce" and that "*If Reformation be not Established in England in the present yeere, three great plagues shall fall vpon it*" (sig. C3^v). Hacket's disciples were convinced that he "indured" all the "torments" that conjurers and "Deuils in hell … could practise against him" in order to prevent him from "establishing the Gospell," after which "all Kings and

44 Ibid.; Matthew Sutcliffe, *An Answere to a certaine libel supplicatorie* (London, 1592), 72.
45 D. G. Allan, "The Risings in the West 1628–31," *Economic History Review*, 2nd series, vol. 5 (1952–3), 76–85.
46 Josias Nichols, *The Plea for the Innocent* (Middleburg, 1602), sig. D5^r.
47 Richard Cosin, *Conspiracie, for pretended reformation* (London, 1592), sig. I3^r. Subsequent references in this paragraph are to this.

Princes should ... yeelde their sceptors vnto him" (sig. E3). Twelve days after the deluded puritans' announcement of the second coming, Hacket's brief "reign" ended as he hung from the scaffold and had his "traytors heart" taken "foorth, and showed out openly to the people" (sig. L3ʳ), but only after he had screamed delusional, "blasphemous and hellish wordes" (sig. L1ʳ), threatening that if God did not deliver him from his enemies he would "fir[e] the heauens, and teare [Him] from [His] throne" (sig. L3ʳ), as well as railing treasons to the horrified onlookers. To the puritans' embarrassment (according to Nichols in 1602), the shocking performance recalled the earlier Anabaptists' revolt in Munster.

This 1591 episode also echoed the lurid anti-puritan propaganda John Bancroft had been promoting since Marprelate. Seizing another opportunity to link puritans to the Anabaptists, Bancroft was able to make the sensational incident "the logical climax of his literary exposure of the puritan movement" thereafter.[48] Cosin did likewise in his *Conspiracie, for pretended reformation* (1592), writing that through Hacket the puritans were, like "the Anabaptists in *Germainie*: who pretended like puritie, and intended also a dangerous Reformation" (sig. M4ᵛ) to tempt "the common multitude" (sig. I3ʳ) into sedition. Cosin claimed that after Hacket's arrest and subsequent investigation, authorities discovered seditious pamphlets in the chamber of puritan leader Wiggenton (of *May-game of Martinisme* fame). One pamphlet entitled *The Fooles bolte* purportedly included the verse, "A Christian true although he be a clowne, / May teach a king to weare scepter and crowne," which Hacket was said to have confessed was framed for the occasion, and, apparently, was intended to refer to himself (sig. F3ᵛ). Just as Martin did, radical puritans like Hacket seemed – or at least were *made* – to confirm a dangerously ignorant, yet clownish stereotype drawn from the Anabaptists.

Puritan intellectual and rational capacity was further called into question via associations with religious radicals' claims to divine inspiration and hence constant references to "the spirit," which anti-puritan satirists portrayed as mere irrationality and outright madness. (The insane Hacket himself was believed to have been "mooued ... inwardly

48 Collinson, *Elizabethan Puritan Movement*, 424.

by the spirit," being "indued with an extraordinarie and singular spirite."[49]) In one anti-Martinist tract Lyly jeered that no place would suit puritans better than "Bedlam …, so mad they are, and so bad they are," since "all proceedes of the spirit. I thinke thou [Martin] art possest with the spirites of Iacke Straw and the Black-smith, who, so they might rent in peeces the gouernment, they would drawe cuts for religion."[50] So, too, Nashe's depiction of the Anabaptists in Munster in his *The Unfortunate Traveller* (1594) portrayed inspiration as ignorant madness:

> Why, inspiration was their ordinary familiar, and buzzed in their ears like a bee in a box every hour what news from heaven, hell and the land of whipper-ginnie … They would vaunt there was not a pea's difference betwixt them and the apostles: they were as poor as they, as base trades as they, and no more inspired than they."[51]

Likewise, one of the most famous Renaissance stage puritans, the zealous, hypocritical madman Zeal-of-the-Land Busy, repeatedly speaks of the "spirit" (3.6, 79; 4.6, 93; 5.5, 38; 5.5, 52) until, in a fit of inspired enthusiasm, he tears down what he believes to be idolatrous gingerbread and puppet stalls before, infamously, losing a debate with a puppet. In yet another example of satire against inspiration, George Chapman's *The Memorable Masque* (1613) features the puritan Capriccio, a fraudulent subversive who describes himself a number of times as a "man of wit"[52] but who is really "a buffoon" (ll. 261 and 263) who wears bellows on his head, symbolic of the "inspiration" which puffs up his brain:

> Sinful? and damnable? What, a puritan? Those bellows you wear on your head shew with what matter your brain is puffed up, Sir; a religion-forger I see you are and presume of inspiration from these bellows; with which ye study to blow up the settled governments of kingdoms. (ll. 255–8)

49 Cosin, *Conspiracie, for pretended reformation*, sigs. K2ᵛ, C2ʳ.
50 Lyly, *Pappe with an hatchet*, in *Works of John Lyly*, 3: 409.
51 Nashe, *The Unfortunate Traveller* (London, 1594), in *Works of Thomas Nashe*, 2: 233.
52 George Chapman, *The Memorable Masque of the Two Honourable Houses or Inns of Court* in *Jacobean and Caroline Masques*, ed. Richard Dutton, 2 vols, (Nottingham, n.d.), 2: 19–32, ll. 200, 220, 245.

Throughout the early modern period, such mockery of inspiration as madly deluded ignorance would be a conventional feature of anti-puritan comedy.[53]

"BOMINATION LEARNING": THE PURITANS' HEAVENLY ACADEMY AS COUNTER-RENAISSANCE

However humorous, what was at stake in attacks on inspiration was nothing less than the basis for authority of interpretation – for what Bancroft called the "authoritie and libertie of judging"[54] – and thus the very stability of authority itself. Oliver Ormerud, writing in *Picture of a Puritane*, questioned in particular the assertion of spiritual authorization underscoring what Cosin had already characterized as the "opinion of equality of authority"[55]: "[A]re all Prophets? are all teachers? doe all speake with tongues? do all interprete?"[56] The satirical journalist Nashe reported of "an assemblie of the brotherhood" that he had observed:

> [A] roome full of Artificers ... sat rounde about uppon stooles and benches to harken to ... I. Cor. 3, ... [Then,] the reader began first to utter his conceit upon the Text, ... then it came to his next neighbors course, and so in order Glosses went a begging, and Expositions ranne apace.[57]

If, in the words of Thomas Cranmer, the faithful had once been advised in their pursuit of scriptural interpretation to "expound it no

---

53 By the mid-eighteenth century, "enthusiasm" was "often associated, in Fielding's work, with the Methodists." Henry Fielding, *Tom Jones*, ed. John Bender and Simon Stern (Oxford, 1998), 878 n. 83. After all, John Wesley authored "a logic textbook vaguely reminiscent of Ramism" and Ramism would ultimately gain in prestige through its influence on Harvard. Walter J. Ong, SJ, *Ramus, Method, and the Decay of Dialogue* (Cambridge, 1983, 1958, 12, 15, 302; quote at 304.

54 Robert Weimann, *Authority and Representation in Early Modern Discourse* (Baltimore, MD, 1996), 81.

55 Cosin, *Conspiracie, for pretended reformation*, 83.

56 Oliver Ormerud, *Picture of a Puritane* (enlarged edn, London, 1605), 70.

57 Nashe, *The Returne of the Renowned Cavaliero Pasquill of England* (London, 1589), in *Works of Thomas Nashe*, 1: 89.

further, th[a]n you can plainly understand it," many Elizabethan observers found not such restrained interpretation but the unbridled "Expositions" of asses at full gallop. Mainstream Protestants objected above all, Robert Weimann observes, that the sole basis for authority among the puritans was inspiration,[59] and therefore, as Nashe would have it, the irrational "violence of long babling praiers."[60] Thus, puritan exegesis was portrayed as self-authorizing enthusiasm, as opposed to the relative rationality of the hierarchical authorities' learned tradition.

The conformists' hostility to inspiration supports John Morgan's assessment in his important study, *Godly Learning*, that the Renaissance was a period marked by an ongoing "struggle between 'enthusiasm' and 'reason' for dominance in religion."[61] In this struggle, the puritans were suspicious of – and most strongly opposed – "human reason," "natural reason," and all that was a product of "humane" arts and learning. In lieu of the reason promoted by the "humane learning" of ensconced Humanist education, puritans advocated an infusion of the Spirit (i.e., inspiration), which would, they believed, allow what they deemed "right reason," that is, a divinely-augmented, "regenerate reason." Thus, mainstream Elizabethan puritan icon William Perkins insisted that he who wished to be wise

> must reject his owne naturall reason, and stoppe up the eyes of his naturall minde, like a blinde man, and suffer himself wholly to be guided by Gods spirit in the things of God, that thereby he may be made wise unto salvation.[62]

Richard Greenham likewise defended spiritual revelation in opposition to reason by proclaiming that "there are many things to be learned, which we cannot attaine unto by naturall reason onely, without

58 John N. King, *English Reformation Literature: Tudor Origins of the Protestant Tradition* (Princeton, NJ, 1982), 132.
59 Weimann, *Authority and Representation in Early Modern Discourse*, 68–82.
60 Nashe, *Unfortunate Traveller*, in *Works of Thomas Nashe*, 2: 234.
61 Morgan, *Godly Learning*, 50.
62 William Perkins, *The Works of That Famous and Vvorthy Minister of Christ in the Vniversitie of Cambridge, M. VVilliam Perkins*, 3 vols (London, 1608–31), 2: 464.

spirituall revelation." Richard Capel was blunter still in his attack on reason – in defense of enthusiasm – in claiming:

> And as our reason is carnall, it is a secret friend to Satan, takes part with him against us.... Because it hath the Divell for its dam ... downe with reason, away with our owne wit, let faith doe all, else faith will do nothing.[64]

In many respects, such puritan opposition to learned reason, what Morgan characterizes as a sort of "Counter-Renaissance," was fundamentally anti-intellectual, indeed a "revolt against intellectualism."[65] This is true because, for all their study, the learned had little to tell the puritan; Humanist intellectuals could only theorize about abstract knowledge (through "carnal" as opposed to spiritual or divine reason) whereas puritans *knew* – or certainly felt – they were right, both in their hearts and by what they deemed divinely inspired experience:

> The knowledge of the reprobate is like the knowledge which a mathematicall geographer hath of the earth and all the places in it, which is but a generall notion, and a speculative comprehension of them. But the knowledge of the elect is like the knowledge of a traveller which can speake of experience and feeling, and hath beene there and seene and knowen the particulars.[66]

Similarly, a puritan such as Thomas Granger had little use for bookish learning when he insisted that "if a man be not guided by the Spirit, his observations are but superstitious, and false rules, his readings erroneous, yea, though he hath read all Bookes ..., he wants wisdome, he hath no learning."[67]

After all, as Francis Rous explained in *The Heavenly Academie: Or the*

---

63 Richard Greenham, *The Workes of the Reverend Richard Greenham*, ed. Henry Holland (London, 1612), 757.

64 Richard Capel, *Tentations: Their Nature, Danger, Cure* (London, 1635), 106–7.

65 Morgan, *Godly Learning*, 62; here quoting Hiram Haydn's *The Counter-Renaissance* (New York, 1950), 84–5. Morgan notes here that "[o]n only one occasion, however, did Haydn specifically mention that puritans fitted the patterns of the 'Counter-Renaissance.' "

66 Arthur Dent, *Pastime for Parents* (London, 1606), n.p.

67 Thomas Granger, *A Familiar Exposition or Commentarie on Ecclesiastes* (London, 1621), 40–1.

Highest School, whereas "the head being captivated by humane reason [was] subject to errour, ... yet the heart ..., [informed] by the Spirit" was never wrong, instilling a resolute conviction of certainty into those so enlightened.[68] What was more, such learning "taught in the schoole of Christ," where the "Master ... is Truth it selfe," provided "an unknowne kind of knowledge, which cannot be taught by man."[69] In fact, the "knowledge taught by God in his heavenly schoole," to which only the puritans had access, was infallible in that it came from an omniscient source.[70] Not surprisingly, then, the "knowledge thus taught of God, doth give such an assurance of an understanding ... and doth so seale upon the soule the truth ... that all objections ... cannot blot out the stamp and character of this seale."[71] What could even the best reason and logic or any amount of evidence do in the face of such unwavering, faith-based certainty? For all those who were not so "illuminate," learned university wits and brilliant Humanists like Nashe and Lyly among them, "right reason" was the worst sort of self-righteous, self-serving enthusiasm.

The learning advocated by "godly" puritans and other radical reformers did in fact constitute a virtual Counter-Renaissance, then, in so far as it was opposed to the Humanist project of advancing learning and rationality. The puritan attack on learning went well beyond the Humanist attacks by Erasmus and Rabelais on the medieval Scholiasts and Scotists for sophistic obscurantism, since the Humanists were themselves scholars who had advocated *real* learning, and particularly the study of biblical and classical texts in their original languages, context, and hence "spirit." By contrast, the puritans denounced such Humanist-oriented "humane" learning as they came to regard all non-inspired learning, including (often) study of ancient languages, the use of learned logic (except, as we shall see, Ramist logic), any use of rhetoric that was not plain-style, and in fact any nuance, complexity, or subtlety with suspicion as hair-splitting nonsense, or, worse, diabolical deception. Notably, the puritans denounced those learned men for

---

68 Francis Rous, *The Heavenly Academie: Or the Highest School. Where Alone is that highest Teaching, the Teaching of the Heart* (London, 1638), 44–5.
69 Ibid., 30, 42.
70 Ibid., 42.
71 Ibid.

whom theology was not a matter solely of inspiration but partly an intel lectual matter and all those who approached the Gospel using their training in (especially Aristotelian) logic, that is, in what puritans viewed as an earthly, "meere ... carnall manner."[72]

Elizabethan Brownists and Barrowists, moreover, actually believed that universities were "the very guard of Antichrist's throne."[73] Robert Browne, father of Brownism, denounced the university curriculum for its emphasis on "those trifling bookes of Aristotle and of all that vaine Philosophie" and claimed that the Bible "expresly sett downe, all necessarie & general rules of the arts & all learning."[74] Likewise, Henry Barrow attacked university curricula as "profane, curious, [and] unfit for a Christian" for the inclusion of "the curious and heathen artes, prophane and vaine bablings and oppositions of science falsely so called ... wherewith they ... corrupt al[l] the youth of the land."[75] Barrow responded to the reasonable enough objection that he was opposed to learning with the less-than-comforting fundamentalist assurance that "I with my whole heart allow of any art or science that is consonant to the word of God, and to the doctrine which is according to godliness"[76] – biblical texts and puritan doctrine, nothing classical or Humanist, and certainly no diversity of opinion. Browne and Barrow were not out of the mainstream of puritan thought in this respect, however, since in general "the puritan, of course, saw the Bible as containing *all* necessary knowledge."[77] We cannot agree, then, with William P. Holden's utter dismissal of anti-puritan satire focusing on godly attitudes toward learning in his conclusion that "[t]he charge of opposition by the Puritans to learning is not easily supported; it can, however, be said that they opposed *various aspects* of education in the universities."[78]

72 Richard Sibbes, *Light from Heaven* (London, 1638), 20–1.
73 Christopher Hill, *The World Turned Upside Down: Radical Ideas During the English Revolution* (1972; rpt New York, 1973), 243.
74 Robert Browne, *Treatise upon the 23. of Matthewe* (Middelburg, 1582), 181.
75 *A Brief Discoverie of the False Church* (Dortmund [?], 1590), in *Writings of Henry Barrow*, ed. Leland H. Carlson (London, 1962–1966), 539.
76 Ibid.
77 Morgan, *Godly Learning*, 75.
78 William P. Holden, *Anti-Puritan Satire, 1572–1642* (New Haven, CT, 1954), 55; emphasis added.

Knowing just what "aspects" even mainstream puritans opposed and supported requires that we take anti-puritan criticisms seriously.

The response to the haughtiness of such fundamentalist anti-intellectualism was, not without reason, alarm and indignation. While attacks on puritanism were painted with a broad brush, it is nonetheless true that the puritans' grand promises of a more learned, less "dunsticall" religion were problematic and dubious to the conformists in the large majority; the notion that religiously inspired "godly learning" was in fact superior to "humane learning" was entirely a matter of inspiration. Due to their suspicion of learning and opposition to reason, puritans' incessant boasting about their own intellectual superiority seemed to many critics outrageous and, perhaps understandably, gave rise to the kind of epithets we saw at the outset – "proud Coxcombs" and "a herd of ... proud ignorants." To the anti-puritan satirist Taylor, the puritans' pride in their intellect seemed topsy-turvy logic:

> Each Ignorant, doe of the Spirit boast,
> And prating fools brag of Holy Ghost,
> When Ignoramous will his Teacher Teach,
> And Sow-Gelders and Cobblers dare to preach;
> This shows men's wits are monstrously disguised,
> Or that our country is Antipodised.[79]

It is with similar palpable indignation that the Humanist Nashe would describe puritans as "Verie deuout Asses ... dunstically set forth"[80] and as "transported with the heate & ignorance of [their] zeale."[81] Nashe went further in purporting to describe, first hand, the effects of the puritan abridgement of Humanist learning: "I frequented the Churches of the Pruritane [sic] Preachers that leape into the Pulpet with Pitchfork, to teach men, before they have learning, judgment, or wit enough to teach boyes."[82] Many contemporaries shared this dim view of puritan learning.

In response to puritan attacks on human reason and "humane"

---

79 John Taylor, *The World Turn'd Upside Down* (London, 1647), sig. A3^r.
80 Nashe, *Unfortunate Traveller*, in *Works of Thomas Nashe*, 2: 233.
81 Nashe, *Returne of Pasquill*, in *Works of Thomas Nashe*, 1: 78–9.
82 Ibid., 73.

learning, satirists portrayed puritans as having an absurd, self-righteously arrogant antipathy toward all literacy and learning. Anti-puritan propagandists such as the aforementioned Sutcliffe claimed that among puritans "[l]earning hath lost almost all reputation," since "these unlearned and unwise consistorians declame against learning."[83] And so, Stupido scorns those who "learne these artes in the laborious schools" and recommends the counsel of his uncle: "Studie not these vaine arts of Rhetorique, Poetrie and Philosophie; there is noe sounde edifying knowledge[e] in them."[84] Once again, Stupido appears to reflect fears of puritan anti-intellectualism fueled by the populist Martin Marprelate when he had actually railed against the bishops' sly, "bomination learning."[85]

Post-Marprelate, satirists had begun to mock and echo puritan hostility to learning in just such terms. Nashe, for instance, imagined puritans railing against education by drawing, dubiously, on New Testament precedent:

> 'Sir Peter [and] Sir Paul were ... Fisher-men .... They were none of these ... Graduates, nor Doctors, therfore why should we tie our Ministrie to the prophane studies of Vniuersitie? What is Logicke but the highe waie to wrangling, containing in it but a world of bibble-babble? Neede we anie of your Greeke, Latine, Hebreue, or anie such gibberinge, when we haue the word of God in English? Go to, go to, you are a great companie of vaine men that stand upon your degrees and tongues, with tittle tattle, I cannot tell what, when ... the Apostles knew neare a Letter of the booke.[86]

Here, the Apostles' humble origins are appropriated in opposition to ancient languages (including Hebrew), an approach Taylor echoed in making the puritans rationalize ignorance based on Christ's choice of simple fishermen as followers: "And God still being God (as he was then) / Still gives his Spirit to unlearned men."[87] Illiteracy, according to such absurd use of biblical precedent, would be most Christian. Again as

83 Sutcliffe, *An answer*, sig. A2^{v}.
84 *Pilgrimage to Parnassus*, 12.
85 Marprelate, *Hay any worke for Cooper?*, 3.
86 Nashe, *Almond for a Parrat*, in *Works of Thomas Nashe*, 3: 350.
87 John Taylor, *A Swarme of Sectaires, and Schismatiques* (London, 1641), sig. B3^{v}.

Nashe had, Thomas Overbury included a portrait of the puritan as self-righteously ignorant in his *Characters* (1614):

> His ignorance acquits him of all science ... and of all language but his mother's .... Anything else, ... he cannot abide ...: Latin the language of the beast, Greek the tongue wherein the heathen poets wrote their fictions, Hebrew the speech of the Jews that crucified Christ, ... logic ... the subtleties of Satan.[88]

Likewise, in *Swarme of Sectaries, and Schismatiques*, Taylor, echoing Overbury, depicted puritans railing that "The Latine is the language of the Beast" (sig. B3ᵛ), so that classical learning is, again, actually Satanic. Ridiculing the puritans' belief that "the Spirit is the only teacher," Taylor could declare them to be " 'Gainst Schooles, and learning. ... Tongues, Science, Logick, Rhetorick" (sig. B3ᵛ), so that his puritans rationalize their ignorance on the following grounds:

> All humane knowledge ... they detest
> Th' unlearn'd (they say) do know the Scriptures best:
> That humane learning breeds confusion,
> ...
> And that the learned ones were, are, and shall
> Be ignorant of human learning all. (sig. C3ᵛ)

Ignorance and a stout opposition to learning, knowledge, and literacy were, in short, among the most consistent attributes of the Renaissance puritan stereotype.

A stereotype of humorous opposition to literacy itself as profane gibbering and vanity often constituted a grotesque caricature of the puritans' familiar insistence upon a *preaching* rather than a so-called *reading* ministry as a sign of learning. The puritans' hostility to reading the orthodox Book of Common Prayer was evident in the famous puritan tract, *A View of Popish Abuses Yet Remaining in the English Church* (1572):

---

[88] Sir Thomas Overbury (and others), *Characters, Together with Poems, News, Edicts, and Paradoxes Based on the Eleventh Edition (1622) of* A Wife Now the Widow of Sir Thomas Overbury (1614), ed. Donald Beecher (Ottawa, 2003), 239.

By the word of God … they make [an office of preaching] an office of reading: Christ said go preach, they in mockery give them the Bible …. And that is not the feeding that Christ spake of …. Reading is not feeding, but it is as evil as playing upon a stage, and worse too. For players yet learn their parts without book.[89]

Although puritans presented their demand for more preaching in the context of an avowed insistence on a more learned ministry, because they voiced their opposition to a "reading ministry" in such extreme terms, opponents burlesqued their position as the ridiculous, elided extreme, "Reading … is … evil," a comic trope that even appears in Shakespeare.

In the midst of his examination of the troubled, divisive place of religious extremism in politics in his first tetralogy (written between 1589 and 1593), featuring the fanaticism of the Catholic Joan la Pucelle (Joan of Arc), the excessive piety of King Henry VI, and the manipulation of the appearance of piety by the Duke of Gloucester before becoming Richard III, Shakespeare included his own satiric portrait of puritan zeal; that is, during a period of intense anti-puritan satire in the wake of Marprelate and Hacket, Shakespeare employed the ignorant, self-righteous puritan radical according to the then-conventional associations with godly rhetoric, clownishly irrational inspiration, lower-class radicalism, and hostility to learning in his brilliant, largely ahistorical portrayal of a carnivalesque Jack Cade in *Henry VI Part 2* (*c.* 1591–92). In his first appearance in 4.2, the zealous rebel Cade's second line, with its biblical echoes of scripture from Leviticus, Ezekiel, and Luke (scripture that had "provided a revolutionary agenda for the Anabaptist leaders"),[90] would have reminded audiences not so much of the

---

89 *A View of Popish Abuses Yet Remaining in the English Church* is excerpted in David Cressy and Lori Anne Ferrell (eds), *Religion and Society in Early Modern England: A Sourcebook* (London, 1996), 84.

90 See *King Henry VI Part 2*, ed. Ronald Knowles (Walton-on-Thames, 1999), n. 31–2 (300): "Cf. Leviticus, 26.8, 'and your enemies shall fall before you upon the sword' …. Texts like Ezekiel, 21.26, 'Remove the diadem, and take off the crown … exalt him that is low, and abase him that is high', and Luke, 1.52, 'He hath put down the mighty from their seats, and exalted them of low degree', provided a revolutionary agenda for the Anabaptist leaders." Knowles, however, does not argue that Cade and his followers are puritan. All references to this edition unless noted.

historical figure as of contemporary puritan caricatures: "For our enemies shall fall before us, *inspired with the spirit* of putting down kings and princes" (4.2, 30–1). Cade's artisan or mechanic followers are also depicted as the godly when they echo puritan cant, speaking of their "vocation" (" 'Labour in thy vocation,' " [l. 14]) as well as of "sin" and "iniquity" ("Then is sin struck down like an ox, and iniquity's throat cut like a calf" [ll. 24–5]).[91] Resembling Cosin's depiction of Hacket in *Conspiracie, for pretended reformation,* Cade even invokes the cause of puritanism as he "vows *reformation*" (4.2, 57–8). He shares, moreover, the puritans' – and especially Hacket's – suspicion of devils when he accuses an opponent of having "a familiar under his tongue" (4.7, 98), claims to be "[i]n despite of the devils and hell" (4.8, 201–2), and boasts that he could defy "ten thousand devils" (4.10, 60) in possible allusions to Hacket's boasts that he constantly endured all the torments that "Deuils in hell" could cause him. More to the point, he cites the biblical authority of the lack of hierarchy in Eden to support his cause ("And Adam was a gardener" l. 121) as he zealously "pray[s] God" (4.9, 37), "beseech[es] God" (4.9, 36), invokes "God's curse" (4.8, 31), and piously objects when a man "speaks not i' God's name" (4.7, 101). And like the leveling "Anabaptisticall Brother[s]"[92] who envisioned an essentially communist society, Cade promises that "All the realm shall be in common" (4.2, 60–1). He claims, too, that in one universal livery all "may agree like brothers" (4.2, 67), while referring to his followers as "Fellow-kings" (4.3, 148–9) and declaring that wives shall be "in common" too, since, he adds, "we charge and command that their wives be as free as heart can wish or tongue can tell" (4.7, 113–15). As he does so, he evokes orthodox propagandists' fears such as those stated in the famed *Homily of Obedience* (1560): "Take way kings, princes, rulers, … and such estates of God's order, … no man shall keep his wife, children,

---

91 In the Arden edition Knowles includes the following note for these lines: "reminiscent of Old Testament rituals of atonement for 'sin and 'iniquity' using various beasts, including the calf and bullock. See Leviticus, 9 and 16" (299). Likewise, when Cade praises the Butcher saying, "They fell before thee like sheep and oxen" (4.3, 3), Knowles notes: "There is possibly an allusion here to the Israelites fighting the Philistines: see 1 Samuel, 14.32" (311).

92 Nashe, *Unfortunate Traveller,* in *Works of Thomas Nashe,* 2: 232.

and possessions in quietness, all things shall be in common." In an Elizabethan context, therefore, there can be little doubt that Shakespeare recast the historical rebel Cade in terms of the contemporary clownish, radical puritan stereotype.

Most importantly, in terms of this ignorant, leveling puritan type, Cade is characterized as embodying the distorted, stereotypical puritans' Counter-Renaissance antipathy toward literacy. In fact, Shakespeare characterizes Cade as an arrogant, illiterate zealot, violently declaiming against literacy as a profane enormity, thereby evoking contemporary figures such as Browne, Barrow, or Hacket. Cade's suspicion of Latin in particular ("Away with him, away with him! He speaks Latin" [4.7, 53]) recalls anti-puritan parody of puritan opposition to "prophane studies" and, especially, Latin as the diabolical language of "the Beast." And, in 4.2, when informed that the clerk of Chatham "can write and read" (l. 75), for instance, Cade exclaims, "O, monstrous!" (l. 78). The Clerk's literacy also makes him "a villain" (l. 79) and a diabolical "conjuror" (l. 81). After Cade examines the clerk with "Dost thou use to write thy name? Or hast thou a mark to thyself like an honest plain-dealing man?" (ll. 89–91) and the rebels learn that the Clerk can indeed write, Cade's ignorant followers explode, "He hath confessed – away with him! He's a villain and a traitor" (ll. 94–5), and Cade orders, "Away with him, I say, hang him with his pen and inkhorn about his neck" (ll. 96–7). Later, Cade denounces Lord Saye's literacy on conspicuously strict moral grounds:

> Thou hast most traitorously corrupted the youth of the realm in erecting a grammar school; and, whereas our forefathers had no ... books ... thou hast caused printing to be used .... It will be proved to thy face that thou hast men about thee that usually talk of a noun and a verb and such abominable words as no Christian ear can endure to hear .... Moreover, thou hast put [poor men] in prison, and because they could not read thou hast hanged them, when indeed only for that cause they had been most worthy to live. (4.7, 30–42)

As real-life radical reformers like Barrow did,[94] and in keeping with the

---

93 Christopher Hill, *Change and Continuity in 17th-Century England* (New Haven, CT, 1991), 189.
94 See page 119 above.

stereotype of puritans as opposed to learning, Cade views literacy as corrupting, so that grammar schools and knowledge of grammar are abominations, education itself becomes un-Christian, and ignorance and illiteracy are a matter of pride, indeed a type of election.

"PLAINE AND EASIE":
THE RAMIST METHOD ... OF CLOWNING

In a context of stereotypical puritan anti-intellectualism, anti-puritan satirists were able to draw further fuel for their stupid-puritan stereotype from a celebrated academic controversy at Cambridge involving the "reformed" rhetoric, logic, and all-encompassing "method" of Calvinist academic Peter Ramus, who was martyred in 1572 at the St Bartholomew's Day Massacre at Paris, and who was thereafter the intellectual hero and primary academic authority of the puritan faction at Cambridge. In *1 Parnassus*, the puritan Stupido marks his ignorance not merely through his identification with Marprelate but, from his first lines, through his equal devotion to Ramus:

> Welcome, my welbeloved brethren! trulie (I thanke God for it!) I have spent this day to my great comfort. I have (I pray God prosper my labours!) analised a peece of an hommelie according to Ramus, and surelie in my minde and simple opinion Mr Peter maketh all things verie plaine and easie. (ll. 322–7)

Like Martinism or puritan hostility to reason, belief in Ramus's authority contributes to the stereotype of puritan stupidity. As we shall see, the Cambridge satire echoes the standard criticism of Ramus, that is, that he had dumbed down learning by making it "simple," "plaine and easie" for simple understandings.

Born *c.* 1515 into poverty (with a charcoal burner for a grandfather and a humble farmer as a father), Pierre de la Ramée did not have an auspicious start as an academic. Rather, because economic hardships forced him to interrupt his studies twice, he was, somewhat embarrassingly, older than the other boys in college, and there were also "stories that young Pierre was slow in learning and found it hard to reason to the point."[95] Nevertheless, a determined Ramus finally earned his Master of

---

[95] Ong, *Ramus, Method, and the Decay of Dialogue*, 19.

Arts degree at the then-tardy age of twenty-one. Undaunted by his late start, he soon ambitiously set to work on "a savage and sweeping attack on Aristotle and Aristotelians" in his *Remarks on Aristotle*,[97] in which he claimed to have found "no division of logic in the *Organon*" and argued that "the chaos" he found needed to be simplified and set "into order"[98] – indicating the marked fixation with order that was to become characteristic of Ramism. But when Ramus's early work was put on trial in the first controversy of his career, he "seems to have held against Aristotle chiefly the fact that he did not start each book of the *Organon* with a definition" so that on March 1, 1544, a royal commission denounced Ramus as too poorly versed in philosophy to teach it and forbade the publication of his attacks on Aristotle, which contained things which were "faulses et estraunges," for "les grand bien et prouffit des lettres et sciences" because of his demonstrable incompetence in attacking Aristotle's dialectic both in obvious bad faith ("mauvaise voulente") and "without giving evidence of understanding it."[99] Most humiliating of all, prior to Henry II's accession, Ramus was forced to teach math – hardly a strength – rather than his beloved logic, a pathetic detail which satirists would exploit.

In his aim of simplifying and re-ordering Aristotle, Ramus was concerned that his counter-method be easy for schoolboys to memorize. Although memorization was already deemed centrally important to understanding in his day, throughout Ramus's work, reason (*ratio*) is "practically *identical* with memory," so that "[t]he memorization process for Ramus [became] virtually synonymous with understanding."[100] Ramus was frank therefore in boasting that "however simple and few the precepts"[101] in which it was rendered, his method was superior because "it is the best possible method for enabling the schoolboy to memorize the twenty-eight lines of Ovid in question."[102] And, for all his attacks on Aristotelian syllogisms, Ramus and his English

96 Ibid., 21.
97 Ibid., 197.
98 Ibid., 44.
99 Ibid., 24.
100 Ibid., 194; emphasis mine.
101 Ibid., 193.
102 Ibid., 194.

followers – among them, William Perkins and Martin Marprelate him self – were, in practice, themselves fixated on syllogisms and "epitomes" (simplified, brief summaries) in keeping with Ramus's counsel:

> When you have cut out from the parts of the continuous discourse the many syllogisms therein (after having found them, for they are often concealed), take away all the amplifications, and, after making brief headings to note the arguments used, form into one syllogism the sum total of the discourse, this sum total being ordinarily self-evident, although it may be swelled to undue proportions by accumulations of ornaments.[103]

Like Ramus's humble origins and his muddled attack on Aristotle, the vaunted "simple ... precepts" of Ramist method presented an easy target for Ramus's relentless opponents.

Those traditionalists most hostile to Ramus and his followers discredited the authority of Ramism in much the same fashion as they degraded Martinism and puritanism generally, that is, by way of repeated associations with ignorance, the lower classes, and clowns. As a result of Ramus's biography, his self-avowed aim of simplifying or reducing logic and rhetoric into forms more easily memorized by schoolboys, his reputation among his critics for dilettantism and misunderstanding the subjects he treated,[104] and the unsubtle application of Ramist method by puritan devotees (including unlearned autodidacts), Ramism came to be associated with paradoxically ignorant pedantry among the Aristotelian, anti-puritan faction. For example, satirists such as the Cambridge-educated Nashe mocked the puritan Ramist faction for their "thredde-bare knowledge" and claimed that "these men make no other vse of learning but to shewe it ... [and] seeme learned to none but to Idiots, who with a coloured shew of zeale, they allure ... to their [i]llusion."[105] Moreover, no doubt observing Martin's use of syllogisms and "epitomes," Nashe concluded by 1590 that Marprelate himself was once part of the Ramist faction at Cambridge: "Who then such an vnnatural enemie to *Aristotle*, or such a

---

103 Ibid., 191.
104 Ibid., 18–20.
105 Nashe, *Anatomie of Absurditie*, in *Works of Thomas Nashe*, 1: 20, 21.

new-fa[n]gled friend vnto *Ramus*?"   Martin had in fact gone so far in his enthusiasm for Ramus as to insist that his opponents "should write syllogistically ... because [their] stile [was] rude and barbarous,"[107] and Lyly had retorted that the tinkerly Martin "hath sillogismes in pike sauce."[108]

Nashe furthered the connection between Ramism, ignorance, and Martinism by mocking mercilessly the somewhat rustic background of one of Ramus's most outspoken advocates at Cambridge, that is, the pedantic, quarrelsome, sometime Cambridge don, Gabriel Harvey, the son of a rope-maker, who patterned himself after his hero Ramus.[109] Referring dismissively to Harvey during the Nashe–Harvey pamphlet war, Nashe writes, "for what can bee made of a Ropemaker more than a Clowne?"[110] Nashe would also rail against Harvey, that "peruerse *Ramisticall* hereticke,"[111] for "abusing of *Aristotle*, & setting him vp on the Schoole gates, painted with Asses eares on his head," asking, "is it any discredit for me, thou great *babound*, ... to be censured by thee that hast scorned the Prince of Philosophers?"[112] It was likewise the puritan Ramist faction that Nashe had in mind when he mused: "I know not how it commeth to passe, by the doting practice of our Diuinitie Dunces, that striue to make their pupills pulpit-men ... those yeares which should bee imployed in *Aristotle* are expired in Epitomies."[113]

In failing to appreciate Aristotle, Ramus, like his disciple Harvey, was mocked as an ignorant dilettante. For example, in making Ramus a character in *The Massacre at Paris* (*c.* 1590), Christopher Marlowe, witness to the conflict between Ramists and Aristotelians during his Cambridge years, gives voice to the conventional criticisms of a

---

106 Nashe, *Almond for a Parrat*, in *Works of Thomas Nashe*, 3: 368.
107 Marprelate, *Epistle*, 53.
108 Lyly, *Pappe with an hatchet*, in *Works of John Lyly*, 3: 411.
109 Harvey had described Ramist "method" with religious fervor as "a heavenly virgin who directs the goddesses of all the Arts" in his *Ode Natalititia* (1574), an elegy to the martyred Ramus. Kendrick W. Prewitt, "Gabriel Harvey and the Practice of Method," *Studies in English Literature* 39. 1 (winter 1999), 19–39; 19, 21.
110 *Works of Thomas Nashe*, 1: 286–7.
111 Nashe, *Have with you to Saffron-Walden* (London, 1596), in ibid., 3: 136.
112 Nashe, *Pierce Penilesse*, in ibid., 1: 196.
113 "To the Gentlemen Stvdents of Both Vniversities," in ibid., 3: 318.

dilettante Ramus "having a smack in all, / And yet ... never sound[ing] anything to the depth" (1.7, 25–6):

> Was it not thou that scoff'st the *Organon* ...?
> ...
> He that will be a flat dichotomist,
> And seen in nothing but epitomes,
> Is in your judgement thought a learned man. (1.7, 27–31)

To this accusation, Ramus retorts that "I knew the *Organon* to be confus'd, / And I reduc'd it into better form" (1.7, 46–7) and, referring to one of his critics, boasts, "my places, being three, contains all his" (1.7, 44–5). Such a response did little to quell concerns that Ramus had "reduc'd" the body of knowledge, that he was arrogantly uninformed and notoriously reductive.

Although the use of dichotomies as a means of systematizing or ordering logic and rhetoric was not exclusive to Ramists, as Marlowe succinctly suggests, Ramus and his followers were recognizably "flat dichotomist[s]," and Walter Ong notes that Ramist method is indeed "definitely committed to the dichotomy."[114] Thus, the division of all topics into two parts took little effort for satirists to reduce, in turn, such conspicuous reduction in logic to *reductio ad absurdum* as when the persona of the Shakespearean comic actor Will Kemp appears in the third part of the Cambridge *Parnassus* trilogy (1601–2) instructing Philomuses in how to be a stage clown by parroting Ramist dichotomies. In Act 4, observing his pupil Philomuses, "Kemp" first remarks, "your face me thinkes would be good for a foolish Mayre or a foolish iustice of peace" (ll. 1849–50). Then, Kemp demonstrates how to be such by employing Ramist rhetoric:

> [M]arke me – Forasmuch as there be two states of a common wealth, the one of peace, the other of tranquility: two states of warre, the one of discord, the other dissention .... I am determined not onely to teach but also to instruct, not onely the ignorant, but also the simple, not onely what is their duty towards their betters, but also what is their dutye towards their superiours. (ll. 1852–6, 1866–9).[115]

---

114 Ong, *Ramus, Method, and the Decay of Dialogue*, 201.
115 Compare the obvious Ramist rhetoric here to that used by non-comformist

Here, the Cambridge author uses the persona of "Kemp" to expose Ramus's dichotomization as arbitrarily imposed upon any and every subject, so that Ramists end up simply repeating themselves and forcing false dichotomies. The satire reflects the fact that "the evolution toward greater and greater dichotomization gathers momentum" in Ramus's work until, incredibly, it "spreads ... ultimately to all reality."[116]

The part "Kemp" recommends to Philomuses, the "foolish Mayre or ... foolish iustice of peace," is of course also part of a broad attack on puritan incorporations, for, as Felicity Heal and Clive Holmes have demonstrated, "There were a sufficient number of zealous magistrates to form a recognisable type ... [and] the zealous justice guyed in the theatre was very likely to be a Puritan."[117] We see a conspicuous use of this zealous puritan magistrate type in a play staged by Paul's Boys, *Blurt, Master Constable*, where the Dogberry-like Constable Blurt often refers reverently to God, such as when he says, "For your serving God I am not to meddle" (1.2, 61), and he speaks in moralizing, puritanical terms as when he is outraged by the "Curtizans" who "are about some ungodlie Acte" (4.3, 152–3). Blurt demonstrates as well a penchant for speaking in malapropisms with the puritans whom Nashe described as suited to be "misterming Clowne[s] in a Comedy." He speaks, for instance, of his duty "in any fray or resurrection [i.e., *insurrection*]" (4.3, 119–20). Blurt also preaches against "baudie house[s], or sincke[s] of wickedness" (1.2, 76–7) and fervently admonishes, "[P]ray take heede with what dice you passe, I meane what company, for Sathan is most busie, where he findes one like himselfe" (1.2, 141–3). This puritan magistrate type and even the religiously inspired "resurrection" malapropism would later appear in Taylor's jestbook *Wit and Mirth* (1629) when a country mayor says:

puritan Cambridge don William Perkins in his *A Golden Chain, or, the Description of Theologie*: "Predestination hath two parts: election and reprobation .... The degrees are in number two: the love of God and the declaration of his love .... The declaration of God's love is twofold. The first, towards infants elected to salvation, the second, towards men ...." Quoted in Cressy and Ferrell, *Religion and Society in Early Modern England*, 114.

116 Ong, *Ramus, Method, and the Decay of Dialogue*, 200–1.

117 Felicity Heal and Clive Holmes, *The Gentry in England and Wales, 1500–1700* (Stanford, CA, 1994), 181.

My Brethren and Neighbors, I do hear that the Queen is dead, where
fore I thought it exceeding fit we should despair to this place, that
being dissembled together we might consult … for … I stand in great
fear that the people will be unrude, so that we shall be in danger of
strange Resurrection.[118]

Clearly, the zealous, ignorant, "misterming" puritan magistrate was
often a figure of fun in Renaissance England.

KEMP'S "APPLAUDED MERRIMENTES":
THE APPEAL OF A SPECIALIZATION IN GODLY CLOWNING

As we have seen, evidence surfaces in the third *Parnassus* play suggesting
that puritan clowns were a specialty of the famous Shakespearean actor
Will Kemp, since he is presented as teaching an amateur actor, in effect,
to "watch me and do it like I do it" (i.e., "marke me –"). Indeed, with
"[h]is reputation as a clown … already established in London by
1590,"[119] being subsequently known as the "head-Master of Morrice-
daunters,"[120] Kemp was staging comic jigs mocking puritans during the
Marprelate controversy in 1588–89,[121] since Martin was skewered on the
stage, Patrick Collinson observes, "within the generic conventions of …
the jig."[122] Harvey gives the titles for two such anti-Martinist jigs: *The
Holie Oath of the Martinistes, That, Thinking to Sweare by His Conscience,
Swore by his Concupiscence* and *The Zelous Love-Letter, or Corinthian
Epistles to the Widow.*[123] Recall that one Marprelate war pamphlet,
Martins Months Minde, complained bitterly about Martin being "made a
May game upon the stage," specifying the stage of Shakespeare's
company before their move to the Globe in 1599, "The Theatre."[124] As
we saw in the previous chapter, one of Nashe's pamphlets actually refers

---

118 *A Nest of Ninnies*, 129.
119 Nunzeger, *Dictionary of Actors*, 216.
120 William Kemp, *Kemps Nine Daies Wonder. Performed in a Daunce from London
to Norwich*, ed. Rev. Alexander Dyce (1860; rpt New York, 1968), 3.
121 See Nicholl, *Cup of News*, 68; Poole, *Radical Religion*, 34, 201 nn. 69, 74.
122 Collinson, "Ben Jonson's *Bartholomew Fair*," 167.
123 Ibid.
124 Chambers, *Elizabethan Stage*, 4: 230.

to a stage portrayal of puritan leaders taking part in the riotous *May-game of Martinisme*.[125] Because of allusions to *The May-game of Martinisme*, "mentioned separately in three anti-Martinist pamphlets,"[126] it would seem that an anti-Martinist *May-game* actually took the stage as a jig, with Kemp likely in the lead role of Martin. Kemp was, after all, identified with the Morris dance, so much so that he danced a sort of marathon Morris from London to Norwich in 1599, a feat he memorialized in *Kemps Nine Daies Wonder* (1600), where he claims in the dedication that he is "such a one as ... hath spent his life in mad Iigges and merry iestes."[127] So known for jigs was Kemp that his name was sometimes attached to them for publication, though he did not author them. Between 1591 and 1595, for instance, the Stationer's Register includes the following advertised "Kemp" jigs: *The Third and Last Part of Kemp's Jig*, *Kemp's Pleasant New Jig of the Broomman*, and *Master Kemp's New Jig of the Kitchen-Stuff Woman*.[128]

The fact that Kemp had participated in attacks on Martin is demonstrated by the 1590 commendatory dedication by Nashe in one anti-Martinist tract to "Brother Kempe" (with the puritan cant endearment "Brother" in addressing fellow "brethren" here reflecting Kemp's anti-puritan comic line), "that most Comicall ... Cavaleire Monsieur du Kempe, Jestmonger and Vice-regent generall to the Ghost of Dicke Tarlton," which suggests the commendation of one comedic anti-Martinist "Cavalier" to another.[129] Kemp had evidently been mocking Marprelate's appropriation of Tarlton's "dual role as Clown and Vice."[130] Likewise, in *Strange News* (1592), during the Nashe–Harvey pamphlet war, "a re-run of the Marprelate controversy,"[131] referring as we have seen dismissively to puritan-sympathizer and Ramist Gabriel Harvey, Nashe writes: "for what can bee made of a Ropemaker more

125 Nashe, *Returne of Pasquill*, in *Works of Thomas Nashe*, 1: 83; see p. 000 above.
126 Nicholl, *Cup of News*, 68, 288–9 n. 27.
127 Kemp, *Kemps Nine Daies Wonder*, 2.
128 Richard Helgerson, *Forms of Nationhood: The Elizabethan Writing of England* (Chicago, 1992), 224–5.
129 Nashe, *Almond for a Parrat*, in *Works of Thomas Nashe*, 3: 339, 3: 341; Nicholl, *Cup of News*, 68.
130 de Grazia, *Hamlet without Hamlet*, 180.
131 Rhodes, *Elizabethan Grotesque*, 92.

than a Clowne? *Will Kempe*, I mistrust it will fall to thy lot for a *merri ment*, one of these dayes."[132] Nashe's remark perpetuates the anti-Martinists' tactic of constructing puritans as low-class, ignorant clowns, but it also reveals Nashe's recognition that, like his own satire, Kemp's "merriments" were often topical and were also targeting clownish puritans. Such references to the clown Kemp, therefore, demonstrate not merely that he had become famous by 1590 but that he had first achieved his fame by acting in anti-puritan comedy.

In fact, even Kemp's so-called "applauded Merrimentes," as advertised on the title page to *A Knacke to Know a Knave* (1592), based upon a Catholic play, were markedly anti-puritan – the play ends with "Honestie" refusing to amend the death sentence imposed on the two puritan villains with the bitter jest, "Trulie no, the spirit doth not mooue me therunto" (G4ᵛ). In the play's lone, brief clown scene, featuring the "mad men of Goteham," Kemp likely took the conventional anti-puritan part of Jeffrey the cobbler, who is the misterming mayor of Gotham. In a mere thirty-nine lines of scripted dialogue (one suspects Kemp improvised more in performance to warrant advertising his connection to the play on the title page), the mad aldermen of Gotham are depicted as having several of the stereotypical features (even beyond ignorance) of the stage puritan. As the clowns debate who shall deliver their petition to the king, they invoke God's name, as when the Miller prays "Jesus blesse him" (l. 1367), or when the Smith hypocritically tries to invoke the "vertue of [the] godhead" of the "god of [his] occupation" (ll. 1374–5), the pagan god Vulcan, at which the cobbler Jeffrey rebukes, "But soft you, your God was a Cuckold, and his Godhead was the horne, and thats the Armes of the Godhead you call upon" (ll. 1376–8). Furthermore, lines such as "nay, neighbor, be not angrie" and "O neighbor, I can not beare it, nor I will not beare it" (ll. 1369, 1388–9) show these clowns using the typical puritan reiteration, the biblical negative imperative, and the chiding, biblical "O." Evidently, then, as in the *Parnassus* play, Kemp's stock "applauded merriments" were anti-puritan comedy that enacted such conventional puritan types as the "ecclesiastical cobbler" and the foolish puritan magistrate.

---

[132] *Works of Thomas Nashe*, 1: 286–7.

It is within the particular context of Kemp's celebrated anti-puritan clowning, which almost undoubtedly also included his appearance as Jack Cade when *Henry VI Part 2* was staged *c.* 1591–92,[133] and of the stupid puritan stereotype generally, that Shakespeare wrote his own strict, stupid puritan clown for Kemp – for whatever reason, Kemp's last Shakespearean role – in 1598. Like the "foolish Mayre or … foolish iustice" that a fictional "Kemp" presented as his comic line in the *Parnassus* play, in *Much Ado About Nothing*, Master Constable Dogberry,[134] the "learned constable" (5.1, 213), is – anticipating that "kind of puritan" Malvolio's (2.3, 140, 147) trick of singularity in *Twelfth Night*[135] – an arrogantly officious, pedantic "officer, … and which is more … a rich fellow enough, go to, … and one that hath two gowns, and everything handsome about him" (4.2, 72–7). Not only does Dogberry preach (e.g., "I think they that touch pitch will be defiled"

---

133 I include a possible composition date of 1592 to reflect the fact that not all are agreed on the 1591 date for *Henry VI Part 2*. See, for instance, Hanspeter Born, who argues for a date "between March and August 1592" (334) in "The Date of *2, 3 Henry VI*," *Shakespeare Quarterly* 25 (1974): 323–34. The earlier date would make Kemp's appearance as Cade likely and the latter certain. Jean Howard conjectures that Kemp "may have played the part of Cade," *The Norton Shakespeare Edition*, ed. Stephen Greenblatt (New York, 1997), 207. Other critics have shared this hypothesis. See T. W. Baldwin, *The Organisation and Personnel of the Shakespearean Company* (Princeton, NJ, 1927), 268; E. W. Talbert, *Elizabethan Drama and Shakespeare's Early Plays: An Essay in Historical Criticism* (Chapel Hill, NC, 1963), 56–60; Longstaffe, "'A Short Report," 13–35. Kemp's connection to the Morris and the jig (Cade is described as "caper[ing] upright like a wild Morisco" [3.1, 365]), the Marprelate war allusions to Kemp's anti-puritan merriments, and Kemp's fame before 1590 make his performance as Cade (*c.* 1591–92) all the more likely.
134 In the Quarto of *Much Ado*, printed in 1600, Kemp's name appears as the speech heading for Dogberry in 4.2, partly perhaps in order to prevent confusion between the speech headings for Constable and Conrade (the latter listed as *"Con."* in the scene): sigs. G4ᵛ–H1ᵛ. See *Shakespeare's Plays in Quarto: A Facsimile Edition of Copies Primarily from the Henry E. Huntington Library*, ed. Michael J. B. Allen and Kenneth Muir (Berkeley, CA, 1981), 514–15. The speech heading for Kemp here is generally taken, rightly I think, as clear evidence that the part was composed for Kemp before he left Shakespeare's company after the 1598 season.
135 For discussion of Malvolio as a type of worldly puritan, see Paul Yachnin, "Reversal of Fortune: Shakespeare, Middleton, and the Puritans," *English Literary History* 70.3 (2003): 757–86.

[3.3, 52–3]), but his diction is zealously puritanical. Notably, he speaks consistently of God – a remarkable *twenty-three* times in his appearance in a mere *four* scenes (3.3, 3.5, 4.2. and 5.1), including, to offer but a few instances, "God's a good man" (3.3, 32–3); "God is to be worshipped" (l. 35); "Gifts that God gives" (l. 38); "write 'God' first, for God defend but God should go before such villains" (4.2, 17–18); "God save the foundation" (l. 301); "if a merry meeting may be wished, God prohibit it" (ll. 305–7). While calling upon God is not in itself unusual, such incessant invocations (an average of six per scene) make Dogberry sound self-consciously pious, stereotypically zealous, or "godly," as does another tic, appropriation of the puritan habit of referring to other godly folk as "neighbors" (3.3, 7, 12, 77, 80; 4.1, 1, 16, 32, 36; 5.1, 308), a leveling, communal epithet akin to "brother."[136]

Dogberry also employs a "characteristically puritan trick of style," that is, "the quasi-Hebraic use of repetitive clauses with amplification."[137] Thus, in his accusation against Borachio and Conrade he declares, "Marry, sir, they have committed false report, moreover they have spoken untruths, secondarily they are slanders, sixth and lastly they have belied a lady, thirdly they have verified unjust things, and to conclude, they are lying knaves" (3.1, 202–5). His marked style of repetition also resembles that of Jonson's famous puritan Zeal-of-the-Land Busy – "it were not well, it were not fit, it were abominable, and not good" (1.6, 72–3) – and both speakers reflect the cramming repetition of synonyms that was, according to Eugene E. White, recognizable puritan-speak. The two major, mutually reinforcing methods in puritan rhetoric, White demonstrates, were reiteration and cumulation, "the method of developing an item of support by either restating it in a somewhat different form or repeating it in the same words" and

---

136 Heywood comments on such sayings: "His [the puritan's] phrase is, Verily; By yea and nay, / In faith, in truth, good neighbor, or good brother." Thomas Heywood, *Troia Britanica: Or, Great Britaines Troy* (London, 1609), 89, stanza 51.

137 Leah S. Marcus, "Of Mire and Authorship" in *The Theatrical City: Culture, Theatre and Politics in London, 1576–1649*, ed. David L. Smith, Richard Strier, and David Bevington (Cambridge, 1995), 173–4. Marcus does not refer to Dogberry.

the method of securing magnification of impact by presenting a tightly structured series of related items in support of an idea – the cumulated effect of the series being greater than the thrust warranted by the logical and psychological merit of the items as individual pieces of support.[138]

Of course, when asses like the illiterate Dogberry or the magistrate modeled by the persona of "Kemp" use such rhetoric, they merely sound illogical, though pedantic, echoing conventional satire.

Above all, Dogberry and neighbor Verges often sound not just ignorant but puritanically pious even in their famous malapropisms. Consider Verges's conclusion that men who are not "good men and true" should "suffer salvation [i.e., *damnation*], body and soul" (3.3, 2–3). Lapsing similarly into fervent sanctimony, Dogberry exclaims in strict judgment, "O villain! Thou wilt be condemned into everlasting redemption [i.e., *damnation*] for this" (4.2, 50–1), followed by, "No, thou villain, thou art full of piety [i.e., *impiety*]" (4.2, 70–1). Thus, Dogberry and Verges regularly misuse words that (were they real people) they might have overheard from the puritans' famous preaching ministry, as when Dogberry claims that the Sexton "hath reformed [i.e., *informed*] Signor Leonato of the matter" (5.1, 238) or when he prays that God may "prohibit" (i.e., *permit*) a "merry meeting" with Leonato in the future (5.1, 307). Apparently, Shakespeare implies, the unlettered Dogberry, for whom "writing and reading" are "vanity" (3.3, 18–19), has encountered weighty words such as "reformed," "redemption," "salvation," "piety," and "prohibit," while gadding to sermons. Dogberry, too, thus recalls the conventional type of "misterming Clowne in a Comedy" that Nashe claimed puritan preachers resembled. There was some truth to Nashe's attack, since puritan admissions suggest that actual godly malapropisms were an all too common fault in puritan speech because sermons frequently "over-r[a]n [the people's] understandings": "Many ... have that in their minds which is not ripe for utterance; and through ill education and disuse, they are strangers to the expressions of those things which they have some Conceptions

---

138 Eugene E. White, *Puritan Rhetoric: The Issue of Emotion in Religion* (Carbondale, IL, 1972), 187. White does not refer to Dogberry.

of." One would, I believe, be hard-pressed to find a better explanation of Dogberry's pious-impious malapropisms.

Though it is not necessary to the conclusion that Dogberry was recognizably of the proud ignorant puritan type in the tradition of Marprelate, Stupido, or Kemp's merriments elsewhere, Dogberry's attempts at pedantry (i.e., he is humorously referred to as the "learned constable" [5.1, 213]), as performed by that occasional mocker of the French scholar Ramus, "Monsieur du Kempe" (here, too, recall Dogberry's affected "Adieu. Be vigitant" [3.3, 83]), may even have taken on a decidedly Ramist flavor for an Elizabethan audience. In particular, Dogberry employs the puritans' rhetorical use of the Ramist method of ordering by numbered lists – "secondarily they are slanders, sixth and lastly they have belied a lady, thirdly they have verified unjust things" (3.1, 203–5) – and his absurd "sixth and lastly" may even allude to Martin Marprelate's and martyrologist John Foxe's somewhat overblown yet homely "sixtly and lastly."[140] Whether employing a dichotomy or a list, Ramist method was based primarily on the importance of ordering logic; indeed, Ramist dialectic is, essentially, order. Ramus had boasted, for instance, that the basis for his dialectic was the "order found within things themselves,"[141] and he had attacked Aristotle for failing to consider that most important question, for him, of "what is first, what second, what third."[142] Likewise, in his first treatment of "method" in his *Training in Dialectic,* first published pseudonymously in 1546, Ramus had defined method as "the arrangement of many good arguments."[143] And, in the final revision of his *Dialectic* (1572), Ramus would write more expansively: "Method is the intelligible order of various homogeneous axioms ranged one before the other according to the clarity of their nature."[144] In Dogberry's attempt at intelligibly ordered Ramist method, however, his inability to count

---

139 R. Baxter, *The Reformed Pastor* (London, 1656), 357, 431–2.

140 Marprelate, *Hay any worke for Cooper?,* 12; John Foxe, *Acts and Monuments* (1583 edition); available online at www.hrionline.ac.uk/foxe/, accessed: 03.27.2006.

141 Ong, *Ramus, Method, and the Decay of Dialogue,* 195.

142 Ibid.

143 Ibid., 245.

144 Ibid., 251.

prompts Claudio's jest, "Rightly reasoned, and in his own division" (5.1, 198–9) – a probable gibe at Ramus once being forced to teach math. The arrogant Dogberry was not merely generically pretentious in his attempted transitions and numbered lists, then, but rather he was pedantic in a manner that some would have recognized as a burlesque of the Ramist learning valorized by puritans ranging from the fictional Stupido and Marprelate to the historical Perkins.

Indeed, given that, in Ramism, order was synonymous with method, and memorization equivalent to understanding, Dogberry's illogical reasoning constituted a subtle satiric rebuttal to Ramist method. Dogberry is illogical not, as Ramus would have it in his attack on Aristotle, because his discourse lacks order; instead, as we have seen, the "learned constable" painstakingly *attempts* to order his rhetoric not just in his "sixth and lastly" speech but also when he conscientiously insists, "write God first, for God defend but God should go before such villains" (4.2, 18–19). Nor does Dogberry fail to understand because he cannot remember things (recall that for Ramus "reason" is "practically *identical* with memory" and "memorization … is virtually synonymous with understanding"),[145] since Dogberry's memory is, ironically, elephantine and obsessive (e.g., "But masters, remember that I am an ass. Though it be not written down, yet forget not that I am an ass" [5.1, 69–70]), but rather because he orders and remembers without first *understanding*, and thus takes things out of context, zealously imposing form divorced from content and meaning. This idiosyncrasy, of course, matches precisely the anti-Ramists' charge against Ramus, who as we saw, according to his critics and the royally commissioned censors, had attacked Aristotle's supposed lack of organization without giving evidence of understanding the content first.

More broadly, we might also consider the ways in which Dogberry's susceptibility to mis-hearing and zealous malapropisms, like Cade's exaggerated misinterpretations of the puritan opposition to the reading ministry, reflects ironically on what Bryan Crockett has called the puritan "cult of the ear,"[146] the belief not simply that preaching was

---

145 Ibid., 194.
146 Bryan Crockett, *The Play of Paradox: Stage and Sermon in Renaissance England* (Philadelphia, PA, 1995), especially 5, 50, 55–6, 69.

edifying but that *hearing* the word of God was the best path to salvation and enlightenment. After all, "The usual Protestant claim [was] that biblical ideas are imparted not primarily by reading but by the spoken word."[147] And, as Crockett further notes, "Protestant reformers frequently support their position by quoting Paul's statement, 'Then faith is by hearing, and hearing by the word of God' (Rom. 10:17)."[148] But as "Protestant 'logolatry' supplant[ed] the idolatry of which the reformers accuse Catholicism,"[149] Shakespeare's stupid puritans point to what was potentially dangerous about the cult of the ear. That is, puritans' absolute faith that hearing would be edifying did not adequately account for rampant individual misinterpretation. As with the satire of Ramism and inspiration, the basis for authority of puritan interpretation was once again called into question.

And yet, I hasten to add, even if Dogberry deflates the proud ideals of puritan logolatry, interpretation, learning, and rhetoric, our response to Dogberry is more complex than seeing him solely as a figure of fun at the puritans' expense, in part because he is such a delight. We also learn that Dogberry is well meaning, a good "neighbor" and friend to his partner Verges, and, ultimately, an essential part of the community, one who plays a key role in unraveling the villains' plot. It may also be instructive that we find ourselves more frustrated with Leonato's arrogance and impatience in dismissing Dogberry in 3.5 than we are with Dogberry's self-satisfied delays. And, on another level, Dogberry's mis-hearing malapropisms subtly reflect the theme of overhearing in the play as a whole – as in the punning title *Much Ado About Nothing*, where "nothing" would have been pronounced like "noting," a term for hearing, as in music. Dogberry's mistaking, ironically, is analogous to the mistakes other, supposedly wiser, characters make. Shakespeare thus represents Dogberry – a type of the ignorant puritan – as anything but ostracized in the play. As a result, for all of many puritans' antipathy to the professional theatre, Shakespeare's humorous take on puritanism seems decidedly more tolerant, patient, inclusive, and generously amused than that of other satirists.

147 Ibid., 55.
148 Ibid., 9.
149 Ibid., 55.

In the end, there were many rationales for staging the puritan minority as "Stupidos." Representations of stupid puritan clowns could serve a variety of functions, ranging from the shoring up ideological boundaries and the debunking of the spiritual claims and mode of education avowed by an extreme wing of Protestantism to buttressing the authority of existing modes of interpretation. Moreover, Martin Marprelate's populist adoption of a low-class, clown-preacher persona (provoking the anti-Martinists' satire and Kemp's on-stage merriments) led conformist opponents to stereotype puritans as ignorant, "Anabaptisticall," "ecclesiastical cobblers," who were irrationally inspired by the spirit and unable to exercise reason. Similarly, Ramus's attack on Aristotle and his boasts of producing a simplified method allowed depictions on stage and in print of puritan learning as dumbed-down pedantry, and the arrogance of godly magistrates and their vaunted "learned ministry" opposed to the "reading ministry" and "humane learning" contributed further to a prevalent Renaissance English stereotype of puritans as, above all perhaps, "proud ignorants." At the same time, the interplay between the university drama (with its delight in the professional actor Kemp's puritan clowns) and public theatre author Shakespeare's awareness of Ramist rhetoric and the educational and religious controversies regarding reason and authority of interpretation is significant both in that it suggests ways in which interest in such concerns cut across the culture and in that it demonstrates that "academic" and "professional" drama were not so separate as critical tradition assumes.

An examination of the stupid clown typology also points to ways in which humorous portrayals could require layered responses from audience members, thereby complementing Grace Tiffany's analysis of yet another Kemp role,[150] Sir Jack Falstaff's embodiment of once-familiar puritan traits (including, again, puritan rhetoric[151]) in *Henry IV, Parts 1 and 2.* Tiffany demonstrates that Shakespeare's puritans "were never unsympathetically rendered or wholly unattractive."[152] Instead, as we

---

150 Wilson notes that the Quarto edition of *Henry IV Part 2* reads "Enter Will" at Falstaff's apparent entrance "early in the Doll scene (2.4)"; *The Fortunes of Falstaff,* 124. Compare to my note 144 above.
151 Here see also Poole, *Radical Religion,* 34–7.
152 Tiffany, "Puritanism in Comic History," 257.

have seen via Dogberry and the simultaneously grotesque, charismatic, and sympathetic Cade, the audience experiences in performance what Tiffany characterizes as a kind of shared "delight"[153] in the Shakespearean puritan. However satirical such puritan characterizations no doubt were, it would be foolish to ignore "the audience sympathy generated for"[154] them, something which "probably softened the anti-Puritan attitudes of mainstream playgoers."[155] Indeed, we cannot dismiss the sympathy evoked by the banished Falstaff, the duped and defeated Cade, or the notoriously abused wits of the foolishly vain Malvolio of *Twelfth Night*, since such characterizations all emphasize the costs of ostracizing puritans. Even as the proud ignorance of Shakespeare's devout asses participated in satire aimed at exposing the dangers of zealously inspired folly, it could also compel fellow-feeling. What is finally most certain, though, is how mistaken the dominant critical narrative has been in claiming that professional drama in the Renaissance rejected the religious concerns of the medieval drama or that the clown Tarlton had "completely secularized the vice" tradition.[156] In fact, in Shakespeare's company, a more secular brand of clowning was late in coming in the persona of the witty "artificial" fool in *King Lear* (1605), as played by Kemp's successor Robert Armin, though elsewhere, as in *Twelfth Night* (1601–2), he had jested about "liv[ing] by the church" (3.1, 3) in a play in which he disguises as a curate and mocks a puritan, details suggesting that his clowning too had often touched upon religious satire.

---

153 Ibid., 266, 275, in reference to Falstaff.
154 Ibid., 266.
155 Ibid., 279.
156 Weimann, *Shakespeare and the Popular Tradition*, 187.

Chapter 4

THE FOOL "BY ART":
THE ALL-LICENSED "ARTIFICIAL" FOOL IN
THE *KING LEAR* QUARTO

I TURN, in this chapter, to another clown type in the professional theatre, the fool proper. Here, I begin with an examination of the logical underpinnings of criticism addressing the two texts of *King Lear* as they affect the character of the Fool(s) there, with the ultimate goal being a better understanding of historical fool types and lingering confusion about this iconic character as we have come to know him, typically, from conflated editions of the play. That conflated figure is a strange product for, as a number of Renaissance textual scholars argued persuasively in the 1980s, most notably in *The Division of the Kingdoms*,[1] the Quarto and Folio versions of *King Lear* are quite different texts often producing remarkably distinct literary and theatrical effects. Any interest in this discovery was effectively and, unfortunately, insistently quelled by the vast majority of "revisionist" critics who, determined in part to prove that the Folio was authorial and definitive, argued that the Folio text was simply an improved or perfected version of the earlier and, they assumed, therefore necessarily inferior, Quarto text. Because most of their work amounted to an extended attempt to demonstrate that the Folio renderings of characters were superior to artistically deficient counterparts in the Quarto, the earlier text has never been fully appreciated. Oddly, the chief victim of an attack on the relative artistry of the Quarto was the Fool, a character revisionist critics found to be

---

1 Gary Taylor and Michael Warren (eds), *The Division of the Kingdoms: Shakespeare's Two Versions of King Lear* (Oxford, 1983).

either too satirical or, conversely, not as satirical as the Folio version. Critical interpretations of the part elsewhere continue to swing between blathering idiot and bitter sage, whereas stage tradition preferring either the Folio or conflated editions has tended to favor the pathos of the former interpretation. The puzzling history of the Fool – including his shocking excision for over 150 years (1681 to 1838), initiated for political and aesthetic reasons under the mutually censorious influences of neoclassicism and the "crisis years of 1678–82," particularly in the wake of the trumped-up Popish Plot of 1679[2] – suggests that perhaps we are missing something in the Quarto, for all the critics' dismissal of it as inferior.

One purported deficiency in the Quarto, according to one revisionist critic, was Shakespeare's occasionally inartful "impulse to comment on contemporary abuses,"[3] something nowhere more evident than in satirical passages involving the Fool. Without any consideration of the history of the heretofore conventional satirical role played by the theatrical clown, Gary Taylor, one of those who most advanced a recognition of two texts, shifted the discussion of the Fool's part to considering whether or not censorship accounts for textual variants. Taylor himself remained anxiously opposed to any notion of censorship as a motive for Folio revisions in an evident attempt to re-establish a stable, inviolable text. He defended Folio changes, for instance, on what he called "purely artistic grounds," since "censorship imposes the political restraints of a particular time and place upon a potentially timeless work of art." He assumed that Shakespeare instead employed a sort of self-censorship as he revised the play, always having "half a mind's eye on the censor";[4] accordingly, Shakespeare was cast in the role of an artistically maturing reviser and was thus supposed to have practiced an artistic restraint in seeking "to play down the mocking tone [evident in the Quarto] …, and to remove frankly topical exchange[s]" throughout the Folio revision.[5]

---

2 Sandra Clark (ed.), *Shakespeare Made Fit: Restoration Adaptations of Shakespeare* (London, 1997), xlvi.
3 Gary Taylor, "Monopolies, Show Trials, Disaster, and Invasion: *King Lear* and Censorship," in *The Division of the Kingdoms: Shakespeare's Two Versions of King Lear*, ed. Gary Taylor and Michael Warren (Oxford, 1983), 77–119; 109.
4 Ibid., 75, 80, respectively.
5 Ibid., 85.

As even Taylor conceded, James's censor George Buc, rather than Shakespeare, may nonetheless have censored the Quarto Fool's famously biting gibes in 1.4 which muse on the fact that the king has given all of his titles away except that of fool and that monopolies at court are now rampant – apparent references to two notorious abuses under James, the wholesale creation of new knighthoods for Scottish favorites and, particularly, the granting *en masse* of monopolies: "[T]he Fool's reference to the granting of monopolies would, without a doubt, have been politically sensitive. The King's granting of monopolies was debated in Parliament in 1604 and 1606 (*as well as in 1610, 1614, and 1621*) ...."[6] Here, nonetheless, Taylor's New Critical bent, which assumed, as Annabel Patterson notes, that historical topicality cannot be characteristic of a great artist,[7] forced him to conclude that, "by curbing [the] impulse" to "comment upon contemporary abuses," the "censor ... may actually ... have done the timeless work of art a service."[8] Taylor's critical tastes, it would seem, do not tend toward satire because, for him, the contemporary and the topical are shallow. Others may perhaps wonder whether one critic's "timeless" or "universal" art may not, sometimes, be another's shallow artistry.

Happily, in her landmark analysis of Renaissance attitudes about the grounds for censorship, Patterson was necessarily much more amenable to satirical topicality in the Fool. She stressed that an "implied analogy of all kinds, but especially between this time and episodes from past history" was often key to the vitality of the theatre in this era. In terms of topicality, Renaissance contemporaries were, as Patterson underscored, quite evidently not "at all bothered by the inexactness or the incompleteness of the parallel," but were "far more flexible on this issue than many modern critics, who have argued against the presence of topical allusion on the grounds that one-to-one correspondences cannot be found." Instead, it was indeed "the very inexactness of the analogies so produced that made them useful, by providing writers with an escape

---

6 Ibid., 102; emphasis added. If censorship occurred due to monopolies, it may have been as late as 1621.
7 Annabel Patterson, *Censorship and Interpretation: The Conditions of Writing and Reading in Early Modern England* (Madison, 1984), 69.
8 Taylor, "Monopolies, Show Trials, Disaster, and Invasion," 70.

route" – a notion that proves relevant to the satire in the *King Lear* Quarto.

If censorship of the politically topical in the Quarto did conceivably motivate the many cuts, changes, and few odd additions that appear in the Folio, one can only speculate as to when the play might have been censored. But the difficulty of determining such a hypothetical dating increases once we recognize that the 1608 Quarto advertised its performance before the King: "As it was played before the Kings Maiestie at Whitehall upon S. Stephans night in Christmas Hollidayes," which the Stationers' Register for November 26, 1607 specifies as having been "Christmas Last." Given that the 1608 Quarto purports to represent the version performed for the king in 1606, one must wonder if and when James, or his censor Buc, would have balked at any of the play's politically charged topics. That James might have been offended is, in some respects, hard to imagine; on one hand the king seems to have been relatively uninterested in the drama, but this play on the other hand may have interested him as potentially complementing his pet project, the union of England and Scotland as "Great Britain." Glynne Wickham, for one, has read the play as "active propagation" of James's plan, with Lear serving as a disastrous antitype to James, that is, as a divider, not a uniter.[10]

Yet, in the Quarto, we may be witnessing a case of inexactitude paving an open escape route, since the Quarto text evidently got past Buc's suspicious eye in the wake of scandal surrounding *Sejanus* in 1603 and *Eastward Ho* in 1605 and the subsequent May 1606 "Act to Restrain Abuses of Players" prior to the royal performance. Buc would thereafter not likely have smiled upon the King's Men's subsequent publication of a play – advertising its connection to no less a person than the king himself – if he or the king had deemed it offensive. Furthermore, a divided kingdom seems so obviously foolish, as we shall see, in the Quarto that it may have appeared to be offering overt praise for the project of union. It is thus not at all clear that the Quarto *was* censored, but if so it now seems most likely that such censorship would have taken place considerably after the 1606 royal performance or the 1608

9   Patterson, *Censorship and Interpretation,* 55.
10 Glynne Wickham, "From Tragedy to Tragi-comedy: *King Lear* as Prologue," *Shakespeare Survey* 26 (1973): 33–48; 36–43.

publication advertising it. In fact, for all the revisionists' concern to establish the revision as authorial, if current events were a motive, perhaps debate about monopoly in Parliament as late as 1614 and 1621 prompted the hypothetical censorship.[11]

Prior to that, especially when union rather than monopoly was the most prominent issue, seemingly obvious praise might initially have provided a sort of "stalking horse," a harmless-looking cover affording opportunities for the exercise of wit – especially under the additional cover of the "all-licensed fool." After all, as Patterson has noted, parallels to James were both many and striking in the Quarto version of *King Lear*:

> [T]he case for reading Lear not as an antitype but a type of James is based on such well-documented characteristics of the new king as his absolutist rhetoric, his abandonment of the cares of government to the pleasures of hunting, on the prominence of his court fool Archie Armstrong, and on the fact that from the beginning of the reign there was dissatisfaction with his use of the prerogative, his lavish creations of knighthoods for his Scottish followers, for example, and his grants of monopolies.[12]

As Taylor does, Patterson notes the special importance of the Fool in Quarto-only passages, where he is given such biting, topical lines as "No, faith, lords and great men will not let me [have the title of Fool to myself]. If I had a monopoly out, they would have part on't"[13] (Q 1.4, 142–3). It seems undeniable that the Quarto Fool possesses some politically satirical quality, one that even such diametrically opposed critics as Patterson and Taylor have acknowledged.

Many readers may, nonetheless, still be inclined to dismiss the politically satiric as topical in the sense of superficial. Thus, rather than inviting the kind of discontent one has come to expect from a New Historical "local reading" of the play,[14] I want to demonstrate in this

---

11 Taylor, "Monopolies, Show Trials, Disaster, and Invasion," 102; emphasis added. If censorship occurred due to monopolies, it may thus have been as late as after the Parliament of 1621.

12 Patterson, *Censorship and Interpretation*, 68.

13 Ibid.

14 Leah Marcus, *Puzzling Shakespeare: Local Reading and its Discontents* (Berkeley, CA, 1988).

chapter that critical dismissal of Quarto Fool variants buries not simply politics but a complex set of related and attendant conventions, an elevated and ironic aesthetic, and a philosophical ethos that adds tremendous depth to the play as a whole.

TOWARD RECOVERING THE QUARTO FOOL: THE THEATRICAL AND PERFORMATIVE CONTEXT

Recognition of the Quarto Fool's merit was quashed by other strands of revisionist criticism which granted the artistic value of the Fool's satiric voice (unlike Taylor), but then consequently aimed to ascribe *to the Folio* any satirical resonances detected in the composite text passed down through generations of editors and performers. Notably, John Kerrigan employed a theory of revision that assumed "to revise" simply meant "to perfect," so that he deemed the Quarto a rough draft at best, a failed attempt to produce the supposedly more refined Folio.[15] Drawing upon a general impression that in the conflated composite text the Fool often seems witty, bitter, wise, and indeed to be a kind of self-conscious critic and satirist, Kerrigan fell into the revisionist critic's trap as he presupposed that the Folio Fool must exhibit these qualities to a greater degree than did the earlier Quarto Fool. Kerrigan therefore asserted that the Folio Fool is a professional, "consistently a wise and worldly jester, deliberately needling Lear,"[16] and he found it simply "indisputable" that the Folio Fool was in all ways "dramatically superior to his Q equivalent," simply "better in F than Q."[17] Here we have the palpable irony that the Quarto Fool was now dismissed by a revisionist textual scholar

---

[15] Assuming that, because the Quarto version was apparently revised, Shakespeare must have been "dissatisfied with it," Roger Warren and Gary Taylor argue one goal of the critic becomes "guessing at the sources of that dissatisfaction." Taylor, "Monopolies, Show Trials, Disaster, and Invasion," 101; Roger Warren, "The Folio Omission of the Mock Trial: Motives and Consequences," *The Division of the Kingdoms: Shakespeare's Two Versions of King Lear*, ed. Gary Taylor and Michael Warren (Oxford, 1983), 45–57; 45.

[16] John Kerrigan, "Revision, Adaptation, and the Fool in *King Lear*," in *The Division of the Kingdoms: Shakespeare's Two Versions of King Lear*, ed. Gary Taylor and Michael Warren (Oxford, 1983), 195–245; 230.

[17] Ibid., 230.

not as *too much* the topical satirist, as Taylor believed, but as *too little* the needling critic.

A more sensible turn in the criticism occurred thereafter when many, fully persuaded that the texts were indeed quite different, also rejected the subjective argument that authorial perfection was the sole motivation for substantive textual variants. Yet even here, scholars such as R. A. Foakes, who would seem to have had the last word in debate about the differences between the Quarto and Folio Fools in *King Lear*, only appeared to disagree with Kerrigan's conclusion that the Folio version of the character was enhanced by the author. While he outwardly disputed such logic, Foakes did not actually disagree with Kerrigan's essential interpretation. In point of fact, he too fell prey to the same revisionist logic of authorial perfection or improvement when he concluded that the Folio Fool is "*more consistently* a bitter one"; the Folio, he further argued, "*enhances* the acerbic quality" of the Fool as it produces "a sharp mature professional, *deliberately needling Lear.*" Such a conclusion was thus not substantively different from Kerrigan's assertion that the F Fool is "*consistently* a wise and worldly jester, *deliberately needling Lear.*"[18] Even Foakes's word choice echoes Kerrigan's. In the end, therefore, minimal qualifications aside, textual critics arrived at an explicit consensus that the F Fool is "enhanced," more definitive, and, in short, more of a good thing, rather than simply different.

Even more damning to considerations of the merits of the Quarto Fool may well have been Jonathan Goldberg's dismissal of all "character criticism" in a much noted 1986 essay entitled "Textual Properties," subsequently revived in his partially retracted collection of previous essays, *Shakespeare's Hand* (2003). Combining deconstructionist theory with research demonstrating the instability of the Shakespearean text due to performance cuts, sophisticators, and compositors, Goldberg claimed that since "the stability of the word is in question, so, too, is the stability of character," which "cannot be assimilated to an authorial intentionality." Even as he staked a claim to a more "rigorous" brand of "historicism" that was more responsive to

---

18 Ibid.; R. A. Foakes, "Textual Revision and the Fool in King Lear," *Trivium* 20 (1985): 33–47; 37; see also *King Lear*, ed. R. A. Foakes, Arden Shakespeare edition (Walton-on-Thames, 1997), 134, 137, emphasis added.

the history or the "materiality" of texts, his decontextualizing approach, which viewed play-texts and characters alike as always already circumscribed by the page, never the theatre, also quite clearly offered a dismissal of drama as theatre. Shakespearean drama itself, like its author, was lifeless, a dead thing to be dissected by "free play," but it was, and is, never *a* play.[19]

The dismissal of all so-called "character criticism" cannot really be defended on historical grounds, since any approach to Renaissance drama that denies absolutely the relevance of theatrical/dramatic contexts and considerations is itself only very selectively historical, particularly in light of the increased awareness of the importance of theatre history in Renaissance studies over the last decades. In this study, concerned as it is about historical contexts, what is perhaps more desirable than a dismissal of theatrical concerns is that, when possible, we try to attend to character in Renaissance terms and consider it, and dramatic revisions, within the context of theatre culture as well. Such attention to the theatrical and historical context is precisely what was lacking in previous analyses of Fool variants.

Perhaps the most important context usually overlooked by those who have examined *Lear*'s Fool and attendant variants has been the historical distinction between so-called "natural" and "artificial" fool types, a distinction, according to Enid Welsford, "so often made in Elizabethan times."[20] Given pervasive modern ignorance and/or misconceptions about the existence of, or differences between, natural and artificial fools, and because no one has previously done so in any detail, it may be useful to offer briefly some criteria for distinguishing between the two types, especially since artificial fools stood essentially in opposition to the thing itself, the "very fool" or "natural," whose folly was real in that it came "by nature," not by pretended artifice or art. While the natural

---

[19] Jonathan Goldberg, "Textual Properties," *Shakespeare Quarterly* 37.2 (1986): 213–17; 215, 214, 216; in his more recent collection, *Shakespeare's Hand* (Minneapolis, 2003), Goldberg now concedes many of his theoretical excesses, admitting that "Textual Properties" was a "somewhat polemical piece" among a collection of essays which now "seem routinized" and which betray "an inattention to historical differences that matter" as well as a failure "to recognize that historical limits impinge upon theoretical possibility" (ix, xii, xviii).

[20] Welsford, *The Fool*, 119.

fool, who first emerged in this study in the discussion of early blackface, was an "innocent," a butt who was generally laughed at for mental deficiencies, the artificial fool distinguished himself and his fooling with his clever, bitter wit, as he provoked laughter at others. Thus, whereas the innocent natural fool was helplessly dependent, and consequently could often be depicted as sweet and pathetic even when he was unintentionally insulting, the artificial fool was capable and characterized by his consistent and intentional bitterness. Similarly, while the natural was demonstrably irrational and so was often painstakingly characterized by nonsensical or disjointed logic, the artificial fool was just as clearly distinguished as rational by his ordered, and occasionally even artfully formal, or syllogistic, logic. And, while the natural was most foolish in that he lacked self-knowledge, the artificial fool was, like Feste in *Twelfth Night*, "wise enough to play the fool" (3.1, 60)[21] and even philosophical in that, "profit[ing] in the knowledge of [him]self" (5.1, 19–20), he harped upon the Humanist, Socratically inspired themes of *nosce te ipsum* ("know thyself") and of the universality of folly, for, as Feste would have it, "Foolery, sir, does walk about the orb like the sun – it shines everywhere" (3.1, 38–9). Finally, whereas the natural or "innocent" was an unconsciously transgressive social deviant who innocently flouted customary rules and thus unwittingly turned the world upside down, the "fool by art" regularly self-consciously flouted such transgression, exposing the socially deviant as natural fools. Therefore, while the natural fool's unintended humor could be inversive and anarchic, the artificial fool's purposeful comedy was instead typically satiric and even "normative" in character in that it defended, promoted, and constructed social norms by mocking transgression and unwitting folly.[22]

The persistent use of artificial fools such as Touchstone, Feste, Lavatch, Thersites, Carlo Buffone, and Passarello rather than ignorant,

---

21 Unless otherwise specified in the case of quotations material to my discussion of differences between Q and F Lear, quotations from Shakespeare's other plays refer to *The Riverside Shakespeare edition*.

22 On artificial fools, see Charles S. Felver, *Robert Armin, Shakespeare's Fool: A Biographical Essay*, Kent State University Bulletin (Kent, OH, 1961); Wiles, *Shakespeare's Clown*, 150; and Theodore B. Leinwand's "Conservative Fools in James's Court and Shakespeare's Plays," *Shakespeare Studies* 19 (1987): 219–34.

carnivalesque rustic or mechanic clowns (which we have seen had dominated the 1580s and 1590s as performed by Tarlton and Kemp) in plays by Shakespeare, Jonson, and Marston indicates that playwrights were self-consciously participating in an artificial fool fad in the years following 1599. For more than a decade thereafter the artificial fool rather than the natural became the most prominent comedic role in Shakespeare's company. The Shakespearean actor famed for playing these artificial fools, Robert Armin, the self-proclaimed "Clonnico del Mundo" ("Clown of the Globe")[23] after *c.* 1599 and author of *Fool Upon Fool or Sixe Sortes of Sottes* (1605), was himself extremely self-conscious about the distinction between fool types as he wrote, for instance, in *A Nest of Ninnies* (1608) that "Fools artificial with their wits lay wait / To make themselves Fools, liking the disguise / To feed their own minds and the gazers['] eyes."[24] Armin was, moreover, unmistakably aware of his popular role as scourge of folly, so much so that he explained on the title page to his satirical *Quips Upon Question* (1600): "[I]t is my profession, / To jest at a jester [i.e., a fool], in his transgression." To sum up, then, the self-conscious artificial fool type played by Armin had foils "to jest at" to set himself apart as he distinguished himself from his peers' foolishness through his rational logic and idiom, wise self-knowledge, demonstrably bitter, often satiric wit, which he employed in jesting at the transgressions of those whom he proved to be naturals.

Far from being mere arcane trivia, this historical distinction between fool types and comic functions so familiar in Shakespeare's day can be applied not only to an analysis of the textual variants of the Fool in Q and F *Lear*, but also to scholarly and dramatic interpretations of the Fool's part more generally (and to that of other Shakespearean fools as well). By keeping in mind the Renaissance distinction between artificial and natural fool types in each text, my argument thus addresses one source of the confusion surrounding the Fool in *King Lear* in the critical and theatrical tradition. Since his return to the stage in 1838, after an absence precipitated by the editorial excision of the Fool by Nahum Tate in 1681, the Fool in *King Lear* has been an enigma.[25] Critical interpretations of the

---

[23] Nungezer, *Dictionary of Actors*, 17.
[24] *A Nest of Ninnies*, 26.
[25] In 1681 Tate's adaptation, entitled *The History of King Lear*, appeared with a number of significant changes, among them the addition of a love plot between

character "have swung wildly between the extremes" of "blathering natural" and "canny rationalist"[26] – that is, between natural and *artificial* fool. But such wild "swings" are sometimes less evident in production. In fact, although the Fool, as he has evolved in conflated editions of the play, often has bitter moments, most actors and scholars have, though typically unconsciously, traditionally tended to interpret the Fool as a natural, as a sweet, comic butt, a sad, pathetic clown who is laughed at but pitied. Surprisingly few critics have been aware of the historical distinction at all, but those who have been have usually assumed that, as Harry Levin argued in the influential, conflated *Riverside Shakespeare* edition, "the nameless Fool in *King Lear* is a natural, a half-witted mascot, a simpleton inspired with the intuitive wisdom of nature."[27] In contrast to the critical tradition, I am prepared to show that the pathos of a sweet, natural Fool consistently derives from the Folio text, while the Fool in the Quarto, as an analysis of the Quarto text reveals (including evidence based on the few actual recorded performances), is a funnier, wiser, and more bitter artificial fool. The earlier version, then, is a comic figure consistent with both the broad tradition of satiric clowns we have been examining and the particular emphasis on satiric wit within the artificial fool tradition, whereas the later version is ultimately a pathetic, tragic figure, not a clown per se at all.

And yet, although I am certainly concerned to draw attention to the Quarto's long-dismissed and misunderstood artificial fool on its own grounds, I hasten to add that, far from arguing that one text is superior to the other, I instead argue that the textual variants in both texts can effectively produce, and in fact actually have successfully produced, markedly different theatrical effects, which are radically different than what critics have expected to find.[28] For that reason alone I would

---

Cordelia and Edgar and a happy ending, as well as the expunging of the Fool. Tate's adaptation held the boards until 1756, when Garrick's version began the process of restoring Shakespeare, although he retained the omission of the Fool. The first production to restore the Fool was Macready's in 1838, after a hiatus of 157 years.

26 Kerrigan, "Revision, Adaptation, and the Fool in *King Lear*," 218.
27 Harry Levin, "General Introduction," in *The Riverside Shakespeare* (1974; rpt Boston, 1997), 1–25; 21.
28 On the Quarto's effects in performance, I refer to David Richman's useful

actually prefer to see versions of *either* text's Fool staged rather than the hodge-podge conflation, but I have absolutely no intention of imposing a new division of the kingdom by maintaining that *one* text is inviolable and definitive, while the other is therefore necessarily artistically inferior. My hope, rather, is that an increase in understanding of the variants between the two texts might allow more informed choices for production. However appealing the enigmatic fool as he appears in conflated editions and in the performances of such may be to some post-modern critics, an appeal based on ignorance is, however, not a solid ground for refusing to assume alternate possibilities, and the idea that Shakespeare was a proto-deconstructionist who artfully produced a brilliantly ambiguous muddle is utter fantasy. What I hope to show instead is that both Q and F Fools are extraordinary, surprisingly differentiated, creations – brilliant in quite different ways.

It is worth pointing out that revision was not as exceptional in the early modern theatre as most revisionist critics had assumed. Standout plays from the repertory were occasionally revised for revival. Contemporary theatre impresario Phillip Henslowe, for instance, referred in his financial records to such revision as providing "new adicyones" or "altrynge." Contrary to revisionists' logic, this "altrynge" was not undertaken because plays were deemed unsatisfactory (since only initially successful plays were revived and worth the expense of revising), but rather, as Eric Rasmussen argues, to "keep pace with current theatrical trends."[29] Roslyn Knutson has suggested that the dynamics of company repertory more generally often operated according to "the principle of duplication by way of sequels, serials, and spin-offs" to capitalize on theatrical successes.[30] The Quarto Fool variants published in 1608 indeed make most sense when situated within the context of one specific, ongoing theatrical trend of "spin-offs," that

analysis in "Shakespeare on Stage: The *King Lear* Quarto in Rehearsal and Performance," *Shakespeare Quarterly* 37.3 (autumn 1996): 374–82.

[29] For an insightful discussion of revision in terms of English Renaissance theatre practice, see Eric Rasmussen, "The Revision of Scripts," in *A New History of Early English Drama*, ed. John D. Cox and David Scott Kastan (New York, 1997), 441–60, especially 448–9.

[30] Roslyn L. Knutson, "The Repertory," in *A New History of Early English Drama*, ed. John D. Cox and David Scott Kastan (New York, 1997), 461–80; 471.

favoring the artificial fools played by Armin, while the subsequent Folio Fool is a more pitiable or pathetic natural Fool in keeping with a later trend, the increasing taste for pathos already evident in Shakespeare's latest plays and, especially, in works associated with the more neoclassical playwright John Fletcher. The latter took Shakespeare's place as the foremost playwright in the King's Men and radically altered their comic aesthetics. The *Lear* Quarto and Folio texts thus not only encode the distinguishing characteristics of the two Renaissance fool types but they also reflect distinct theatrical trends which had significant impact on the history of the comic.

Given evidence of the fad involving Armin's brand of artificial fools, determining when Armin (d. 1615) retired, taking his last exit from Shakespeare's "great stage of fools" (Q 4.6, 171; F 4.5, 176),[31] may help us date the Folio revision. It is clear that Armin was still playing his popular fool roles at least as late as 1610, two years after the publication of the Quarto, since in that year John Davies's *Scourge of Folly* commends – using the present tense – "honest-gamesome Robin Armin" who "*playest* both" a "foole and [a] knave," urging him to continue to "do *as thou dost*, wisely play the foole."[32] Armin, therefore, was still playing his signature brand of wise, knavish fools (Lear's Fool is called "more knave than fool" [Q 1.4, 301; F 1.4, 84] and also "pretty knave" [Q 1.4, 89; F 1.4, 91]) as of 1610, shortly before Shakespeare's retirement. In 1613, by contrast, Shakespeare's and Fletcher's *Henry VIII* included a remarkable prologue justifying the absence of the legendary fool Will Somers from the play:

> I come no more to make you laugh; things now
> That bear a weighty and a serious brow,
> Sad, high, and working, full of state and woe:

---

31 Here and throughout, for the reader's convenience, my quotations from Q and/or F *Lear* texts refer to *King Lear: A Parallel Text Edition*, ed. René Weis (London, 1993). In cases of significant variants, I include as well the "Through Line Number" (TLN) from *The First Folio of Shakespeare*, Norton Facsimile edition, ed. Charlton Hinman (London and New York, 1968). Where Weiss's parallel text edition obscures notable variants in Q, I have included page signatures from *Shakespeare's Plays in Quarto*.

32 John Davies, *The Complete Works of John Davies of Hereford*, ed. Alexander B. Grossart (Edinburgh, 1878), II, 60–1; emphases added.

Such noble scenes as draw the eye to flow,
We now present ....

...

　　　　... Only they
That come ... to see a fellow
In a long motley coat guarded with yellow,
Will be deceivd. For, gentle hearers, know,
To rank our chosen truth with such a show
As fool ...

...

Will leave us never an understanding friend. (ll. 1–5; 13–22)[33]

The absence of such a well-known, well-liked character as Henry VIII's
fool, one the "under-standers" or groundlings in the audience expected
to see, justified as it is on the basis of a neoclassical decorum that is atyp-
ical for Shakespeare, is now taken not only as an indication of the influence of Fletcher's aesthetics but also as a sign that Armin had retired by
June of 1613, and, I would emphasize, *recently enough that such
commentary was still deemed necessary.* As John Southworth observes,
"[B]etter perhaps no Will [Somers] at all than a Will played by anyone
other than ... the outstanding player of fools in his time," Armin.[34] That
the fool role could not so easily be filled in *King Henry VIII* suggests that
the earliest probable time of revision for the *Lear* Folio was shortly after
Armin's retirement, likely some time in 1613. If the Fool's part in *Lear*
was indeed revised for another actor following Armin's retirement,
there is a strong possibility that Shakespeare (also largely retired by the
end of 1613 and dead in 1616) did not undertake the revision extant in F
at all.

In any case, as remarkable as it may seem to modern commentators,
such rapid, *actor-specific* revision and initial creation of parts was characteristic not only of Shakespeare's practice but that of the Renaissance
theatre generally and of the King's Men in particular. It already had a
precedent in 1598–99, for instance, when Shakespeare himself suddenly
shifted from writing the rustic "ass" Dogberry specifically for Will

---

33　Of course, the artificial fool often appropriated the "fools coat" to mark his pro-
　　fession and give him license. As Wiles notes, "Anyone could be an artificial fool
　　by dressing up in the motley uniform of the natural." *Shakespeare's Clown*, 150.
34　Southworth, *Fools and Jesters*, 136.

Kemp to creating the witty fool Touchstone specifically for Armin, while Jonson wrote the part of the bitter-witted Carlo Buffone for the latter actor in *Everyman Out of His Humor* in the same year.[36] Likewise, Armin wrote the parts of the witty artificial fool Tutch, the star of his play, and the contrasting bit-part of the natural fool John of the Hospital for himself in 1599 in *History of the Two Maids of Moreclacke* (printed 1609), whose title page depicts Armin, atypically, as a natural wearing a "muckender" (a handkerchief appended to a natural to wipe his nose or mouth [Figure 5]). Also in 1599, as Southworth observes, because of the clown Kemp's departure from the company before Armin's arrival, Falstaff could not appear as promised in *Henry V*.[37] But if there has been scholarly acceptance of the fact that Shakespeare and other professional playwrights obviously wrote characters with particular actors in mind, revisionist critics have been curiously reluctant to explore the possibility that revisions and "new adicyones" of the updating kind to which Henslowe referred were also written for this purpose. The ignoring of such a possibility is all the more remarkable given that we know that actor-specific revision for the resident clown actually occurred when John Marston added the artificial fool Passarello for Armin to his revision of *The Malcontent* when the King's Men acquired the play from a boy company in 1604,[38] a year before Shakespeare authored the part of the Fool for him in *King Lear*.

In aligning Armin with the Quarto Fool I am clearly rejecting the wholly subjective argument, most recently evident in Southworth's otherwise excellent work, that Armin must have played Edgar rather

---

35 In the Quarto of *Much Ado*, printed in 1600, Kemp's name appears in the stage directions and as the speech heading for Dogberry in 4.2, perhaps in order to prevent confusion between the speech headings for "Constable" and "Conrade" (the latter listed as "*Con.*" in the scene); sigs. G3v–G4v. See *Shakespeare's Plays in Quarto*, 514–15. The speech headings for Kemp are evidence that the part was composed for him before he mysteriously left Shakespeare's company in the year 1598–99.

36 Further evidence of a fad for Armin's type of fool is suggested by the title of Chapman's last Admiral's comedy, *All Fools but the Fool* (*c*. 1599, lost), which strongly suggests immediate competition with Armin's popularity.

37 Southworth, *Fools and Jesters*, 132.

38 For discussion of the revision for Armin, see Felver, *Robert Armin, Shakespeare's Fool*, 65–6.

THE
History of the two Maids of More-clacke,

With the life and simple maner of IOHN
in the Hospitall.

Played by the Children of the Kings
Maiesties Reuels.

Written by ROBERT ARMIN, seruant to the Kings
most excellent Maiestie.

LONDON,
Printed by N.O. for *Thomas Archer,* and is to be sold at his
shop in Popes-head Pallace, 1 6 0 9.

Figure 5. Title page, Robert Armin, *History of the Two Maids of More-Clacke* (1609). Atypically, Armin appears here as a natural fool. By permission of the Folger Shakespeare Library.

158

than the Fool. As the argument goes, the part of Edgar is better suited to Armin because it is, supposedly, a better part than the Fool, "a more demanding role in which, for the greater part of the play, he is required to disguise himself as a madman," and Armin was a skilled mimic. Yet, by such logic, Armin must also have played the lead roles in *Hamlet* and *The Malcontent*, since both of these roles also require an ability to play the persona of a madman or natural, but, of course, Burbage seems to have played both roles quite successfully. More to the point, the subjective modern assumption that Edgar is a better part ignores the popularity of Armin's fools at the time, not to mention what a rewarding, scene-stealing role the Fool is (in either text). Thus, when *King Lear* was first performed, probably in 1605, a year after Armin's enormous popularity had necessitated the addition of the artificial fool's part in *The Malcontent*, as well as a year in which he was capitalizing on his popularity with the pamphlet *Fool Upon Fool* – that is, at the very height of his popularity – Armin would definitely have played the role for which he was famous. Such casting is all the more likely since the Fool is the most challenging, iconic fool part in Shakespeare's repertoire – again, in either text. But while the part of the Fool in the Quarto was tailor-made for Armin's celebrated line of artificial fools, as we shall now see, the Folio revision was clearly not.

FOOL VARIANTS AND THEIR EFFECTS

Far from making the Fool more acerbic as previous critics argued, the Folio revisions instead make the Fool a sweetly pathetic figure. To Act 3.4, for instance, one of the storm scenes, the F text adds lines for Lear in which he expresses concern for the Fool: "*Lear.* In boy, go first. You houseless poverty. / Nay, get thee in. I'll pray and then I'll sleep" (F only, 3.4, 26–7; TLN 1807–8). This added expression of concern for the Fool's condition in F, combined with Lear's prior concern for the Fool's exposure to the cold extant in both texts ("How dost my boy? Art cold? … Poor fool and knave, I have one part in my heart / That's sorry yet for thee" [Q 3.2, 68–73; F 3.2, 68–73]), creates an emphasis and, thus, a distinct impression that the Fool's health is waning in F. The Folio's additional lines also make the Fool there seem sweet and loyal since he possibly resists going in out of the cold ahead of Lear. Alternatively, the Folio lines may suggest that its natural Fool does not always have the proverbial "sense to come in out of the rain," suggesting that, consistent with the stage tradition of Lear affectionately fondling the Fool like a pet or a child, he is dependent on Lear for care, as was typical of the pathetically dependent natural fool.

Perhaps the Folio variant that most makes the Fool the pitiable natural, however, is the addition of the poignant statement, "And I'll go to bed at noon" (F only, 3.6, 41; TLN 2043), as the Fool's last line. This Folio-only line is the Fool's response to the mad Lear's inversionary claim, "we'll go to supper i' the morning" (Q 3.6, 78; F 3.6, 40). In his last line in F, not only does the Fool acquiesce to Lear's inversion of custom, but he also identifies himself pathetically with a flower that shuts itself away after the passing of the noon-day sun. According to John Gerard's description in the famous book *The Herball* (1597), the "Go to bedde at noone" was a flower "which shutteth it selfe at twelve of the clocke and sheweth not his face open vntill the next daies sunne do make it flower anew, whereupon it was called Go to bed at noone."[39] The allusion suggests the Folio Fool's pathetic resignation: since the failing king will not return to glory, the Fool will "shew … not his face" again, but rather, he will shut up or even die.

The standard presupposition that the F Fool must be the more bitter fool has led revisionist textual scholars to read his Folio-only line as a "mocking exit line" or as an expression of the "Fool's determination to leave *King Lear* with its course half run …. So he resolves to call it a day at noon, to abandon the action at its midpoint, to absent himself from half the story."[40] But this is not how the line has usually been interpreted in performance. When the Fool was first restored to the play in 1838 following his excision by Tate, Priscilla Horton, playing the Fool as a sweet boyish natural, one previously lovingly "fondled" with "earnest care,"[41] was said to have found pathos in the line:

---

39 John Gerard, *The Herball* (London, 1597), 594–5.
40 Kerrigan, "Revision, Adaptation, and the Fool in *King Lear*," 229.
41 *King Lear*, edited with a theatre commentary by John Russell Brown (New York, 1996), 41.

When all his attempts have failed, either to soothe or outjest [Lear's] injuries, he sings, in the shivering cold, about the necessity of going to bed at noon. He leaves the stage to die in his youth, and we hear of him no more till we hear the sublime touch of pathos over the dead body of the hanged Cordelia.[42]

Likewise, Antony Sher interpreted the line as his Fool's death knell, a line "which would make perfect sense coming from a mortally wounded man."[43] Olivier's television production found the line equally pathetic:

Here [in 3.6] pathos is the dominant note. Lear's "Well go to supper i' th' morning" is immediately followed by a close up of the stricken Fool for his "And I'll go to bed at noon." The bustle of Gloucester's urgent return still permits the camera to linger over the sleeping Lear and his tender removal by Kent and Edgar to the litter. But the end of the scene is given to the Fool.... We first see him from the rear sitting alone on the bale of hay as the others leave. After the cut to Edgar [exiting], the angle is reversed for the camera's zooming return to the abandoned and shivering figure. That last shot is of the Fool's face, mouth twitching and eyes shut against the pain of approaching death.[44]

While assumptions of authorial perfection have prompted textual critics to view the Folio Fool's final line as a bitter one, performances have most often found pathos in it instead as they have shown him dying or being abandoned.

The Quarto text, by contrast, makes the Fool's death or abandonment very difficult to justify, since in Q the scene concludes with Kent commanding the Fool, "Come, help to bear thy master; / Thou must not stay behind" (Q 3.6, 93–4), which F cuts, followed by Edgar's soliloquy, which F also cuts ("When we our betters see bearing our woes. ... Lurk, lurk!" [Q 3.6, 95–108]). Kent's command here might suggest that the

---

42 John Forster reviewing W. C. Macready's *King Lear* at the Theatre Royal, Covent Garden, London, from *The Examiner*, 14 February, 1838, reprinted in Stanley Wells (ed.), *Shakespeare in the Theatre: An Anthology of Criticism* (1997; rpt New York 2000), 76.

43 Antony Sher, "The Fool in *King Lear*," in *Players of Shakespeare 2*, ed. Russell Jackson and Robert Smallwood (1988; rpt Cambridge, 1993), 151–65; 163.

44 James P. Lusardi and June Schlueter, *Reading Shakespeare in Performance*: King Lear (Rutherford, NJ, 1991), 103–4.

Quarto Fool may actually be acting out of self-interest, trying to stay behind to detach himself from Lear's company. This detachment would, of course, be well within the powers of an artificial fool capable of independence and self-sufficiency. Edgar's soliloquy in Q, moreover, makes any staging of the Fool's death extremely awkward to manage, in terms of stage business, because, unless the Fool exits, Edgar will not be left alone on stage to soliloquize.

Performances such as Linda Scott Kerr's natural Fool, for the Royal Shakespeare Company's 1990 production, have in fact had to follow the Folio's cutting of Kent's line and of Edgar's soliloquy alike to achieve a pathetic interpretation: "Closely following the Folio text, the production showed the Fool abandoned at the end of 3.6, mouthing inaudible nonsense as Kent and Gloucester hurried the sleeping Lear away."[45] Likewise, in Granville-Barker's 1950 production, Alan Badel, playing a "cringing" Fool to John Gielgud's Lear,[46] "was suddenly to find himself alone on the stage, the others all gone; and like a frightened dog to look about for the scent, and cry Nuncle Lear, Nuncle Lear to the emptiness."[47] The Folio's abandoned Fool is certainly effective dramatically precisely because an emphatically shivering Fool seems either to be dying or to be an utterly dependent natural unable to care for himself – as with the extreme pathos Alec Guinness's Fool evoked at the New Theatre, London, in 1946, via "the queer, still, frightened fancy of a whipped menial poignant as a puppy in pain."[48]

Such pathos is only enhanced by the Folio text's cutting of the Beckett-like mock trial in 3.6. Without that episode, the Folio's natural Fool offers no resistance to Lear's lapse into madness. In marked contrast, as the scene appears in Q, as was typical of Armin's artificial fools, the Fool bitterly calls attention to the transgressive irrationality of Lear's raving about the imaginary defendant Goneril when he refuses to see what Lear sees:

45 *The Tragedy of King Lear*, ed. Jay L. Halio, New Cambridge Shakespeare edition (Cambridge, 1992), 53.
46 *King Lear*, ed. Russell Brown, xix.
47 Marvin Rosenberg, *The Masks of King Lear* (Berkeley, CA, 1972), 238.
48 *King Lear*, ed. Russell Brown, xix.

Lear	Arraign her first. 'Tis Goneril: I here take my oath before this honourable assembly she kicked the poor King her father.
Fool	Come hither, mistress. Is your name Goneril?
Lear	She cannot deny it.
Fool	Cry you mercy, I took you for a joint-stool.

(Q 3.6, 43–8)

The final line of this Quarto-only exchange, the Fool's last line in the Quarto text, shows him to be, as was typical of Armin's artificial fools, refusing to humor the mad Lear. Thus, the Fool's destruction of Lear's illusion that the stool is not empty and that Goneril is actually there prompts Lear's angry outburst, as if the Fool had let her escape: "Stop her there. / Arms, arms, sword, fire, corruption in the place! / False justicer, why hast thou let her scape?" (Q 3.6, 50–2). David Richman's rare account of the Quarto in performance at the University of Rochester is instructive here: "The audience invariably laughed when the Fool remarked of Goneril, 'took you for a joint-stool.' But in the best tradition of tragic farce, it was a pained laugh …. In our production, the mock trial achieved stunning effects. It was indeed an epicenter."[49] Therefore, contrary to claims that in the trial scene the Quarto Fool "overlaps with Edgar and Lear" in "[trying] harder to please the King" and that the mock trial generally "flattens out the distinction between the Fool and Poor Tom,"[50] in Q, Tom and Lear serve as foils to the Fool, since the Quarto Fool separates himself from both, distinguishing himself as an artificial fool by insisting bitterly on reality rather than merely joining in the madness. In other words, the Quarto Fool is insistently and bitterly sane, that is, an emphatically artificial fool.

In fact, contrary to F's additional expression of concern for the natural Fool, Q's Fool is recognizably an artificial fool as he bitterly pursues a stinging attack on Lear's folly in several lines which the Folio text omits entirely: in the Quarto alone, the Fool answers his riddle, "Dost know the difference, my boy, between a bitter fool and a sweet one?" (Q 1.4, 127–8; F 1.4, 129–30). Prompted by Lear's "No, lad, teach

---

49 Richman, "Shakespeare on Stage," 382.
50 Kerrigan, "Revision, Adaptation, and the Fool in *King Lear*," 230, 226; *King Lear*, ed. Foakes, 135.

me" (Q 1.4, 129; F 1.4, 131), the Q Fool begins a famous exchange with Lear that appears *only* in the Quarto text:

> *Fool*   That Lord that counselled thee
> To give away thy land,
> Come, place him here by me;
> Do thou for him stand.
> The sweet and bitter fool
> Will presently appear,
> The one in motley here,
> The other found out there.
>
> *Lear*   Dost thou call me fool, boy?
>
> *Fool*   All thy other titles thou hast given away; that thou wast born with.
>
> *Kent*   This is not altogether fool, my lord.
>
> *Fool*   No, faith, lords and great men will not let me. If I had a monopoly out, they would have part on't; and ladies too: they will not let me have all the fool to myself; they'll be snatching. (Q 1.4, 130–45)

Prior to Kent's interjection, like Armin's other artificial fools Feste, Lavatch, and Thersites, the Quarto Fool distinguishes himself, an artificial fool, a professional court jester in motley who is wise enough to play the fool, from a foil, Lear, who "wast *born*" a natural fool. In Q, then, we see the typical pairing of Armin's artificial fool with a foil (e.g., Touchstone with Corin or Will, Feste with Sir Andrew or Malvolio, Lavatch with Parolles, Thersites with Ajax, Carlo Buffone with Sogliardo, Passarello with Bilosio, etc.) whose folly becomes increasingly obvious. As an artificial fool appearing with a foolish foil, the Quarto Fool boldly calls Lear a fool to his face for giving away his lands and titles, bitterly reducing Lear to a "sweet," abject natural fool. The interjection by the truth-telling Kent, "This is not altogether fool, my Lord," which softens the blow of the Fool's own bitter truth-telling while simultaneously acknowledging the wisdom of a pointed gibe, further signals the truth of the artificial Fool's shrewd observation.

Apart from the Quarto's bitter insult here, it is significant that only in the Quarto do we see an artificial fool assuming the role of teacher to a simple-witted natural fool; only in Q does the Fool take up Lear's invitation ("No, lad, teach me") to teach him "the difference ... between a bitter fool and a sweet one." The Q-only passage thus shows an artificial fool making logical, ordered substitutions ("do thou for him stand"), rationally explaining and clarifying his logic, and pressing home the conventional maxim of the wise, Socratically inspired artificial fool: "Know thyself; know thy folly." The Fool in the Quarto cleverly illustrates, therefore, that Lear has foolishly "given away" all "[his] other titles," and is now left only with the title of fool – "that thou wast born with." This is, of course, a tragic lesson that Lear, who "hath ever but slenderly known himself" (Q 1.1, 280–1; F 1.1, 290–1), must learn – particularly in the Quarto.

The Q-only exchange in 1.4 in fact provides a central, unifying focus for the fundamental thematic opposition, evident in both of the double plots, of ignorant/unwise folly (i.e., that of the natural fool) and the wise-folly or *moro-sophy* of the artificial fool or the Socratic/Erasmian wise man. Whereas Lear has only ever "slenderly known himself," in the Socratic philosophy popularized by Erasmus, Rabelais, and other Humanist thinkers and humorists, limited "human wisdom" requires "examining both myself and others," so that, famously, "life without this sort of examination is not worth living";[51] the king's foolish choices require him, especially in the original Quarto text, to undertake such often painful self-examination ("Who is it that can tell me who I am?" [Q 1.4, 218; F 1.4, 203]) and to journey from being an utter fool to a wiser one. Similarly, Socrates, in Plato's *Apology*, while maintaining that he is "only too conscious that [he has] no claim to wisdom, great or small," nonetheless defines the limited extent of his own famous wisdom (and, he insists, of all human wisdom) in terms that illuminate the original conceptions of the Fool and the theme of folly throughout *King Lear*:

> Well, I am certainly wiser than this man. It is only too likely that neither of us has any knowledge to boast of; but he thinks that he knows something which he does not know, whereas I am quite conscious of my ignorance. ... I am wiser than he is to this small extent, that I do not think that I know what I do not know.[52]

---

51 Plato, *The Apology*, in *The Last Days of Socrates*, trans. Hugh Tredennick and Harold Tarrant (New York, 2003), 66.
52 Ibid., 44–5.

As the play was originally conceived, the telling Quarto exchange in 1.4 makes meaningful pervasive references to folly elsewhere, as when the Fool observes, "I am better than thou art now; I am a fool, thou art nothing" (Q 1.4, 180–2; F 1.4, 167–8); "thou wouldst make a good fool" (Q 1.4, 35; F 1.4, 33); and "Thou shouldst not have been old before thou hadst been wise" (Q 1.5, 40–1; F 1.4, 38–9).[53] Given the Quarto Fool's philosophical ethos, it is little wonder that Armin was a favorite of "the youthful … generous Gentlemen of Oxenford, Cambridge, and the Inns of Court" to whom he appealed in the dedication to *Nest of Ninnies* in 1608.[54]

In the face of such a wise Fool's reproving, Lear cannot help but begin to see his folly ("O Lear, Lear! / Beat at this gate that let thy folly in / And they dear judgment out" [Q 1.4, 257–9; F 1.4. 240–2]) but does not want to look into it, preferring to see himself rather as simply the unwitting victim of his daughters' cruelty, the gods, or fortune ("I am e'en / The natural fool of fortune" [Q 4.6, 177–8; F 4.6, 183–4]). (By contrast, in the mirror subplot, Gloucester sees his foolish culpability within moments after his blinding, exclaiming, "O my follies! Then Edgar was abused" [Q 3.7, 88; F 3.7, 88].) Ultimately, however, Lear begins to find his own humanity by identifying with the foolish "Poor Tom," whom he calls "this philosopher," "Noble philosopher," and "my philosopher" (Q 3.4, 142, 156, 160; F 3.4. 142, 160, 164). And he recognizes that he foolishly allowed himself to be deluded by flattery, trappings of state that hid his faults, and his very office, mistaking the role and authority of kingship for a personal identity. Through his cathartic madness, Lear thus crawls toward wise-folly, recognizing that we all play similarly foolish roles on "this great stage of fools" (Q 4.6, 171; F 4.5, 176), a Socratic-sounding insight that helps him to know himself and claim his own folly when he is reunited with the wronged Cordelia ("I am a very foolish fond old man" [Q 4.7, 58; F 4.6, 54]; "Pray now, forget and forgive, I am old / And foolish" [Q 4.7, 82–3; F 4.6, 77–8]).

Because the original conception of the play extant in the Q text so

---

53 Other characters likewise note Lear's foolishness, with Kent rebuking his king by remarking that his "majesty stoops to folly" (Q 1.1, 139; F 1.1, 147) and Goneril coldly saying that he "must needs taste his folly" (Q 2.4, 261; F 2.4, 280).

54 *A Nest of Ninnies*, 17.

emphatically establishes Lear's folly in dividing the kingdom, abdicating his throne, and banishing Cordelia, especially in 1.4, the Fool's many later invocations of inversion also have an artificial fool's typically biting irony in Q. Subsequent gibes recall a readily recognizable theme in the culture of early modern Europe found in illustrations since at least the mid-sixteenth century, that of the world turned upside down. As Peter Burke has shown, the "reversal between man and beast: the horse turned farrier" and the age and status reversal where the child "is shown beating [the] father" were familiar themes in these early prints.[55] As was typical of parts written for Armin, who claimed it was his very "profession / To jest at … transgression," in the Quarto the Fool's attacks in 1.4 on the folly of abdicating provide a context that clarifies and motivates the Fool's choric use of inversionary imagery to demonstrate that Lear has foolishly transgressed. Lear's foolish decision, the Fool rails, has turned the world topsy-turvy by reversing power and status: "When thou clovest thy crown i the middle and gavst away both parts, thou borest thine ass o th back oer the dirt" (Q 1.4, 149–51; F 1.4, 135–7); "[T]hou madst thy daughters thy mother … when thou gavst them the rod and puttst down thine own breeches" (Q 1.4, 160–2; F 1.4, 146–8); and "May not an ass know when the cart draws the horse?" (Q 1.4, 211; F 1.4, 197). In associating Lear's abdication with the world turned upside down, the bitter artificial Fool puts down carnivalesque inversion as represented in the foolish natural Lear. In Q it is Lear rather than the Fool who foolishly turns the world upside down, and it is an artificial Fool who repeatedly points out Lear's natural folly and inversion in an attempt to set things right again. But whereas the Q Fool self-consciously harps on carnival-esque, topsy-turvy imagery in order to *continue* an attack on Lear's transgressive folly begun lines earlier in 1.4, the F Fool's verbal inver-sions – lacking the motivation of lines in the Quarto (Q 1.4, 130–44) presenting an actual attack on, or explicit criticism of, Lear's abdication and division of the kingdom – seem to be nonsensical, the standard humor characteristic of a natural who turns the world upside down, not out of any satirically motivated logic, but merely "by nature."

In their discussions of the Quarto-only exchange in 1.4, however, revisionist scholars assume that the Fool must necessarily be assigning

55 Peter Burke, *Popular Culture in Early Modern Europe* (New York, 1978), 188–9.

the title of "bitter fool" to the king, so that consequently the Folio version of the Fool, lacking these lines, is "more consistently a bitter one" than the Quarto Fool.[56] Only by lifting the lines out of the insulting context of the Quarto Fool's overtly acerbic criticism, as well as from the theatrical context of Armin's specialization in strikingly bitter-witted artificial fools,[57] can one confidently dismiss the fact that the Q Fool is actually proving Lear a fool. Thus, even if the Quarto Fool were disingenuously suggesting that *he*, rather than Lear, is the sweet fool, we cannot ignore the bitterly ironic implications or audacious humor of such fooling. If this artificial Fool does appropriate the title of sweet fool, he does so only to point out the bitter truth that he has lost the monopoly to the title of fool to others, who have not only adopted foolishness, but who do so more "naturally."

That the Folio's omission of the 1.4 exchange in Q was clearly not intended to make the Fool "more consistently a bitter one" is also demonstrated by audience responses to the Fool's attack in the Quarto-only exchange on stage; in performances of the Quarto at the University of Rochester, noted above, Richman observed that

> in our performance this was one of the Fool's most successful sequences. "All thy other titles thou hast given away; that thou wast born with" elicited a strong reaction from the audience throughout the run. Every night the spectators laughed and gasped, fully understanding the comedy and growing pain of Lear's situation.[58]

The shock, laughter, and awareness of Lear's pain indicate that an artificial Fool's obviously bitter humor in the Quarto was certainly not lost on its modern audience.

Why, if they are so effective in performance, were the lines cut in 1.4 of the Folio? The changes cannot be said to make the Folio Fool a more

---

56 *King Lear*, ed. Foakes, 134.
57 Equally bitter jesting is, of course, characteristic of Armin's other artificial fool roles, as with the bitter Thersites of *Troilus and Cressida*, a self-described "rascal, a scurvy railing knave" (5.5, 28), who jests that Ajax has "not so much wit ... [a]s will stop the eye of Helen's needle" (2.1, 78–80) and calls Achilles "thou full dish of fool" (5.1, 9) and Patroclus "Achilles male varl[e]t" (5.1, 15). When Achilles instructs him to bear a letter to Ajax, Thersites retorts, "Let me bear another to his horse, for that's the more capable creature" (3.3, 306–7).
58 Richman, "Shakespeare on Stage," 381.

consistently bitter and deliberately needling figure. What, then, moti
vated cuts of some of the Fool's wittiest and most biting comic material?
As we have seen, one possibility is that the Quarto Fool's biting claim
that others are snatching at his monopoly on foolishness (Q 1.4, 166–9)
may have been cut due to censorship of politically charged gibes.
Although censorship of the Q-only lines is surely possible, I want to
emphasize that the cuts in the Folio in to 1.4 are equally consistent with
other revisions throughout that cumulatively work to make the Fool
more simply foolish or irrational even as they make the king less so and
enhance our sympathy with Lear, who becomes less blameworthy, and
thus more pitiable. F also adds lines for Lear in 1.1 which, by providing a
rational motive for his otherwise rash action in dividing the kingdom
and by inviting sympathy for his age, substantially mitigate his responsibility for the chaos that ensues:

> … while we
> Unburdened *crawl toward death*. …
> We have this hour a constant will to publish
> Our daughters several dowers, *that future strife*
> *May be prevented now*.
> (F only, 1.1, 39–44; TLN 45–50; emphasis added)

Not only does F's addition here make Lear's death sound imminent,
because he figuratively "crawl[s] toward death," but, as Thomas Clayton
argues, it "lays a strong foundation for the development of sympathy
and admiration by providing Lear with a creditable, rational, and regal
motive for his division of the kingdom" – to prevent "future strife."[59] In
F, Lear's motivated choice to divide the kingdom and publish his daughters' dowers in order to prevent future conflict does not appear to be so
patently foolish.

In marked contrast, the Quarto Lear's abbreviated announcement of
his rash retirement – as Clayton notes, "his sole stated motive in the
Quarto" – is blatantly foolish because Lear's decision to divide the
kingdom in the early text "appears arbitrary and unexplained."[60] As

---

59 Thomas Clayton, "'Is this the promis'd end?' Revision in the Role of the King," in
The Division of the Kingdoms: Shakespeare's Two Versions of King Lear, ed. Gary
Taylor and Michael Warren (Oxford, 1983), 121–41; 125.

60 Ibid., 125; *King Lear*, ed. Foakes, 137.

Richman records in his account of the Quarto performances at Roch ester, although the Quarto "presents a clear, strong image of the king," it nonetheless "lacks the king's sense of the political consequences of his actions." Thus, Richman observes, the Folio King has more "political savvy" than the rash Quarto King.[61] What I want to add to Richman's deft analyses is that the Q King's markedly foolish lack of savvy can hardly be considered a mistake, given the original focus on the need for Lear to recognize his demonstrable folly.

The Folio's omission in 1.4 of the lines referring to the king's folly (from "That lord that counselled thee" to "they'll be snatching" [Q 1.4, 130–45]), combined as it is with the addition of lines that make the king more politically astute, not only affects the motivation of lines alluding to the world upside down later on, but also inevitably affects perceptions of the Fool's reasoning. Apart from the fact that his inversive logic is unmotivated throughout, he suddenly makes less sense because the Folio Fool skips jarringly from an offer to prove the difference between a sweet and bitter fool to a non sequitur:

> Fool   Dost know the difference, my boy,
>   between a bitter fool and a sweet one?
> Lear   No, lad, teach me.
> Fool   Nuncle, give me an egg and Ill give thee
>   two crowns.   (F 1.4, 129–31; TLN 667–71)

Again, revisionists' response to this variant has been largely one of befuddlement because few have entertained the possibility that the earlier Fool could be more rational than the later one. Even some critics who assume authorial perfection are thus forced to concede that "to those acquainted with the full Quarto text, the Folio's train of thought appears nonsensical" so that this is "one of the few clumsy cuts in the Folio text" since the compositors had "to resort to the settling of nonsense."[62] Nevertheless, some have gone so far as to find that the cut makes the Folio less "set" and "monotonous" and that the illogical leap

---

61 Richman, "Shakespeare on Stage," 376.
62 Taylor, "Monopolies, Show Trials, Disaster, and Invasion," 107; Steven Urkowitz, *Shakespeare's Revision of* King Lear, (Princeton, NJ, 1980), 155, n. 21 and 13

in conversation, a "disjunction" or "dislocation" in the Fool's logic, makes the Folio Fool the "more urbane and more oblique" one.

Although the Folio's later insertion of a song in the scene in which Lear discovers Kent in the stocks ("Winter's not gone yet" [F only, 2.4, 40–8; TLN 1322–7]) "seem[s] distressingly irrelevant" and illogical, the assumption that the revised Fool must be wiser and wittier nonetheless leads to the view that such non sequiturs or "disjunction[s]" are evidence that the Folio Fool is "hard-headed" and clearly "disengaged from the King" in keeping with "the Fool's psychology."[63] Yet, such irrelevant, disjointed and disordered logic is characteristic of the psychology not of a rational artificial fool but of an irrational natural fool like the mad Jailer's Daughter in Shakespeare's and Fletcher's collaboration, *The Two Noble Kinsmen* (1613).[64] The artificial fool's logic is, after all, typically ordered, rational, explicit, sometimes even mock-formal and pedantic.[65]

The possibility that the Folio's excision of the Fool's logically ordered, biting critique in 1.4 may actually have been intended to affect percep-tions of his mental capacity is underscored by variations elsewhere in the Fool's idiom. Here, it is illuminating that Jay L. Halio, basing his commentary on his Folio-only New Cambridge edition, has argued that the F Fool's "characteristic idiom suggests he is a natural fool, not an

---

63 Kerrigan, "Revision, Adaptation, and the Fool in *King Lear*," 219, 220.
64 For example, see the following Jailers Daughters lines:

        I am very hungry.
    Would I could find a fine frog – he would tell me
    News from all parts o' th' world, then would I make
    A carrack of a cockle-shell, and sail
    By east and north-east to the King of the Pygmies,
    For he tells fortunes rarely. (3.4, 11–16)

65 Artificial fools often make outrageous claims that bait their listeners into saying, "How prove you that?" "Derive this; come," or "Tell me thy reason," so that they may take on the persona of a logician. Thus, Passarello (another Armin role) in *The Malcontent* can "prove anything" (5.1, 52) as when he proves a "valiant" quarreler a coward: "Why thus. He that quarrels seeks to fight; and he that seeks to fight, seeks to die; and he that seeks to die, seeks never to fight more; and he that will quarrel and seeks means never to answer a man more, I think he's a coward" (5.1, 47–51). John Marston, *The Malcontent*, ed. George K. Hunter (Manchester, 2000). All subsequent citations refer to this edition.

artificial one." While the differences might initially be dismissed as merely the result of printing house practice, the Fool's idiom in the Folio does indeed seem like a natural's. The Folio Fool uses contractions more consistently and characteristically than the Quarto Fool, a speech habit that makes the Quarto's artificial Fool in performance sound more educated and articulate by comparison. To cite but a few instances, the Folio substitutes "thou'lt" for "thou wilt" (F 1.4, 157; TLN 696; Q sig. D1ʳ); "o'thing" for "of thing" (F 1.4, 159; TLN 698; Q sig. D1ʳ); "em" for "them" (F 1.5, 30; TLN 908; Q sig. D3ʳ); "that's" for "that is" (F 1.5, 48; TLN 923; Q sig. D3ʳ); "thou'dst" for "thou hadst" (F 2.4, 44; TLN 1338; Q sig. E4ʳ); and "t'is" for "this is" (F 3.4, 98; TLN 1891; Q sig. G2ᵛ). The Folio text also omits or changes words that make the Quarto's artificial Fool's syntax sound polished, sophisticated, and logical by comparison. For instance, in the Folio text, the Quarto's line "Truth is a dog that must to kennel" (Q 1.4, 103) becomes the rougher "Truth's a dog must to kennel" (F 1.4, 105; TLN 641) and the line "He that keeps neither crust nor crumb" (Q 1.4, 185) in the Quarto text becomes "He that keeps nor crust not crumb" in the Folio (F 1.4, 171; TLN 710). While Folio variants may, again, merely reflect printshop practice, they have certainly encouraged actors to use more alien dialects and even half-witted voices in performance. Notably, in Adrian Noble's famous 1982 Royal Shakespeare Company production, Antony Sher used what he characterized as a "goonish" lower-jaw underbite that he himself believed made him sound "slightly retarded," and Linda Scott Kerr played a "babbling" natural with a somewhat alien Glaswegian accent in the 1990 RSC production.[67] Following the speech habits of the favored Folio text, then, performers have definitely concurred with Halio's interpretation that the Fool's "characteristic idiom [there] suggests he is a natural fool."

Beyond the effects on the Fool's motivation and logic that the Folio achieves by cutting the iconic passage in 1.4 and the impact of essentially degrading the Fool's idiom, other revisions also systematically make the F Fool an irrational natural. It is, after all, only in the Folio that the Fool

---

66 *The Tragedy of King Lear*, ed. Halio, 7.
67 Both productions followed the Folio more than the Quarto. Sher provides an excellent account of his performance in "The Fool in *King Lear*"; here 154, 157.

makes the strange "prophecy" (F only, 3.2, 80; TLN 1749) in which he predicts that "the realm of Albion" (F only, 3.2, 91; TLN 1745) will one day be an ideal world suffering through "great confusion" (F 3.2, 92; TLN 1746). Here, as the Fool predicts that Renaissance England will fall into chaos because things will be just (*"No heretics burned but wenches tutors, / When every case in law is right, / ... Then comes the time, who lives to see[']t, / That going shall be used with feet"* [F only, 3.2, 79–94; TLN 1739–48]), his description takes on the illogical, disjointed quality of the natural so that any ironic critique here is accidental. Most importantly, the Fool says that he actually lives before Merlin ("This prophecy Merlin shall make, for I live before his time" [F only, 3.2, 95; TLN 1749]); in fact, as many in a Renaissance audience would have known, he must: according to Holinshed's popular Renaissance historical account, Lear reigned in the eighth century BCE, whereas Arthur reigned over a millennium later in the sixth century CE. To make such a prophecy, the Folio Fool would have to be "touched" or preternaturally gifted like a natural fool.

A natural's disjointed, enigmatic psychology is also, I would suggest, evident in one of the most effective Folio revisions. In Q, Lear rails in 1.4,

> Who is it that can tell me who I am?
> Lears shadow? I would learn that, for by the marks
> Of sovereignty, knowledge and reason,
> I should be false persuaded I had daughters.
> Fool   Which they will make an obedient father.
> Lear   Your name, fair gentlewoman? (Q 1.4, 218–23)

The Quarto shows Lear's wits beginning "to turn" as he gropes slowly toward self-knowledge, while the Quarto's artificial Fool continues intentionally to harp on the theme we saw earlier: Lear's foolish inversion of the normal social order in abdicating power to his daughters who have assumed the disciplinary role of parent/ruler in treating Lear like a disobedient child/subject. The Folio, on the other hand reads as follows:

> Lear   ... Who is it that can tell me who I am?
> Fool   Lears shadow.
> Lear   Your name, fair gentlewoman?
> (F 1.4, 203–5; TLN 743–5)

173

Although both Fools' lines sting, the F text offers a brilliant revision, one which doubtless even future productions otherwise following the Q text's Fool closely may wish to retain because it is so haunting in performance. But the Folio's line also calls to mind the sometimes surprisingly sage wisdom of a natural fool touched with profound, enigmatic insights that he cannot explain. Here is Levin's nameless natural "inspired with the intuitive wisdom of nature."[68]

In addition to revisions making the Fool appear more irrational, among F's most subtle yet significant revisions to the Fool's character are those that alter speech headings in the Fool's exchanges with Lear and Kent in 1.4 to remove the intentional bitterness characteristic of artificial fools. Combined with the Folio's cuts of the Fool's bitterest attack on Lear's folly there, the F text changes speech headings to ensure that the Fool's remaining bitter lines do not come as a direct response to whomever he is insulting. The resulting shift toward indirection in F mitigates the severity and undercuts the intentionality of the Fool's insults. For instance, after the Fool's first entrance, in 1.4 in the Quarto, the Fool first intentionally mocks the disguised Kent (whom he, therefore, seems to recognize), and only then turns to his next opponent, Lear. After twice offering Kent his coxcomb, the Quarto text has Kent respond, "Why, fool?" (Q 1.4, 91), whereas the Folio text assigns the question to Lear: "Why, my boy?" (F 1.4, 93; TLN 628). Because the questioner is Kent in the Quarto version, the ensuing response pointedly takes place only between the Fool and Kent, while Lear is the one impudently discussed as "this fellow":

Kent   Why, fool? [F: *Lear.* Why, my boy?]
Fool   Why, for taking ones part that's out of favour. Nay, and
          thou canst not smile as the wind sits, thou'lt catch cold
          shortly. There, take my coxcomb. Why, this fellow hath
          banished two on's daughters and done the third a
          blessing against his will. If thou follow him, thou must
          needs wear my coxcomb.
                             (Q 1.4, 91–7; F 1.4, 93–9; TLN 628–34)

Whereas the Quarto's artificial Fool bitterly jests about Kent's folly in following a foolish king, the Folio's choice to replace Kent's question

---

68 Levin, "General Introduction," 21.

174

with Lear's "Why, my boy?" divides the Fool's attention (between Kent and Lear) and makes the Fool's commentary on Kent's folly in serving Lear non-confrontational, apparently innocent and unintentional, since the Fool no longer directly confronts Kent at length before taking on Lear. Thus, the extended exchange with Kent in the Quarto postpones a long-absent, independent artificial Fool's acknowledgement of Lear since it intervenes between the King's earlier greeting to the Fool, "How now, my pretty knave, how dost thou?" (Q 1.4, 89; F 1.4, 91), and the Fool's eventual, pointedly bitter and delayed acknowledgement of Lear; in the Quarto text, it is only after successfully disposing of Kent and impudently ignoring his king as if he were a nobody or a nothing for ten lines that the bitter artificial Fool finally acknowledges the King, "How now, nuncle? Would I had *two* coxcombs and two daughters" (Q 1.4, 97–8; F 1.4, 99–100), whereas the Folio revision makes a natural Fool readily acknowledge Lear by addressing some of his early responses immediately, and therefore more respectfully, to Lear.

Later in 1.4, the Folio changes a speech heading again, effectively decreasing the bitterness and intentionality of a direct criticism once more. After the Fool teaches Lear his rhyming speech ("Have more than thou showest, / Speak less than thou knowest, " etc., Q 1.4, 110–19; F 1.4, 111–20), the Quarto text has Lear respond directly to the Fool's address to him, "This is nothing, fool" (Q 1.4, 120), while F's revision reassigns the line to Kent:

Lear	This is nothing, fool.
Fool	Then like the breath of an unfeed lawyer, you gave me nothing for't. Can you make no use of nothing, uncle?
Lear	Why no, boy; nothing can be made out of nothing.
Fool	*[to Kent]* Prithee tell him, so much the rent of his land comes to; he will not believe a fool.
Lear	A bitter fool. (Q 1.4, 120–6; F 1.4, 121–8; TLN 658–66)

The intentional jesting of an artificial Fool in the Quarto, where the Fool is allowed to respond directly to Lear, is once again diffused in the Folio, diverted away from the Fool's butt (Lear) momentarily by *Kent's* interjection, which now has the effect of validating the impression that the Folio Fool is speaking nonsense rather than riddling. By contrast, in the Quarto, the Fool not only aggressively mocks Lear's foolishness by addressing him directly, but he bitterly harps on the word "nothing." Such self-conscious usage suggests that the Quarto's bitter artificial Fool has knowledge of Lear's earlier exchange with Cordelia, since he pointedly directs his use of the word "nothing" to Lear rather than diffusing the sting of an innocent word choice by deflecting the speech toward Kent. The Quarto Fool's acerbic harping on the painful word "nothing," moreover, is consistent with the Fool's pursuit of this theme later in the scene with Lear, as at "Thou hast paired thy wit o both sides and left *nothing* i the middle" (Q 1.4, 174–5; F 1.4, 160–1); "Now thou art an O without a figure. I am better than thou art now; I am a fool, thou art *nothing*" (Q 1.4, 180–2; F 1.4, 166–8); and "I will hold my tongue; so your face bids me, though you say *nothing*" (Q 1.4, 182–3; F 1.4, 168–9). The Quarto Fool's direct responses in the exchanges at 1.4, 92 and 1.4, 121 make the Fool seem unmistakably aware of the sting the word will inflict throughout the scene as he truly provokes Lear's comment that he is "A bitter fool." The Folio undercuts the bitterness of the Fool's word choice to make him innocent of intentional criticism.

As a rule, revisionist critics have again offered unsatisfying accounts for these changes, arguing that F's alterations of the speech prefixes from Kent to Lear at the earlier F 1.4, 93 (TLN 627; Q 1.4, 91) and from Lear to Kent at the later F 1.4, 121 (TLN 658; Q 1.4, 120) in the Folio break "monotonous" exchanges or offering that the altered speech headings make the Fool more "acerbic" (even though the F Fool only turns his wit directly against Kent at the "unfeed lawyer" line [Q 1.4, 121; F 1.4, 122; TLN 659] rather than more aggressively after Q's "Why, fool?" some thirty-one lines earlier).[69] Instead, the direct address throughout Q makes the Fool's criticism in that version pointed, while the Folio's diffused speech headings have the effect of making the Fool there seem unwitting and thus less persistently biting. The direct attacks against Lear's folly and Kent's foolish faithfulness by the Quarto Fool are, in fact, unmistakably needling since his responses suggest that he rather than Lear orchestrates the scene. Instead of innocently reacting to the other characters as in F, the Q Fool, consistent with Armin's artificial

---

69 Kerrigan, "Revision, Adaptation, and the Fool in *King Lear*," 219; *King Lear*, ed. Foakes, 134.

fools, intentionally provokes them and sets them up with riddles in order to knock them down and prove them fools.

It is only within such a coherent pattern of variants that we are able to appreciate what I would suggest is a subtle variant that also appears in 1.4, which makes the Fool in the Quarto a bitter, pestilent fool rather than simply an irritant, and which reinforces the Q Fool's status as a professional artificial fool. After the Quarto's Fool offers Lear his coxcomb and tells him to beg another of his daughters whom he likens to the dog Lady Brach, the Quarto text has Lear respond, "A pestilent *gull* to me" (Q sig. C4ʳ),[70] "gull" being a synonym for "fool," and "pestilent" marking him as the paradoxically and intentionally bitter artificial one, while the Folio revision has Lear responding, "A pestilent *gall* to me" (F 1.4, 107; TLN 644), typically glossed merely as a source of irritation. Even though this detail could once again be ascribed to printshop misconstructions, an "accidental" in the text, the difference should not be dismissed off-hand as necessarily typographical since the "bitter gull's" consistency with the general tenor of Q's more bitter and aggressive Fool makes this possibility less likely. In the Quarto text, Lear's use of "gull" alludes to the Fool's role as fool, forming a parallel to his irritable retort twenty-four lines later, "A bitter fool" (Q 1.4, 126; F 1.4, 128), since the lines together distinguish him as an artificial fool. The Folio's later "gall" could just as easily be attributed to printshop error, but there too the choice of a word for a natural irritant seems entirely appropriate to F's occasionally unwittingly irritating natural Fool. The Quarto Fool, by contrast, like Armin's fools Lavatch, Passarello, Carlo Buffone, and Thersites, is not merely an unwitting natural irritant but an intentionally biting, "pestilent gull," a bitter Socratic gadfly.[71]

---

[70] In his parallel text edition, Weis apparently takes "gull" as a type-setting error, since he changes it to the Folio's "gall" reading.

[71] Playwrights indeed emphasized the bitterness of Armin's artificial fools. Passarello in Marston's *The Malcontent* would thus be a "pestilent fool!" and a "bitter fool!" (3.1, 126, 142), while Ben Jonson's Carlo Buffone in *Every Man Out of His Humour* (1599) is "an impudent ... common jester, a violent rayler ... belov'd of none" (Induction ll. 351–3). Ben Jonson, *Every Man Out of His Humour*, ed. Helen Ostovich (Manchester, 2001).

Cumulatively, the evidence supports the contention that the Folio revisions tend to cut bitter comedy and create pathos, making the Fool a sweet, pathetic natural. Earlier in this discussion I cited Eric Rasmussen's argument that revision was most often motivated by a desire to "keep pace with current theatrical trends." And we have seen how the Quarto text was consistent with the trend for artificial fools played by the popular clown Armin during his successful tenure with Shakespeare's company. I want now to suggest that the revisions that appear in the Folio were motivated by a desire to keep pace with a later theatrical trend that flowered after Armin's apparent retirement (c. 1613) and was promoted by Fletcher. Although some of the changes in the Folio Fool, such as the critique of excessive monopolies, may have been motivated by "James's attempt to suppress criticism towards the end of his reign,"[72] most of the revisions in the Folio character seem equally attributable to changing theatrical tastes or trends, specifically a purposeful shift toward exploiting more pathos in the drama.

Furthermore, though it is perhaps unwise to place too much significance on the shift in title between the two editions because these differences could easily be ascribed to differing printshop practices, that the Quarto is called a "History" while the Folio is deemed a "Tragedy" is consistent with the general shift in tone between the two versions of *King Lear*. The Folio's "tragic" version is sharply focused on the domestic tragedy of Lear and Cordelia, while the Quarto stresses "the stuff of history," the unfortunate loss of judgment resulting in strife and disorder. F cuts references to a broader historic conflict, the war with France, trims substantially the parts of Kent, Edmund, Edgar, and Albany "in the later acts of the play," and cuts some thirty-three lines developing the relationship between the vindictive Goneril and the sympathetic Albany in 4.2, thereby sharpening the focus on the pathos of Lear's personal tragedy.[73]

---

72 Dillon, "Theatre and Controversy," in *The Cambridge History of British Theatre*: vol. 1, *Origins to 1660,* ed. Jane Milling and Peter Thomson (Cambridge, 2004), 364–82; 376.
73 *King Lear,* ed. Foakes, 132, 143, 145. See also Urkowitz's discussion, "The Role of

The Folio's sharp focus on the pathos of Lear's relationships does indeed seem to reflect a theatrical trend since it makes *King Lear* similar to Shakespeare's latest plays, the romances, in which pathos and sweetness are more essential to the effect. "Sweetness," Marvin Rosenberg observed, "was [also] in the first known portrayal [of Lear's Fool], in Macready's *Lear* of 1838," where Priscilla Horton's sweet, pathetic Fool "set a pattern for later women Fools."[74] I would argue that the popularity of such sweet fools often portrayed by women throughout the nineteenth century further established a pattern for Shakespearean fools in performance generally. Since the Fool's return to the stage in 1838, that is, since Horton's "simple-witted" "half-idiot," "being identified with the pathos and passion of the scene,"[75] actors have often tended to play the character as a sweet, comic butt, a sad clown who is laughed at but pitied. To cite but a few famous modern examples of such an interpretation, Grigori Kozintsev's 1969 film featured an abused but faithful, youthful village idiot; Antony Sher's incredibly influential RSC Fool in 1982–83 was a "goonish" sounding, "crippled outcast," a down-and-out Charlot clown in white face with a red button nose, crumpled bowler hat, tail-coat, over-sized shoes, and baggy worn trousers; and Linda Scott Kerr's 1990 RSC sweet simpleton left the stage "mouthing inaudible nonsense" at the end of the storm scene. Partly as a result of such a well-defined pathetic or sad-clown tradition, the Fool has traditionally tended to come across as only occasionally and unintentionally funny and as pathetic rather than witty and bitter; that is, in Renaissance terminology, he seems to be a natural fool, rather than a sane, witty, bitter, professional artificial fool. Although this dominant portrayal of *Lear's* Fool may be attributed in part to the continuation of an emphasis in a performance tradition that began in 1838, over two hundred years after Shakespeare wrote the play, it is also true that the *textual* basis for the sweet/pathetic Fool tradition was *already* present in the Folio, the supposedly definitive text preferred by editors and thus the theatre.

Albany in the Quarto and Folio" in *Shakespeare's Revision of* King Lear, 80–128, and Michael Warren's "The Diminution of Kent," in *The Division of the Kingdoms: Shakespeare's Two Versions of King Lear*, ed. Gary Taylor and Michael Warren (Oxford, 1983), 59–74.
74 Rosenberg, *The Masks of King Lear*, 107–8.
75 *The Examiner* (1838), in *Shakespeare in the Theatre*, 76.

Interestingly, noted recent productions of the play have achieved a decided compromise between the sweet and bitter Fool, between pathetic natural and acerbic artificial, that is, the *bittersweet* hybrid of the composite text. Notably, playing to Ian McKellen's Lear in the 2007 RSC production by Trevor Nunn, Sylvester McCoy's diminutive Fool was a bittersweet compromise between the two texts' characterizations. Certainly, McCoy hammed it up, coming off as clearly a shrewd professional, but also as a tired old vaudevillian (or even Dickensian music-hall) performer, and, too often, as mere comic relief, singing and saying lines rapidly to his merry playing of spoons or a soldier's accordion. Such a performance choice, as many reviewers noted, unfortunately had the effect of making his lines difficult to hear, even occasionally inaudible, as if noting them was not terribly important to "some necessary question of the play." And, though McCoy's Fool was certainly "wry" and "shrewd,"[76] he was "insufficiently acerbic"[77] and, as "a seedy musical-hall cutup,"[78] he came across, like Sher's tramp Charlot clown, as a decidedly pathetic attempt at comic relief; he was indeed a tired old figure, something underscored as he "scrape[d] away his reddish wig to reveal the grey hair beneath."[79] Finally, in this production's chief innovation, McCoy's Fool was actually hung, strung up by Goneril's soldiers "without a struggle or … protest [from] the obliging Fool,"[80] and left hanging pathetically at the close of the first "act" at the intermission, a choice which made literal the pathos underlying Lear's famous line, "And my poor fool is hanged" (Q 5.3, 297; F 5.3, 279). The dominant note struck by McCoy was indeed a bittersweet one, representing a conflation of and compromise between the two textual

[76] Benedict Nightingale, "King Lear," *The Times* (June 1, 2007). Available online at http://entertainment.timesonline.co.uk/tol/arts andentertainment/stage/theatre/article1867831.ece.

[77] Peter Lathan, "King Lear," British Theatre Guide (2007). Available online at www.britishtheatreguide.info/reviews/RSClear07TRN-rev.htm.

[78] Charles McNulty, "The King of Pain," *LA Times* (October 22, 2007), E1.

[79] John Stokes, "Shakespeare, Performance and Ian McKellen," *Times Literary Supplement* (June 13, 2007). Available online at http://tls.timesonline.co.uk/article/0,25352–2646001,00.html.

[80] John Heilpern, "Shaky and Naked on the Heath," *New York Observer* (September 18, 2007); available online at www.observer.com/2007/shaky-and-naked-heath.

versions of the Fool, whether consciously or not. If many may find that middle-of-the-road approach ideal, the best of both worlds, that compromise seems to me not altogether a happy one; the extraordinary theatrical power of either tradition/text, I would suggest, has thereby been muted by the blurring of distinctly different conventions and personae.

NEW UNDERSTANDINGS AND NEW DIRECTIONS

The Quarto is not, as most revisionist critics assumed, a defective version of F, a failed attempt to achieve the supposedly superior effects that the Folio does; instead, Q is entirely successful in achieving profoundly different, purposeful effects. Specifically, far from being merely an inferior or simply unperfected text, the Quarto has much to tell us about the comedy of Shakespeare's artificial fools. For one thing, if a bitter, funny, satirical Fool is indeed what critics want, he can be found in the older text, the Quarto, not in the later Folio where scholars have looked for him in vain. Here it is illuminating that Richman's commentary on the Quarto Fool in performance indicates that the Folio purposefully cut some of the Fool's best comic material in 1.4 and 3.6. Scrutiny of the variants suggests, in short, that while the Folio was actually revised to cut the comic and to evoke pathos instead, the Quarto *Lear* offers insights into Shakespeare's bitter, witty, wise artificial fools as initially performed by the clown Robert Armin, who according to a contemporary observer "wisely play[ed] the fool." The earlier Quarto text yields a Fool that is more consistent with the fashion for the artificial fool roles written by Shakespeare and other playwrights for Armin. In fact, the Q variants consistently point to a biting artificial fool bent on freeing the world of folly by mocking it in others, one who aggressively attacks or impudently ignores his betters, consistent with Armin's typical fool roles.

The Quarto Fool is, moreover, hostile toward inversion while the pathetic natural Fool in the Folio is not. With the exception of the Folio *Lear*, fools (as opposed to rustic clowns) in Shakespeare's plays do not typically turn the world upside down, but rather, they wisely mock those who do. The comedy of artificial fools, then, is not reducible to any sweeping comic model (e.g., the carnivalesque, festive comedy, subversion-containment). Instead, the Quarto preserves the specific conventions and *modus operandi* of the artificial fool in tending to attack natural folly and transgression and to uphold normalcy by jesting at transgression with wry, bitter humor. The Folio Fool is thus the exception that proves the rule that Shakespearean fools are more normative than we might expect. But if the Q Fool may satisfy some modern tastes for irony, we should not be so jaded as to think that the pathetic natural Fool in the Folio is not itself "artful." Indeed, the Folio revision of the Fool – even if not a "fool by art" in one sense – is remarkably effective. It simply produces a strikingly different artistic effect than critics expected to find, for the Folio successfully makes the Fool there no longer a clown or comic role at all.

Epilogue

LICENSE REVOKED: ENDING AN ERA

I F CENSORSHIP of the Fool is debatable in *King Lear*'s Folio revision, its effects on clowns are all too apparent by the close of the Renaissance. Even before the oppressive censorship of the Interregnum, aesthetic censoriousness had already singled out the clown in the Stuart era. In fact, Armin's retirement from the King's Men in 1613 marked a dramatic turning-point in stage clowning; he is the last specialist in *witty* fools that I have been able to uncover. Making a related claim, Peter Thomson likewise observes that "In an often-forgotten sense, indeed, the clown outlasted the fool as the Jack Pudding of seventeenth-century [fare]."[1] Thomson identifies a major shift away from fools toward dishonest "knaves" like DeFlores in *The Changeling* (1622), signaling "a downgrading of the philosophical significance of folly in Stuart London," so that any foolishness, whether artificial or no, "bec[a]me shameful, and the [Stuart] comedian [had to] accommodate himself to satire"[2] – or, rather, outside of the citizen playhouse, a new *mode* of satire that no longer privileged the clown.

Except at the plebian Fortune and the Red Bull, the comedian increasingly had to accommodate himself to neoclassical ideals. Indeed, when Fletcher announced, in the opening line of the Prologue to *Henry VIII* (1613), that the King's Men "c[a]me no more to make you laugh" (l. 1), he evidently meant it, at least in so far as the company would be less inclined to tolerate the supposedly low laughter of "merry, bawdy" clowns (l. 14). Instead of "rank[ing] our chosen truth with such a show / As fool" (ll. 18–19), which now amounted to "forfeiting / Our own

1   Thomson, "Clowns, Fools and Knaves," 413.
2   Ibid.

brains and the opinion that we bring" (ll. 19–20), the King's Men appealed to "gentle hearers" (l. 17) and the new aim of the company was to produce something neoclassical, more "weighty and … serious," something in fact, like the Folio revision to *King Lear*, "Sad, high, and working, full of state and woe: / Such noble scenes as draw the eye to flow" (ll. 2–4). So serious was Fletcher in this veritable theatrical manifesto that no major comic roles would appear in his plays thereafter.[3] In fact, though the (previously) comic actor John Shank had joined the King's Men not long after Armin's retirement (sometime between 1613 and 1619), Shank is mentioned in the list of principal actors for plays of Beaumont and Fletcher, T. W. Baldwin noted, "*just once,*" and even that mention appears in "a revamped old play, *The Prophetess*" (likely appearing as Geta, the clown, described as "a man of a spare body").[4] The decidedly thin Shank was also forced to play minor female parts, sometimes, as with the maid Patella in *The Wild Goose Chase*, with *no lines whatsoever.*[5]

Baldwin thus observes,

> We have good reason to believe that this omission of the clown parts from Beaumont and Fletcher plays was not accidental. Indeed, the contemporary eulogists of Beaumont and Fletcher take pride in the fact that these authors, in pleasing contrast to Shakespeare, found their humor elsewhere than in the clown.[6]

When clowns do appear in Fletcher's work, they are typically in plays produced in collaboration with more populist playwrights, as in *The Nice Valor* (1616, with Middleton), *The Prophetess* (1622, with Massinger), and *The Maid in the Mill* (1624, with Rowley). And whereas playwright William Cartwright associated Shakespeare's clowns with "scurrility," "obsceaneness," and "bawdry," with Beaumont and Fletcher "mirth

---

3   Baldwin, *Organization and Personnel*, 217.
4   Ibid.; emphasis mine
5   G. E. Bentley did find "clown roles" elsewhere such as Sir Roger in *The Scornful Lady*, Hilario in *The Picture*, and Hodge in *The Soddered Citizen*, and he observed that the latter offers "low comedy, depending on a broad dialect; stupidity, and clownish capering." *The Jacobean and Caroline Stage: Dramatic Companies and Players*, 7 vols (Oxford, 1941–68), 2: 562.
6   Baldwin, *Organization and Personnel*, 218.

came unforced …. Without labour, clean, chaste, and unvex'd." Here, the laughter begotten by clowns is metaphorically linked with rape. In commendatory verses on Fletcher prefixed to the Beaumont and Fletcher Folio edition (1647) Cartwright is less explicit in his use of metaphor but no less squeamish in his judgment of the humor of Shakespearean stage clowns as old-fashioned obscenities:

> Shakespeare to thee was dull, whose best jest lies
> I' th' ladies' questions, and the fools' replies,
> Old-fashioned wit, which walk'd from town to town
> In trunk-hose, which our fathers called the clown;
> Whose wit our nice times would obsceaneness call,
> And which made bawdry pass for comical.[8]

As extreme as such neoclassical resistance to the Shakespearean comic sounds, Cartwright understood Beaumont and Fletcher's banishment of clowns from their plays well enough.

By August of 1635, Armin's successor, the clown Shank, was actually being "restrained" from the stage, as we learn in a petition to the Lord Chamberlain:

> A peticon of *Iohn Shankes* to my L[d] Chamberlaine shewing that according to his Lo[ds] order hee did make a proposition to his fellowes for satisfaccon vpon his assigening [*sic*] of his parts in ye seuerall houses vnto them bet they not onely refused to giue satisfaccon but restrained him from the Stage …. [*Shankes* is seeking] a proportionable & equitable sume of money to bee payd vnto [him] for the two parts which he is to passe vnto *Benfield, Swanston,* & *Pollard* & to cause a finall agreem[t] & convayances to bee settled accordingly.[9]

The company's reason for giving Shank the boot is unclear, but it demonstrated no high regard for stage clowns. By December of the same year, Shank was making his will, bitterly remarking that his estate

> doth consist for the most part in a Lease which I haue for a few years of

---

7 Ibid.
8 Ibid.
9 N. W. Bawcutt (ed.), *The Control and Censorship of Caroline Drama: The Records of Sir Henry Herbert, Master of the Reveals 1623–1673* (Oxford, 1996), "Revels Documents to 1642," # 324, 193–4.

Two Eight parts in the Blackfryers Playhouse, and of a Lease which I am to haue of Three Eight parts in the moity of the Globe Playhouse for the Terme of Nyne years from Christmas last *which I bought, and paid deere for.*"[10]

Renaissance clowns had known a time when they did not have to fight for their share of roles or profits, but the Caroline period was a world away from that heyday.

In a survey of the parts played by Thomas Pollard, one of Shank's rivals in the petition of 1635, T. W. Baldwin found no fools or rustics in Pollard's Caroline comic line, but roles that ranged through courtiers, soldiers, cooks, fat men, and cuckolds.[11] Baldwin was thus unable to discern from these roles any certain comic type other than remarking that "Pollard regularly did light comedy."[12] Pollard was no stage clown, but his comedy was marketable; he is said to have been worth £500 upon his death.[13] To be sure, then, indoor hall playwrights did not utterly banish all comic elements from their works. Rather, their newly penned comic lines differed significantly from those of an earlier era. Baldwin concludes therefore that in Beaumont and Fletcher's repertoire, the "nearest" these authors come to "approach[ing] ... the clown" per se "is to be found in the comic lines performed ... by [William] Eccleston and [Nicholas] Tooley," the former playing "the foibles of youth" and the latter being a character actor of idiosyncratic individuals requiring "queer makeup" or various "foolish gulls," all of which Baldwin found "wholly fitting for ... disciples of Ben [Jonson]."[14] But Eccleston and Tooley, like Pollard, were hardly clowns.

"FAT CLOWN" TO "FATTE BISHOP"

The last notable stage clown of the Jacobean era to specialize in satire, the critically underestimated William Rowley (d. before February 11, 1626, according to the parish records of St James, Clerkenwell),

---

10 Bentley, *Jacobean and Caroline Stage*, 2: 567; emphasis mine.
11 Baldwin, *Organization and Personnel*, 185–6.
12 Ibid., 185.
13 Bentley, *Jacobean and Caroline Stage*, 2: 533.
14 Baldwin, *Organization and Personnel*, 218, 211–12.

performed for the Prince's Men at that bastion of the clown, the Red Bull in Clerkenwell, from about 1610 until 1624. At that point, he appears in the cast and stage directions of such King's Men plays as *The Maid in the Mill* (1623) and *Love's Pilgrimage* (1624). His name appears in the King's Men's patent of June 24, 1625, but that is the latest notice of Rowley in connection with any company. For all his popularity, the player and collaborative playwright Rowley was not able to change the waning esteem for clowning amidst the rising influence of neo-classicism. Disrespect for the comic tradition is reflected in the fact that, aside from the writings of the populist Heywood, so many of the clown roles of the Jacobean period had to be penned (frequently in collaboration, whether with Middleton, Heywood, or even the undoubtedly reluctant Beaumont and Fletcher) by Rowley himself in plays such as *The Birth of Merlin* (1608), *Fortune by Land and Sea* (1609), *A New Wonder, a Woman Never Vexed* (1611), *Wit at Several Weapons* (1613), *The Old Law* (c. 1618), *The Mayor of Queensborough* (c. 1618), *All's Lost by Lust* (c. 1619–20), *The Witch of Edmonton* (1621), *A Match at Midnight* (1622), *The Changeling* (1622), and *The Maid in the Mill* (1623).

Much can be gleaned about the comic repertoire of Rowley from these plays. For example, as T. W. Baldwin found, "Evidently … Rowley was a fat clown"; his known parts often invite laughter at his corpulence and resultant lumbering about. The type first "appears in the Beaumont and Fletcher plays as Bustopha in *The Maid in the Mill*, coincident with Rowley's appearance in the company; and [he] waddles his foolish way through the last of the plays projected during his [brief] membership."[15] Earlier, he had been "Plumporridge" in Thomas Middleton's *Inner Temple Masque* (1619), where he had moved "like one of the great porridge-tubs / Going to the Counter."[16] He also played the fat fool Lollio in Middleton's *The Changeling* (1622) and "Fat Clown" in his own moralizing play, *All's Lost by Lust*.[17] If mere fat jokes appear to make Rowley's success a contradiction to the argument I have laid out

---

15 Ibid., 214.
16 Ibid.
17 Richard Dutton, "Thomas Middleton's *A Game at Chess*: A Case Study," in *The Cambridge History of British Theatre*: vol. 1, *Origins to 1660*, ed. Jane Milling and Peter Thomson (Cambridge, 2004), 424–38; 430.

here that the greatest Renaissance clowns (Tarlton, Kemp, Armin) were masters of satirical comic lines, we need to reconsider "fat" roles such as Plumporridge. This fat clown is, after all, a satirical representation of a puritan noncomformist whose objections to fasting are rendered entirely self-serving:

> With any Fasting Day, persuade me not;
> Nor anything belongs to Ember week;
> And if I take it against a thing, I'm stomachful;
> I was born an Anabaptist, a fell foe
> To fish and Fridays; pig's my absolute sweetheart,
> And shall I wrong my love, and cleave to saltfish,
> Commit adultery with an egg and butter?[18]

Here, this noncomformist dubiously justifies his then stereotypically carnivalesque and hypocritical gluttony for his sweetheart "pig" by way of his hatred of Lenten fasting as Romanism. Fat jokes could have satirical and moral import, then, and be used in the heated climate of religious debate over orthodoxy. But even if Rowley's typical fat-clowning were not ultimately reflective of a marked satirical impulse elsewhere, it would nonetheless be significant that Middleton's authorial impulse was to find a way to use the clown's comic business in a satirically topical way involving religion. That impulse is, apparently, not just characteristic of this particular Calvinist author, however, but rather consistent with an English Renaissance turn of mind – in the popular theatre at least.

It is precisely in such collaborations with other authors, whether as a co-author or simply as an actor, that we may best glimpse Rowley's ideal of clowning. What emerges in such author-actor/author collaborations is an emphasis on social commentary – either sensational topicality or the political – even in Rowley, Dekker, and Ford's *The Witch of Edmonton* (1621), featuring the exuberantly infectious, endearing, dog-loving rustic ass Cuddy Banks, one of the funnier clown roles of the English Renaissance and played by the fat clown Rowley. Here again, his physical size becomes a running gag in the part as when he says of the hobby horse he intends to play, "Let the hobby-horse provide a strong

---

18 *A Book of Masques* (1967; rpt Cambridge, 1980), 260 (ll. 60–6).

back. He shall not want a belly when I am in 'em" (2.1, 90–2), or when he remarks on "A gross lie as big as myself" (4.1, 266). The play itself dealt with a sensational episode in which an Elizabeth Sawyer was accused of witchcraft, leading to her execution in June of the same year. Likewise, his lost Red Bull play with Webster, Dekker, and Ford, *The Late Murder of the Son upon the Mother, or Keep the Widow Waking* (1624), which prompted a lawsuit,[19] reveals another attempt to capitalize on scandalous topicality (recent murders at Whitechapel). Like other sensational "domestic tragedies," both works "possess[ed] a strongly religious and moralistic tone" that verged on the satirical.[20]

The similarly topical *A Game at Chess*, also from 1624, and another product of Middleton–Rowley collaboration, provided one of the most sensational episodes in the Renaissance English theatre. Rowley performed the role of "the Fatte Bishop," an obvious satirical representation of the portly Marc Antonio De Dominis, the notorious archbishop of Spalato (d. September 1624). Prior analyses of revisions to the play argue that "the late edition to the script, and especially the creation of the Fat Bishop," shifted the focus "from essentially serious moral satire … towards topical comedy" after it was approved by the censor.[21] But was the latter really simply a distraction from the former, or did topical comedy enhance the moral – and political – satire? Consistent with the religio-political clowning practiced throughout the era as well as with the actual physique of De Dominis and conventional joking about Rowley's own corpulence, the Fat Bishop makes repeated reference to his own enormity (e.g., "It has lost many an ounce of reputation / Since I came of this side …. / I'd have some round preferment, corpulent dignity" [3.3, 4–7]). But here, as with Plumporridge, Rowley's corpulence targets a particular political figure even as it offers moral symbolism, embodying hypocrisy, corruption, excess, and pride. Aside from the theatrical portrait of the Spanish ambassador Conde Gondomar as the Black Knight (complete with sedan chair fitted with a hole to ease his infamous anal fistula), the portly, hypocritical apostate

---

19 William Rowley, Thomas Dekker, John Ford, *The Witch of Edmonton*, ed. Peter Corbin and Douglas Sedge (Manchester, 1999), 6.

20 Ibid., 7.

21 Dutton, "Thomas Middleton's *A Game at Chess*," 430.

archbishop, De Dominis, "is the only character … to be so transparently identifiable"[22] in the play. The Fat Bishop was also immediately recognized by numerous contemporaries via references to posts De Dominis received in compensation for his initial conversion from Catholicism to Protestantism, before converting back.[23] Furthermore, when this chess piece, called "the turncoat Bishop" (4.5, 10) and a "prepared hypocrite" (3.1, 296), is put into "the bag" with other taken pieces at the order of the White King, the Black Jesting Pawn gibes, "All the bag, I think, / Is room too scant for your *Spalato* paunch" (5.2, 194). Ultimately, the "personation" of Gondomar and the archbishop of Spalato made the play provocative because such mimicry potentially made a mockery of the license granted by the Master of Revels.[24]

It is, actually, unclear that crown or court truly disapproved of the play when it "was Acted nine days to gether" in early August 1624,[25] or that it did not proceed for a time with at least tacit approval. In one account, although James officially ordered the Privy Council to investigate the matter when Spanish representatives complained, it was said that James, Charles, and Buckingham "were all loth to haue it forbidden, and by report laught hartely at it."[26] By the middle of 1624, the long-projected Spanish match between Charles and Isabella (the Infanta of Spain) was dead, restraints upon anti-Spanish and anti-Catholic sentiments had effectively been substantially relaxed, and on May 13, 1624 a proclamation had been issued ordering "that all Jesuites and seminarie priests shold avoide the realme by the 14th of June" (the origins of the Jesuit order being Spanish).[27] With its anti-Spanish, anti-Jesuit, and anti-Catholic focus, and within the specific context of the recent collapse of the Spanish match – an event treated, remarkably, with patriotic fervor recalling the defeat of the Spanish Armada in 1588[28] – as well as increased efforts to promote an intervention in Protestant Germany to restore the Elector Frederick and James's

---

22 Ibid., 434–5.
23 Ibid.
24 Ibid., 437–8.
25 T. H. Howard Hill (ed.), *A Game at Chess* (Manchester, 1993), 17.
26 Ibid., 16, 14.
27 Ibid.
28 Ibid., 16.

daughter Elizabeth to the Palatinate, Janette Dillon finds that "the play becomes a propagandist intervention in support of the Protestant cause."[29] In fact, when the play went through a number of quarto editions *c.* 1625, the title page included an obvious, quite accurate portrait of De Dominis (see Figure 6). Rowley's impersonation of the corpulent turncoat archbishop of Spalato made the anti-papist propaganda all the more relevant, and his performance underscores the fact that the play's "three levels of allegory," "moral, religious and political," are "as inextricably intertwined in *A Game at Chess* as they were in Middleton's England."[30]

If the topical, often religious, clowning of Rowley seems to have met resistance from time to time (e.g., censorship of *A Game at Chess* when a warrant was ostentatiously issued for the apprehension of Middleton when it was reported that he had shifted "out of the way"[31]), it is clear that Rowley was sustaining a characteristically "Renaissance," polemical mode of clowning. As such, recurring hostility to the topical humor reflected in Rowley's career indicates that change was afoot. The fact that his career – and, shortly thereafter, his life – ended near the time of the death of James himself (March 1625) coheres with a perception that the great era of Renaissance English clowning had come to a close by the end of the Jacobean era. Going beyond even "James's attempt to suppress criticism towards the end of his reign,"[32] under the Caroline and Commonwealth regimes, sensational topicality would not be countenanced with the old "license" that had been associated with Renaissance fooling.

"PURGED FROM BARBARISM" VS. "RED BULL PHRASE"

A taste for the art of satirical clowning was clearly on the wane. Alexander Leggatt, for instance, observes a "gentrification of comedy …. [f]rom the 1620s onward," finding that "Caroline comedy follows [Beaumont and Fletcher's] lead in its focus on the gentry," with the

---

29 Dillon, "Theatre and Controversy," 364–82; 376.
30 Howard Hill, *Game at Chess*, 36.
31 Ibid., 22.
32 Dillon, "Theatre and Controversy," 376.

Figure 6. Title page, Thomas Middleton, *A Game at Chaess* [*Chess*], Q1 (1625), featuring "the Fatte Bishop," Marc Antonio De Dominis, Archbishop of Spalato. By permission of the Huntington Library.

satiric element "tamed a little."   It would be more accurate, though, to say that satire was not "tamed" but instead *diffused*, no longer finding its voice through a clown. Consequently, when the "most prolific of Caroline writers, with over thirty plays to his credit," James Shirley,[34] offered his *Doubtful Heir* (1640) first to the Blackfriars, only to have the venue changed to the Globe, he wrote a bitter prologue schooling the amphitheatre playgoers in what *not* to expect from a play originally intended for an indoor hall staging:

> Gentlemen, I am onely sent to say,
> Our Author did not calculate his Play,
> For this Meridian; the Bank-Side he knows
> Is far more skilful at the ebbes and flowes
> Of water than of Wit: He did not mean
> For this elevation of your poles this Scene.
> No shews, no frisk, and what you most delight in, ...
> No Clown, no squibs, no Divells in't; oh now
> You Squirrels that want nuts, what will ye do?
> Pray do not crack the benches, and we may
> Hereafter fit your palats with a Play.
> But you that can contract your selves, and fit
> As you were now in the *Black-Friers* pit,
> And will not deaf us with lewd noise, or tongues,
> Because we have no heart to break our lungs,
> Will pardon our vast Scene, and not disgrace
> This Play, meant for your persons, not the place.[35]

Contrary to expectations at public houses, in this play there would be "No Clown." Though Shirley did include minor clown parts in such works as *The Opportunity* (c. 1634–39), *The Royal Master* (c. 1637–38), *The Martyred Soldier* (c. 1638, with Heywood), *Part 1 Saint Patrick for Ireland* (c. 1639), and *The Arcadia* (1639–40),[36] in most of the plays he

33 Alexander Leggatt, *Introduction to English Renaissance Comedy* (Manchester, 1999), 7.
34 James Bulman, "Caroline Drama," in *The Cambridge Companion to English Renaissance Drama*, ed. A. R. Braunmiller and Michael Hattaway (1990; rpt Cambridge, 2003), 344–71; 346.
35 Andrew Gurr, *Playgoing in Shakespeare's London* (1987; rpt Cambridge, 1994), 188.
36 Of course, indoor hall playwright William Davenant likewise included clown

wrote in the Caroline period for fashionable indoor halls, the new style of proto-comedy-of-manners would render clowns less central to satire than London fashion-mongers, aspirant courtiers, country gentry, or eccentrics played by the likes of the light comedian Tooley.

The relatively more popular and old-fashioned satirical repertoire of Richard Brome, a theatrical Son of Ben, did feature clown parts in such plays as *The City Wit* (1630), *The Queen's Exchange* (1631), *The Sparagus Garden* (1635), and *The Antipodes* (1636–38), but Brome's brand of satiric Caroline comedy more "often include[d] elaborate and theatrical parades of social types" – gallants, prodigals, thieves, bawds, con-artists, and gulls.[37] And, it was Brome who famously made his character Letoy correct the stage clown Biplay's infelicities in the meta-dramatic *Antipodes* by arguing it belonged to "the days of Tarleton and Kemp, / Before the stage was purged from Barbarism, / And brought to the perfection it now shines with" (2.1. 102–4). This attitude toward the old clowns announces the triumph of neoclassical aesthetics and decorum. In his overview of Caroline theatre, James Bulman offers a further rationale for why the role of the stage clown was diminished in most indoor hall plays of the era: "Brome aims his satire more directly at those who can distinguish – the aristocratic Londoners gathered at the Salisbury Court theatre."[38] If so, as Brome held the mirror up to the nature he found in his discerning audience, conventional clown roles – rustics, mechanicals, natural and artificial fools – were not reflected, and consequently were not likely to be depicted on stage.

Not surprisingly, in this Caroline context, the public playhouses, with their plebian, old-fashioned taste for revivals, became virtual sanctuaries for stage clowning. As Bulman thus observes,

> The old-style popular playhouses – the Fortune, the Red Bull, and, in the summer, the Globe – were sustained almost exclusively by a nostalgic and nationalistic diet of apprentice plays, pseudo-histories, chivalric adventures, and low-life farces. With their ... indecorous

parts at least in the proto-comedy-of manners *The Platonic Lovers* (1635), as well as in *Luminalia* (1638) and *The Temple of Love* (1635).

[37] Martin Butler, *Theatre and Crisis 1632–1642* (Cambridge, 1984), 190.

[38] Bulman, "Caroline Drama," 359.

mixture of kings and clowns, such plays appealed to a regressive plebian taste.[39]

The Red Bull playhouse came to be noted reductively for old-style farce, comic devilry, and romance/chivalry, so that it was said that the "red bull phrase" was simply "enter three devils *solus*"; this theatre was admired for its familiar and predictable "Drums, Trumpets, Battels, and Hero's [*sic*]."[40] Martin Butler characterizes the style of drama favored here as embracing not only "the mingling of clowns and kings" but all that was "festive, ranting, traditional, nostalgic, and Elizabethan."[41]

The revival of earlier repertories troubled Caroline authorities because it threatened to make available "a drama that was skeptical, critical and leveling, [one] in which common men rubbed shoulders with kings" irreverently.[42] The old revivals were, in their effect on audiences, perceived to be more politically charged than one might now think, often for good reason. At the public playhouses, the surprising potential of revivals to voice topical religious or class antagonism was audaciously exploited, both pre- and post-closure of the theatres. In 1639, two episodes were particularly scandalous. In May, at the Fortune, a revival of *The Cardinal's Conspiracy* (now lost) appealed to popular animus toward supposed High-Church Romanism. As Edward Rossingham reported by letter:

> Thursday last the players of the Fortune were fined £1,000 for setting up an altar, a bason, and two candlesticks, and bowing down before it upon the stage, and although they allege it was an old play revived, and an altar to the heathen gods, yet it was apparent that this play was revived on purpose in contempt of the ceremonies of the church.[43]

Subsequently, in September, the Red Bull players likewise provoked authorities with a run of "many days together" of the lost play of *The Whore New Vamped*, which targeted new duties on wine and even called alderman William Abell, a wine monopolist, a knave and a drunkard. Council minutes of September 29 record that

---

39 Ibid., 344.
40 Butler, *Theatre and Crisis*, 181.
41 Ibid., 183.
42 Ibid., 185.
43 Gurr, *Playgoing in Shakespeare's London*, 186, 187.

Complaint was this day made to his Majestie sitting in Councell, that Stage players of the Red Bull have lately for many days to gether acted a scandalous and Libellous play wherein they have audaciously reproached, and in a Libellous manner traduced and personated some persons of quality, and scandalized, and defamed the whole profession of Proctors belonging to the Court of the Civill Lawe, and reflected upon the present Government.[44]

Here, the Red Bull company was clearly fueling popular discontent against "the present Government." Key to later developments, however, the citizen playhouses tended to vent "hostility [against] the counselors of the government and its City agents rather than ... the king himself."[45] Ultimately, if Butler sees this episode as evidence that some Caroline "amphitheatre plays had topical commentary seeping into them,"[46] we have seen that such "seeping in" was hardly new; it was revival sustaining an old tradition.

RAZING CANE:
STOPPING "SCANDALOUS AND LIBELOUS PLAY"

Having already suffered theatrical banishment, as well as the coinciding indignities of neoclassical disapproval and Stuart censorship, clowning would experience still more degradations in the wake of extreme assertions of power by the censorious puritan government during the Commonwealth. In September of 1642 it was unclear whether parliament's ban on playing would be permanent or a temporary suspension only "while these sad causes and set times of humiliation do continue."[47] Although the Globe had ostentatiously been pulled down in 1644, the puritan government's moral animus toward the theatre was first unambiguously expressed in a February 1648 decree that commanded that playhouses were to be demolished,[48] with the express

---

44 Ibid.
45 Ibid.
46 Martin Butler, "The Condition of the Theatres in 1642," in *The Cambridge History of British Theatre*: vol. 1, *Origins to 1660*, ed. Jane Milling and Peter Thomson (Cambridge, 2004), 439–56; 453.
47 Ibid., 441.
48 Ibid.

purpose of "the utter suppression and abolishing of all stage-plays and interludes" and the order that all players who disobeyed were to be whipped and the audiences fined.[49] Although the Salisbury Court and the Fortune were soon destroyed, Members of Parliament were said to be attending illegal performances suppressed by the army in 1649,[50] and the Blackfriars and the Hope were not pulled down until 1655–56.[51]

Yet, as of the Restoration, the Red Bull in Clerkenwell, the theatre whose stage clowns would prove most resistant to the puritan government, was still standing and suitable for playing.[52] Perhaps it survived, as has been claimed, merely because it "was somewhat out of the way."[53] Still, the audacious Interregnum playing here hardly escaped notice and repeated censorship, and so it is remarkable that of all the theatres (along with the Cockpit/Phoenix), this playhouse should have survived, being still in use at least through 1659, when Middlesex Sessions of the Peace record in May of that year that actors Edward Shatterel and Anthony Turner were bound over for "the unlawful maintaining of stage plays and interludes at the Red Bull."[54] The survival of the Red Bull is all the more extraordinary given its resilient Interregnum history of activism, whether surreptitious or overt – the latter expressed through stage clowns.

A case in point is to be found in the career of one of the last great stage clowns before the Restoration, Andrew Cane, who first appears in theatrical records in 1622 in association with Palgrave's and Lady Elizabeth's Players, after which time little or nothing is heard of him until he joined Prince Charles's Men in 1631 when he appeared as the humorous gallant Trimalchio in Marmion's *Holland's Leaguer*. After this point, Edwin Nungezer's findings would support the conclusion that his clowning could be quite politically topical, in the line of Tarlton,

49 Janet Clare, "Theatre and Commonwealth," in *The Cambridge History of British Theatre*: vol. 1, *Origins to 1660*, ed. Jane Milling and Peter Thomson (Cambridge, 2004), 458–76; 459.
50 Butler, "Condition of the Theatres in 1642," 443.
51 Ibid., 441.
52 Ibid.
53 Dale B. J. Randall, *Winter Fruit: English Drama 1642–1660* (Lexington, MA, 1995), 47.
54 Clare, "Theatre and Commonwealth," 462.

Kemp, and Rowley, since on September 29, 1639, he and the Prince's Men were summoned for acting a "scandalous and libelous play," *The Whore New Vamped*, in which, the authorities complained, the players had "personated some persons of quality" and Cane especially had libeled the hypocritical wine monopolist alderman.[55] But his political resistance to authorities would grow bolder still, both on stage and off. In fact, on December 12, 1642, while the mayor and his council met at the Guildhall, it is recorded that "Cain the Clown at the Red Bull, and others came in great multitude, and filled the Hall and Yard."[56] Remarkably, other records indicate that Cane coined money for the King in Oxford.[57] Little wonder that anti-royalist, revolution-era puritans disliked players. After the suppression of full-scale plays at public playhouses in 1648, in the satirical work *A Key to the Cabinet of the Parliament* (1648), Cane appears alongside two other noted comedians of the period in mockery of the puritan faction:

> We need not more stage-players: we thank them [the Puritans] for suppressing them: they save us money; for I'll undertake we can laugh as heartily at ... their godly ministers, as ever we did at Cane at the Red Bull, Tom Pollard in *The Humorous Lieutenant*, Robins in *The Changeling*, or any humourist of them all.[58]

But Nungezer found that Cane and his company actually continued to perform surreptitiously at least until January 1650 when soldiers surprised the players and arrested them off the stage of the Red Bull. The royalist pamphlet *Mercurious Pragmaticus* records the episode as follows: "*Andr. Cane* is out of date and all other his complices; alas poor players they are acting their parts in prison, for their presumptions to break a Parliament Crack."[59] A comment on this period of censorship and closure appearing in *Pleasant Notes upon Don Quixot[e]* (1654) offers a bleak assessment: "It was not then ... *Andrew Cane* could pacifie; Prologues nor Epilogues would prevaile; the Devill and the fool were quite out of favour."[60] And so was all clowning.

---

55 Nungezer, *Dictionary of Actors*, 82.
56 Ibid., 83.
57 Bentley, *Jacobean and Caroline Stage*, 2: 398.
58 Nunzeger, *Dictionary of Actors*, 83.
59 Ibid.,84.
60 Ibid., 83.

In this regard, consider even the little that is known about the Caroline-Interregnum actor "Tim Reede the Foole." Mirroring the treatment of Shank by Fletcher, Reade first appeared among Queen Henrietta's Men as a maid in Shirley's *Wedding*, which was performed at the Cockpit in May of 1626.[61] But if Shirley was reluctant to give him a fool's part, other playwrights were less so. Thomas Goffe, to cite one example, praised his comic skill in *Careless Shepherdess* (published 1656; performed *c.* 1625–29):

> There is ne'er a part
> About him but breaks jests. –
> I never saw Reade peeping through the curtain,
> But ravishing joy entered my heart."[62]

What is not altogether clear here is who was breaking jests on whom, but by 1641, Reade was, with Cane, one of the most famous clowns of the era, since he appears as himself in *The Stage-Players Complaint, in a pleasant Dialogue between Cane of the Fortune and Reed of the Friers, deploring their sad and solitary condition for the want of Imployment* (1641).[63] More to the point, Reade was evidently playing the comic part of the coward Bessus in a revival of Beaumont and Fletcher's *A King and No King* when he was arrested from the stage of Salisbury Court on October 6, 1647, as is noted in a letter from Queen Henrietta Maria, dated February 25, to Charles:[64]

> The Sherriffes of the City of London with their officers went thither, and found a great number of people; some young lords, and other eminent persons; and the men and women with the Boxes, [that took monies] fled. The Sherriffes brought away Tim Reede the Foole, and the people cryed out for their monies, but slunke away like a company of drowned Mice without it.[65]

---

61 Ibid., 291.
62 Ibid., 292.
63 Ibid., 291.
64 Terence P. Logan and Denzell S. Smith (eds), *The Later Jacobean and Caroline Dramatists: A Survey and Bibliography of Recent Studies in English Renaissance Drama* (Lincoln, NE, 1978), 33.
65 Nunzeger, *Dictionary of Actors*, 292.

The choice of play here was pointed in so far as *King and No King* would seem to support a royalist agenda. Recalling models from the days of Edward VI, this old play deals with a scheming Lord Protector who wishes to make his own son king. The characterization of the Lord Protector presents him as a great warrior who is otherwise coarse and ignoble because he ultimately proves to be not of royal blood. Such themes in this revival undoubtedly glanced topically at the ambitions of the militaristic, sometimes boorish Cromwell. In any case, note that it was the clown Reade who was mentioned prominently in accounts of the players as defiantly performing in the face of the closure of the public playhouses. Given that Reade was praised in his day as "the most incomparable mimicke upon the face of the Earth,"[66] it seems likely that he employed some topical "personation" akin to that practiced years earlier in *A Game at Chess* and possibly by Cane in *The Whore New Vamped.*

Another popular Caroline-Interregnum clown who proved to be of a decidedly political bent was William Robins (a.k.a., Robinson), getting his start, not surprisingly, at the Red Bull with Queen Anne's company between 1616 and 1619 and, after her funeral in May 1619, with the Players of the Revels at the Red Bull, where he is mentioned as one of the "chiefe players" in 1622. Not long after the sudden death of James at the end of March 1625 and then the subsequent prompt marriage of Charles to Princess Henrietta Maria of France in early May, the company was rechristened Queen Henrietta's Men. When the author of *A Key to the Cabinet of the Parliament* (1648) claimed that "we can laugh as heartily at … their godly ministers, as ever we did at … Robins in *The Changeling*,"[67] as John Southworth observes, he suggests that one of Robins's prime comic parts would have been that of Antonio, the changeling of the title, who pretends to be a natural to gain access to his beloved, imprisoned in a madhouse.[68] Robins seems elsewhere to have actually played naturals, since he is depicted in a conical fool's cap and in a parti-colored fool's long-coat as the diminutive Clown on the title page of Heywood's *A Maidenhead Well Lost* (*c.* 1625–34),[69] part of the

---

[66] Ibid.
[67] Ibid., 83.
[68] Southworth, *Fools and Jesters*, 181.
[69] Ibid.

repertory of Queen Henrietta Maria's company, by then playing largely at the Cockpit. By about 1626 Robins was certainly with Queen Henrietta's Men, where he evidently played the clown Clem the drawer in revivals of Thomas Heywood's *Fair Maid of the West, Part I* (*c.* 1601–2). Robins was thus one of the popular actors who played clowns written by the prolific citizen favorite Heywood, working at the Red Bull and the Cockpit, in such Stuart plays as *Fair Maid of the West, Parts 1 and 2* (*c.* 1601–2, and *c.* 1630), *If you Know not Me you Know Nobody, Parts 1 and 2* (1604, 1605), *The Rape of Lucrece* (1607), *Fortune by Land and Sea* (1609, with Rowley), *The Golden Age* (1610), *The Four Prentices of London* (1615), *The English Traveler* (1627–33), *A Maidenhead Well Lost* (*c.* 1625–34), *Love's Mistress* (1634–35), and *A Challenge for Beauty* (1635–36).

In at least one of Robins's/Robinson's noted clown roles in Heywood's citizen fare, that of Clem, religious politics are invoked. The main action occurs between two key events of the Anglo-Spanish War, England's 1596 raid on Cadiz and its 1597 raid on the Azores, "affairs which were invested by [the English] with a spirit of heroism in excess of their actual achievement."[70] Further enhancing its topical relevance, the play was revived in the era of *A Game at Chess* in the wake of the collapse of the Spanish match and the expulsion of the Jesuits, at a time when Protestant militarists favored war against the Spanish in defense of the German Palatinate. Clem's politics, like those of Heywood, whom Julia Gaspar has called "a first-half-of-the-chapter Calvinist"[71] (i.e., without any subtleties), are also unsubtle, since he appears in a jingoistic, anti-Spanish, and anti-Moorish play (he even appears disguised as a Moor, evidently in blackface in 5.i). At one point, upon capturing the Spanish, Clem slurs "these Spaniards" as "you Don Diegos, you that made Paul's to stink –" (4.110–11), with a taunt that crosses a line into anti-Spanish bigotry as it refers to a Spaniard who was said to have

---

70 Thomas Heywood, *The Fair Maid of the West, Parts I and II*, ed. Robert K. Turner Jr (Lincoln, NE, 1967), xv.
71 Julia Gaspar, "The Reformation Plays on the Public Stage," in *Theatre and Government under the Early Stuarts*, ed. J. R. Mulryne and Margaret Shrewring (Cambridge, 1993), 190–216; 199.

infamously disgraced – and in fact soiled – himself in St Paul's Cathedral, London.[72]

Far more obvious politics were typical of Robins's/Robinson's on-stage persona during the Civil War, and this actor's blatant politics off-stage were even less difficult to discern. He died fighting for the king during the period of the Puritan Revolution, the only clown for whom I know this to be the case. At Basing House in October of 1645, the puritan minister and chaplain to Cromwell reports:

> In the several rooms, and about the house, there were slain seventy-four …. There lay dead upon the ground, … slain by the hands of major Harrison (that godly and gallant gentleman,) … Robinson the player, who, a little before the storm, was known to be mocking and scorning the parliament and our army.[73]

His death is addressed more neutrally, but with some pathos, in *A Diary or an Extract Journall* of 9–16 October, 1645, which reported: "Robinson the Player … was in Drury Lane a Comoedian, but now hee acted his own Tragedy."[74] The author of *Historia Histrionica* (1699) would later add a detail hinting at the ruthlessness of Robinson's death when he claimed that Harrison "refused him quarter, and shot him in the head when he had laid down his arms."[75] As with the reference to Robinson's recent "mocking and scorning [of] the parliament and our army," other contemporary accounts "imply that his comedian's mockery was in part responsible for his death."[76] So died another Yorick, assassinated in cold blood for his political playing. The lengths to which authorities went to silence an old tradition of satiric clowning are a tragic tribute to the power of such mockery. Even the fact that a politically motivated clown's death was exploited for propagandistic purpose underscores the once widely recognized political bent of Renaissance clowning.

To say that more work needs to be done on the clowns briefly outlined here is to say the obvious, since the Renaissance comic, and

---

72 Heywood, *Fair Maid of the West*, 73 n. 110–11.
73 Information in this paragraph is taken from Nunzeger, *Dictionary of Actors*, 298–9.
74 Bentley, *Jacobean and Caroline Stage*, 2: 549.
75 Nunzeger, *Dictionary of Actors*, 299.
76 Bentley, *Jacobean and Caroline Stage*, vol. 2, 548.

particularly the figure of the clown, has much to yield in religious, polemical, political, and satirical contexts. The results of such future analyses, I predict, will find not shallow topicality in the humor of the era but some critical insights which animate the comic, giving it rich significance that we can still recover and appreciate. Close analyses of stage clowns in myriad historical contexts will ultimately prove more productive than ahistoric applications of sweeping, universalizing, generic, and thereby limited and limiting models. The ongoing work of unearthing Yoricks will be worthwhile, for, even if Renaissance clowns do not quite prove to be of "infinite jest" (*Hamlet*, 5.1, 184), their jesting will nonetheless be challenging enough.

BIBLIOGRAPHY

Manuscript Sources

Borthwick Institute, York, High Commission Cause Papers, 1597/12.
Buckinghamshire Record Office, D/A/V4, fol. 53ᵛ.
British Library, MS. Add. 44874, fol. 75.
Inner Temple Library, MS. Petyt 538/47.

Published Works

Allan, D. G., "The Risings in the West 1628–31," *Economic History Review*, 2nd series, vol. 5 (1952–3), 76–85.
Anglo, Sydney, "An Early Tudor Programme for Plays and Other Demonstrations Against the Pope," *Journal of the Warburg and Courtauld Institutes* 20 (1957), 177–8.
——, *Spectacle, Pageantry, and Early Tudor Policy* (1969; rpt Oxford, 1997).
Armstrong, C. D. C., "Gardiner, Stephen (*c.* 1495/8–1555)," in *Oxford Dictionary of National Biography* (Oxford, 2004); available online at www.oxforddnb.com/view/article/10364.
Aston, Margaret, *The King's Bedpost: Reformation and Iconography in a Tudor Group Portrait* (Cambridge, 1993).
Axton, Marie (ed.), *The Queen's Two Bodies: Drama and the Elizabethan Succession* (London, 1977).
——, *Three Tudor Classical Interludes* (Cambridge, 1982).
Baldwin, T. W., *The Organisation and Personnel of the Shakespearean Company* (Princeton, NJ, 1927).
Ball, William, *Lincoln's Inn: Its History and Tradition* (London, 1947).
Barrow, Henry, *A Brief Discoverie of the False Church* (Dortmund [?], 1590) in *Writings of Henry Barrow*, ed. Leland H. Carlson (London 1962–66), 539.
Barthelemy, Anthony Gerard, *Black Face, Maligned Race: The Representation of Blacks in English Drama from Shakespeare to Southerne* (Baton Rouge, LA, 1987).

Baskervill, Charles Read, *The Elizabethan Jig and Related Song Drama* (Chicago, 1929).

Bawcutt, N. W. (ed.), *The Control and Censorship of Caroline Drama: The Records of Sir Henry Herbert, Master of the Reveals 1623–1673* (Oxford, 1996).

Baxter, R., *The Reformed Pastor* (London, 1656).

Bednarz, James P., "William Kemp," in *Fools and Jesters in Literature, Art, and History: A Bio-Bibliographical Sourcebook*, ed. Vicki K. Janik (Westport, CT, 1998), 273–80.

Belkin, Ahuva, "Antichrist as the Embodiment of the *Insipiens* in Thirteenth-Century French Psalters," *Florilegium* 10 (1988–91): 65–77.

Bentley, G. E., The *Jacobean and Caroline Stage: Dramatic Companies and Players*, 7 vols (Oxford, 1941–68).

Berry, Ralph, "*Twelfth Night*: The Experience of the Audience," in *Shakespeare Survey* 34, ed. Stanley Wells (Cambridge, 2002): 111–20.

Bevington, David, *Tudor Drama and Politics* (Cambridge, MA., 1968).

Billington, Sandra, *A Social History of the Fool* (New York, 1984).

Black, Joseph, "The Rhetoric of Reaction: The Martin Marprelate Tracts (1588–89), Anti-Martinism and the Uses of Print in Early Modern England," *Sixteenth Century Journal* 28.3 (fall 1997): 707–25.

Blunt, Richard, "Recreating Renaissance Black Make-Up," dissertation for M.Litt in Shakespeare and Renaissance Literature in Performance (Mary Baldwin College, VA, spring 2006).

Boas, F. S., *University Drama in the Tudor Age* (Oxford, 1914).

Boemus, Johann, *The Manner, Lawes, and Customes of All Nations* (London, 1611).

Bolton, Robert, *Mr Bolton's Last & Learned Worke … Together with the Life and Death of the Author, Published by E[dward] B[agshaw]* (London, 1632).

A Book of Masques: in Honour of Allardyce Nicoll, with introduction by G. E. Bentley (1967; rpt Cambridge, 1980).

Booth, Stephen (ed.), *Shakespeare's Sonnets: edited with analytic commentary* (New Haven, CT, and London, 1977).

Born, Hanspeter, "The Date of *2, 3 Henry VI*," *Shakespeare Quarterly* 25 (1974): 323–34.

Boskin, Joseph, Sambo: *The Rise and Demise of an American Jester* (New York, 1986).

——, "The Life and Death of Sambo: Overview of an Historical Hang-Up," *Journal of Popular Culture* 4.3 (winter 1971), 647–57.

Bradbrook, M. C., *The Growth and Structure of Elizabethan Comedy* (London, 1955).

Brand, John, *Popular Antiquities of Great Britain: Chiefly Illustrating the Origin of Our Vulgar and Provincial Customs, Ceremonies, and Superstitions* (1848–49; rpt New York, 1970).

Brigden, Susan, "Youth and the English Reformation," in *The Impact of the English Reformation 1500–1640*, ed. Peter Marshall (London, 1997), 55–85.

Browne, Robert, *Treatise upon the 23. of Matthewe* (Middelburg, 1582).

Bulman, James, "Caroline Drama," in *The Cambridge Companion to English Renaissance Drama*, ed. A. R. Braunmiller and Michael Hattaway (1990; rpt Cambridge 2003), 344–71.

Burke, Peter, *Popular Culture in Early Modern Europe* (New York, 1978).

Butler, Martin, "The Condition of the Theatres in 1642," in *The Cambridge History of British Theatre*: vol. 1, *Origins to 1660*, ed. Jane Milling and Peter Thomson (Cambridge, 2004), 439–56.

——. *Theatre and Crisis 1632–1642* (Cambridge, 1984).

Callaghan, Dympna, *Shakespeare Without Women: Representing Gender and Race on the Renaissance Stage* (London and New York, 2000).

Capel, Richard, *Tentations: Their Nature, Danger, Cure* (London, 1635).

Carlson, Leland (ed.), *Martin Marprelate, Gentleman: Master Job Throckmorton laid open in his colors* (San Marino, CA, 1981).

Chambers, E. K., *The Elizabethan Stage*, 4 vols (Oxford, 1923).

——, *The Mediaeval Stage*, 2 vols (Oxford, 1903).

Chapman, George, *The Memorable Masque of the Two Honourable Houses or Inns of Court*, in *Jacobean and Caroline Masques*, ed. Richard Dutton, 2 vols (Nottingham, n.d.), 19–32.

The Chester Mystery Cycle, ed. R. M. Lumiansky and David Mills, Early English Text Society, Supplementary Series 3 (London, 1974).

Clare, Janet, "Theatre and Commonwealth," in *The Cambridge History of British Theatre*: vol. 1, *Origins to 1660*, ed. Jane Milling and Peter Thomson (Cambridge, 2004), 458–76.

Clark, Sandra (ed.), *Shakespeare Made Fit: Restoration Adaptations of Shakespeare* (London, 1997).

Clayton, Thomas, " 'Is this the promis'd end?' Revision in the Role of the King," in *The Division of the Kingdoms: Shakespeare's Two Versions of King Lear*, ed. Gary Taylor and Michael Warren (Oxford, 1983), 121–41.

Cockrell, Dale, *Demons of Disorder: Early Blackface Minstrels and Their World* (Cambridge, 1997).

Collinson, Patrick, "Ben Jonson's *Bartholomew Fair*: The Theatre Constructs Puritanism," in *The Theatrical City: Culture, Theatre and Politics in London, 1576–1649*, ed. David L. Smith, Richard Strier, and David Bevington (Cambridge, 1995), 157–69.

——, *The Elizabethan Puritan Movement* (1967; Oxford, 1990).

——, *From Iconoclasm to Iconophobia: The Cultural Impact of the Second English Reformation* (Reading, 1986).

——, "Perne, Andrew (1519?–1589)," in *Oxford Dictionary of National Biography* (Oxford, 2004); available online at www.oxforddnb.com/view/article/21975].

Cosin, Richard, *Conspiracie, for pretended reformation* (London, 1592).

Cox, John D., *The Devil and the Sacred in English Drama, 1350–1642* (Cambridge, 2000).

Crankshaw, D. J. and A. Gillespie, "Parker, Matthew (1504–1575)," in *Oxford Dictionary of National Biography* (Oxford, 2004); available online at www.oxforddnb.com/view/article/21327.

The Creation, and the Fall of Lucifer, in *Everyman and the Medieval Miracle Plays*, ed. A. C. Cawley (1956; rpt London, 1999).

Cressy, David and Lori Anne Ferrell (eds), *Religion and Society in Early Modern England: A Sourcebook* (London, 1996).

Crockett, Bryan, *The Play of Paradox: Stage and Sermon in Renaissance England* (Philadelphia, PA, 1995).

D'Amico, Jack, *The Moor in the English Renaissance Drama* (Tampa, FL, 1991).

Davidson, C., "Carnival, Lent, and Early English Drama," *Research Opportunities in Renaissance Drama* 36 (1997), 123–4.

Davies, John, *The Complete Works of John Davies of Hereford*, ed. Alexander B. Grossart (Edinburgh, 1878).

Davis, David Brion, "At the Heart of Slavery," in idem, in *the Image of God: Religion, Moral Values, and Our Heritage of Slavery* (New Haven, CT, 2001), 123–36.

——, *Inhuman Bondage: The Rise and Fall of Slavery in the New World* (Oxford, 2006).

——, *The Problem of Slavery in Western Culture* (Ithaca, NY, 1966).

Davis, Natalie Zemon, "Women on Top," in idem, *Society and Culture in Early Modern France* (1965; reprint, Stanford, CA, 1978), 124–51.

de Grazia, Margreta, *Hamlet without Hamlet* (Cambridge, 2007).

de Molen, Richard L., "The Boy-Bishop Festival in Tudor England," *Moreana* 45 (February 1975): 17–28.

Dent, Arthur, *Pastime for Parents* (London, 1606).

Devereux, Janice (ed.), *An Edition of Luke Shepherd's Satires* (Tempe, AZ, 2001).

Dictionary of National Biography, vol. XXX, "Johnes–Kenneth," ed. Sidney Lee (London, 1892).

Dillon, Janette, "Theatre and Controversy, 1603–1642," in *The Cambridge History of British Theatre*: vol. 1, *Origins to 1660*, ed. Jane Milling and Peter Thomson (Cambridge, 2004), 364–82.

Donnan, Elizabeth, *Documents Illustrative of the History of the Slave Trade to America*, 4 vols (1930; rpt New York, 1965).

Dormon, James H., "The Strange Career of Jim Crow Rice (with apologies to Professor Woodward)," *Journal of Social History* 3.2 (winter 1969–70): 109–22.

Duffy, Eamon, *The Stripping of the Altars: Traditional Religion in England 1400–1580* (New Haven, CT, 1992).

Dutton, Richard, "Thomas Middleton's *A Game at Chess*: A Case Study," in *The Cambridge History of British Theatre*: vol. 1, *Origins to 1660*, ed. Jane Milling and Peter Thomson (Cambridge, 2004), 424–38.

Edwards, Paul, "The Early African Presence in the British Isles," in *Essays on the History of Blacks in Britain: From Roman Times to the Mid-Twentieth Century*, ed. Jagdish S. Gundara and Ian Duffield (Aldershot, 1992), 9–29.

Ellis, David, *Shakespeare's Practical Jokes: An Introduction to the Comic in His Work* (Lewisburg, PA, 2007).

Felver, Charles S., *Robert Armin, Shakespeare's Fool: A Biographical Essay*, Kent State University Bulletin (Kent, OH, 1961).

Feuillerat, Albert (ed.), *Documents Relating to the Revels at Court in the Time of King Edward VI and Queen Mary* (Louvain, 1914).

Fielding, Henry, *Tom Jones*, ed. John Bender and Simon Stern, Oxford World's Classics (Oxford, 1998).

The First Folio of Shakespeare, Norton Facsimile edition, ed. Charlton Hinman (London and New York, 1968).

Fletcher, Reginald J. (ed.), *The Pension Book of Gray's Inn: 1569–[1800]* (London, 1901–10).

Fo, Dario, *The Tricks of the Trade*, trans. Joe Farrell (New York, 1991).

Foakes, R. A., "Textual Revision and the Fool in *King Lear*," *Trivium*, 20 (1985), 33–47.

Four Morality Plays, ed. Peter Happé (Harmondsworth, 1979).

Foxe, John, *Acts and Monuments* (1583 edition); available online at www.hrionline.ac.uk/foxe/.

Frederickson, George M., *The Black Image in the White Mind: The Debate on Afro-American Character and Destiny, 1817–1914* (New York, 1971).

——, *Racism: A Short History* (Princeton, NJ, 2002).

Freedman, Paul, *Images of the Medieval Peasant* (Stanford, CA, 1999).

Fryer, Peter, *Staying Power: The History of Black People in Britain* (London, 1984).

Fumerton, Patricia, "Introduction: A New New Historicism," in *Renaissance Culture and the Everyday*, ed. Patricia Fumerton and Simon Hunt (Philadelphia, PA, 1999), 1–17.

Gair, Reavley, *The Children of Paul's: The Story of a Theatre Company, 1553–1608* (Cambridge, 1982).

Gairdner, James and R. H. Brodie (eds), *Letters and Papers, Foreign and Domestic, Henry VIII* (London, 1894), vol. XIV.

Gaspar, Julia, "The Reformation Plays on the Public Stage," in *Theatre and Government under the Early Stuarts*, ed. J. R. Mulryne and Margaret Shrewring (Cambridge, 1993), 190–216.

Gates, Henry Louis, *Figures in Black: Words, Signs, and the "Racial" Self* (New York and Oxford, 1987).

"George Bernard Shaw Puts Shakespeare into His Latest Play; But the 'Bard of Aavon' Is Scarcely a Hero in 'The Dark Lady of the Sonnets,'" *New York Times*, December 25, 1910, SM6.

Gerard, John, *The Herball or General Historie of Plantes* (London, 1597).

Gifford, D. J., "Iconographical Notes Towards a Definition of the Medieval Fool," in *The Fool and the Trickster: Studies in Honour of Enid Welsford*, ed. Paul V. A. Williams (Cambridge, 1979), 18–35.

Goldberg, Jonathan, *Shakespeare's Hand* (Minneapolis, MN, 2003).

——, "Textual Properties," *Shakespeare Quarterly* 37.2 (1986): 213–17.

Goldenberg, David M., *The Curse of Ham: Race and Slavery in Early Judaism, Christianity and Islam* (Princeton, NJ, 2003).

Gottschild, Brenda Dixon, *Digging the Africanist Presence in American Performance: Dance and Other Contexts* (Westport, CT, 1996).

Granger, Thomas, *A Familiar Exposition or Commentarie on Ecclesiastes* (London, 1621).

Green, V. H. H., *Religion at Oxford and Cambridge* (London, 1964).

Greenblatt, Stephen, *Hamlet in Purgatory* (Princeton, NJ, 2001).

——, *Shakespearean Negotiations* (Berkeley, CA, 1988).

Greenham, Richard, *The Workes of the Reverend Richard Greenham*, ed. Henry Holland (London, 1612).

Grovett, L. A., *The Kings Book of Sports* (London, 1890).

Gurr, Andrew, *Playgoing in Shakespeare's London* (1987; rpt Cambridge, 1994).

Haigh, Christopher, "Anticlericalism and the English Reformation," in *The English Reformation Revised*, ed. Christopher Haigh (1987; Cambridge, 2000), 56–74.

Hall, Kim F., *Things of Darkness: Economies of Race and Gender in Early Modern England* (Ithaca, NY, 1995).

Halliwell-Phillips, James Orchard, *Tarlton's Jests, and News Out of Purgatory: With notes, and some account of the life of Tarlton* (London, 1844).

Hamilton, Donna B., *Shakespeare and the Politics of Protestant England* (Lexington, MA, 1992).

Happé, Peter, "The Devil in the Interludes, 1550–1577," *Medieval English Theatre* 11.1–2 (1989): 42–55.

Harmer, Harry, *The Longman Companion to Slavery, Emancipation and Civil Rights* (London, 2001).

Harris, Joseph E., *Africans and Their History*, 2nd rev. edn (1972; New York, 1998).

Haydn, Hiram, *The Counter-Renaissance* (New York, 1950).

Haynes, Stephen R., *Noah's Curse: The Biblical Justification of American Slavery* (Oxford, 2002).

Heal, Felicity and Clive Holmes, *The Gentry in England and Wales, 1500–1700* (Stanford, CA, 1994).

Helgerson, Richard, *Forms of Nationhood: The Elizabethan Writing of England* (Chicago, 1992).

Heywood, John, *The Plays of John Heywood*, ed. Richard Axton and Peter Happé (Cambridge, 1991).

Heywood, Thomas, *The Fair Maid of the West, Parts I and II*, ed. Robert K. Turner Jr. (Lincoln, NE, 1967).

——, *Troia Britanica: Or, Great Britaines Troy. A Poem Deuided into XVII. Seuerall Cantons, intermixed with many pleasant Poeticall Tales* (London, 1609).

Hill, Christopher, *Change and Continuity in 17th-Century England* (New Haven, CT, 1991).

——, *Society and Puritanism in Pre-Revolutionary England* (1958; rpt New York, 1997).

——, *The World Turned Upside Down: Radical Ideas During the English Revolution* (1972; rpt New York, 1973).

——, *Writing and Revolution in 17th-Century England*, vol. 1, of *The Collected Essays of Christopher Hill* (Amherst, MA, 1985).

Hill, Errol, *Shakespeare in Sable: A History of Black Actors* (Amherst, MA, 1984).

Holden, William P., *Anti-Puritan Satire, 1572–1642* (New Haven, CT, 1954).

Hornback, Robert, "Blackfaced Fools, Black-Headed Birds, Fool Synonyms, and Shakespearean Allusions to Renaissance Blackface Folly," *Notes & Queries* 55 (2008): 215–19.

——, "The Fool in Quarto and Folio *King Lear*," *English Literary Renaissance* 34.3 (2004): 306–38.

——, "Reformation Satire, Scatology, and Iconoclastic Aesthetics in *Gammer Gurton's Needle*," in *The Blackwell Companion to Tudor Literature and Culture, 1485–1603*, ed. Kent Cartwright (forthcoming, 2009).

Hotson, Leslie, *Shakespeare's Motley* (New York, 1952).

Howard Hill, T. H. (ed.), *A Game at Chess* (Manchester, 1993).

Humphrey, Chris, *The Politics of Carnival: Festive Misrule in Medieval England* (Manchester, 2001).

Inderwick, F. A., *A Calendar of the Inner Temple Records*: vol. 1, *1505–1603* (London, 1896).

Ingram, R. W. (ed.), *Coventry*, Records of Early English Drama (Toronto, *c.* 1981).

Isaac, Benjamin, *The Invention of Racism in Classical Antiquity* (Princeton, 2004).

James I, *The True Law of Free Monarchies and Basilikon Doron of James VI*, ed. Daniel Fischlin and Mark Fortier (Toronto, 1996).

Janson, H. W., *Apes and Ape Lore in the Middle Ages and the Renaissance* (London, 1952).

Jones, Eldred, *Othello's Countrymen: The African in English Renaissance Drama* (London, 1965).

Jones, J. Gwynfor, "Robinson, Nicholas (*c.* 1530–1585)," in *Oxford Dictionary of National Biography* (Oxford, 2004); available online at www.oxforddnb.com/view/article/23860.

Jonson, Ben, *Bartholomew Fair*, ed. G. R. Hibbard, New Mermaid edition (New York, 1997).

——, *Every Man Out of His Humour*, ed. Helen Ostovich (Manchester, 2001).

Jordan, Winthrop D., *White Over Black: American Attitudes Toward the Negro, 1550–1812* (Chapel Hill, NC, 1968).

Kaiser, Walter, *Praisers of Folly: Erasmus, Rabelais, Shakespeare* (Cambridge, 1963).

Kemp, William, *Kemps Nine Daies Wonder. Performed in a Daunce from*

London to Norwich [1600], ed. Rev. Alexander Dyce (1860; rpt New York, 1968).

Kerrigan, John, "Revision, Adaptation, and the Fool in *King Lear*," in *The Division of the Kingdoms: Shakespeare's Two Versions of* King Lear, ed. Gary Taylor and Michael Warren (Oxford, 1983), 195–245.

King, John N., *English Reformation Literature: Tudor Origins of the Protestant Tradition* (Princeton, NJ, 1982).

Knutson, Roslyn L., "The Repertory," in *A New History of Early English Drama*, ed. John D. Cox and David Scott Kastan (New York, 1997), 461–80.

Kurlansky, Mark, *The Big Oyster: History on the Half Shell* (New York, 2006).

Lake, Peter, *Anglicans and Puritans? Presbyterianism and English Conformist Thought from Whitgift to Hooker* (London, 1988).

——, "Defining Puritanism – Again?" in *Puritanism*, ed. F. Bremer (Boston, 1993), 3–29.

Laroque, François, *Shakespeare's Festive World: Elizabethan Seasonal Entertainment and the Professional Stage*, trans. Janet Lloyd (Cambridge, 1993).

Leggatt, Alexander, *Introduction to English Renaissance Comedy* (Manchester, 1999).

Leinwand, Theodore B., "Conservative Fools in James's Court and Shakespeare's Plays," *Shakespeare Studies* 19 (1987): 219–34.

Lennam, Trevor, *Sebastian Westcott, the Children of Paul's, and* The Marriage of Wit and Science (Toronto, 1975).

Levin, Harry, "General Introduction," in *The Riverside Shakespeare* (1974; rpt Boston, 1997), 1–25.

Lhamon Jr., W. T., *Jump Jim Crow: Lost Plays, Lyrics, and Street Prose of the First Atlantic Popular Culture* (Cambridge, 2003).

——, *Raising Cain: Blackface Performance from Jim Crow to Hip Hop* (Cambridge, 1998).

Lockyer, Roger, *Tudor and Stuart Britain, 1471–1714* (New York, 1993).

Logan, Terence P. and Denzell S. Smith (eds), *The Later Jacobean and Caroline Dramatists: A Survey and Bibliography of Recent Studies in English Renaissance Drama* (Lincoln, NE, 1978).

Longstaffe, Stephen, " 'A Short Report and Not Otherwise': Jack Cade in *2 Henry VI*," in *Shakespeare and Carnival: After Bakhtin*, ed. Ronald Knowles (Basingstoke, 1998), 13–35.

——, "What Is the English History Play and Why Are They Saying Such Terrible Things About It?" *Renaissance Forum: An Electronic Journal of Early-Modern Literary and Historical Studies* 2.2 (autumn 1997): available online at www.hull.ac.uk/renforum/v2no2/longstaf.htm.

Lopez, Jeremy, *Theatrical Convention and Audience Response in Early Modern Drama* (Cambridge, 2003).

Lott, Eric, *Love and Theft: Blackface Minstrelsy and the American Working Class* (New York, 1993).

Lowe, Ben, "Lever, Thomas (1521–1577)," in *Oxford Dictionary of National Biography* (Oxford, 2004); available online at www.oxforddnb.com/view/article/16535.

Lusardi, James P., and June Schlueter, *Reading Shakespeare in Performance:* King Lear (Rutherford, NJ, 1991).

Lydgate, Dan John, *A Selection from the Minor Poems of Dan John Lydgate*, ed. James Orchard Halliwell-Phillips (London, 1860).

Lyly, John, *The Complete Works of John Lyly: Now for the First Time Collected and Edited from the Earliest Quartos with Life, Bibliography, Essays, Notes, and Index*, ed. R. Warwick Bond, 3 vols (Oxford, 1902).

——, *Mar-Martine, I know not why a trueth in rime set out maie not as wel mar Martine and his mates, as shamelesse lies in prose-books cast about marpriests, & prelates, and subvert whole states.* (London, 1589).

——, *Pappe with an hatchet. Alias, a figge for my God sonne* (London, 1589)in The Complete Works of John Lyly, ed. R. Warwick Bond, 3 vols (Oxford, 1902), 3:

——, *Puritan Discipline Tracts: Pap with a hatchet: being a reply to Martin Mar-prelate* (London, 1844).

McClintock, Anne, "Soft-Soaping Empire: Commodity Racism and Imperial Advertising," in *Travelers' Tales: Narratives of Home and Displacement*, ed. George Robertson et al. (New York, 1994), 131–54.

MacCulloch, Diarmaid, *The Boy King: Edward VI and the Protestant Reformation* (Berkeley, CA, 2002).

Mann, David, *The Elizabethan Player: Contemporary Stage Presentations* (London, 1991).

Marcus, Leah S., "Of Mire and Authorship," in *The Theatrical City: Culture, Theatre and Politics in London, 1576–1649*, ed. David L. Smith, Richard Strier, and David Bevington (Cambridge, 1995), 173–4.

——, *Puzzling Shakespeare: Local Reading and its Discontents* (Berkeley, CA, 1988).

Marprelate, Martin (pseud.), *The Epistle* (1588)

——, *The Epitome* (1588)

——, *Hay any worke for Cooper?* (1589)

——. *The Marprelate Tracts* [1588–1589], facsimile edition (Leeds, 1967).

The Marriage Between Wit and Wisdom, ed. Trevor N. S. Lennam (1966; rpt Oxford, 1971).

The Marriage of Wit and Science, ed. John S. Farmer, Tudor Facsimile Texts (London and Edinburgh, 1909).

Marston, John, *The Malcontent*, ed. George K. Hunter (Manchester, 2000).

Martin Iuniors Epilogve (1589).

Martin, J. W., "Christopher Vitel: An Elizabethan Mechanic Preacher," *Sixteenth Century Journal* 10 (May 1979): 15–22.

Matthews, Brander, "The Rise and Fall of Negro-Minstrelsy," *Scribner's* LVIII (1915): 754–9.

Moore Smith, G. C., *College Plays Performed in the University of Cambridge* (Cambridge, 1923).

More, St Thomas, *The Confutation of Tyndale's Answer*, ed. L. A. Schuster et al., in *The Complete Works of St Thomas More*, vol. viii (1) (New Haven, CT, 1973).

Morgan, John, *Godly Learning: Puritan Attitudes towards Reason, Learning and Education, 1560–1640* (London and New York, 1986).

Morgan, Philip D., "British Encounters with Africans and African-Americans, circa 1600–1780," in *Strangers Within the Realm: Cultural Margins of the First British Empire*, ed. Bernard Bailyn and Philip D. Morgan (Chapel Hill, NC, 1991), 157–219.

Mountford, William, *The Life and Death of Doctor Faustus Made into a Farce with the Humours of Harlequin and Scaramouche* (London, 1697).

Mullinger, James Bass, *The University of Cambridge: From the Royal Injunctions of 1535 to the Accession of Charles the First* (Cambridge, 1884).

Nashe, Thomas, *An Almond for a Parrat* ([London], 1590).

——, *The Anatomie of Absurditie* (London, 1589).

——, *Christs Teares Over Iervsalem* (London, 1594).

——, *Have with you to Saffron-Walden* (London, 1596).

——, *Pierce Penilesse his supplication to the diuell* (London, 1592).

——, *The Returne of the Renowned Cavaliero Pasquill of England* (London, 1589).

——, *The Unfortunate Traveller, or, The Life of Jacke Wilton* (London, 1594).

——, *The Complete Works of Thomas Nashe*, ed. Alexander B. Grossart, 6 vols (London, 1883–84).

——, *The Works of Thomas Nashe*, ed. from the original texts by Ronald B. McKerrow, 5 vols (London, 1904–11).

Nelson, Alan H. (ed.), *Cambridge*, Records of Early English Drama, 2 vols (Toronto, 1989).

——, *Early Cambridge Theatres: College, University, and Town Stages, 1464–1720* (Cambridge, 1994).

——, "Early Staging in Cambridge," in *A New History of Early English Drama*, ed. John D. Cox and David Scott Kastan (New York, 1997), 59–67.

A Nest of Ninnies and Other English Jestbooks of the Seventeenth Century, ed. P. M. Zall (Lincoln, NE, 1970).

Nicholl, Charles. *A Cup of News: The Life of Thomas Nashe* (London, 1984).

Nichols, John Gough (ed.), *The Diary of Henry Machyn, Citizen and Merchant-Taylor of London, From ad 1550 to ad 1563* (London, 1848).

—— (ed.), *Literary Remains of King Edward the Sixth*, vol. 2 (London, 1857).

—— (ed.), *Two Sermons Preached by the Boy Bishop at St Paul's ... with an Introduction ... by Edward F. Rimbault* (Westminster, 1875).

Nichols, Josias, *The Plea of the Innocent* (Middelburg, 1602).

Niebrzydowski, Sue, "The Sultana and Her Sisters: Black Women in the British Isles Before 1530," *Women's History Review* 10.2 (2001): 187–210.

Nungezer, Edwin, *A Dictionary of Actors and of Other Persons Associated with the Public Representation of Plays in England before 1642* (1929; rpt New York, 1968).

Nye, Russell, *The Unembarrassed Muse: The Popular Arts in America* (New York, 1970).

Ong, Walter J., SJ, *Ramus, Method, and the Decay of Dialogue* (1958; rpt Cambridge, 1983).

Ormerud, Oliver, *Picture of a Puritane* (London, 1605).

Overbury, Sir Thomas (and others), *Characters, Together with Poems, News, Edicts, and Paradoxes Based on the Eleventh Edition (1622) of A Wife Now the Widow of Sir Thomas Overbury (1614)*, ed. Donald Beecher (Ottawa, 2003).

Parker, Matthew, *Correspondence of Matthew Parker*, ed. John Bruce and Thomas Thomason Perowne (Cambridge, 1853).

Patterson, Annabel, *Censorship and Interpretation: The Conditions of Writing and Reading in Early Modern England* (Madison, WI, 1984).

Patterson, Orlando, *Slavery and Social Death: A Comparative Study* (Cambridge, MA., 1982).

Payne, Elizabeth Rogers, Sapientia Solomonis: *Acted Before the Queen by the Boys of Westminster School January 17, 1565/6* (New Haven, CT, 1938).

Perkins, William, *A Golden Chain, or, the Description of Theologie* (London, 1590).

——, *The Works of That Famous and VVorthy Minister of Christ in the Vniversitie of Cambridge, M. VVilliam Perkins*, 3 vols (London, 1608–31).

Pessen, Edward, *Jacksonian America: Society, Personality, and Politics* (1969; rev edn: Urbana and Chicago, 1985).

The Pilgrimage to Parnassus with the Two Parts of the Return from Parnassus. Three Comedies performed in St John's College. (1597–1601), ed. Rev. W. D. Macray (London, 1886).

Plato, *The Apology*, in *The Last Days of Socrates*, trans. Hugh Tredennick and Harold Tarrant (New York, 2003).

Poole, Kristen, *Radical Religion from Shakespeare to Milton: Figures of Nonconformity in Early Modern England* (Cambridge, 2000).

——, "Saints Alive! Falstaff, Martin Marprelate, and the Staging of Puritanism," *Shakespeare Quarterly* 46.1 (spring 1995): 47–75

Prager, Carolyn, "'If I Be Devil': English Renaissance Response to the Proverbial and Ecumenical Ethiopian," *Journal of Medieval and Renaissance Studies* 17.2 (fall 1987): 257–79.

Prewitt, Kendrick W., "Gabriel Harvey and the Practice of Method," *Studies in English Literature* 39.1 (winter 1999): 19–39.

Rael, Patrick, "The Long Death of Slavery," Chapter 4 in *Slavery in New York*, ed. Ira Berlin and Leslie M. Harris (New York, 2005), 111–46.

Randall, Dale B. J. *Winter Fruit: English Drama 1642–1660* (Lexington, MA, 1995).

Rasmussen, Eric, "The Revision of Scripts," in *A New History of Early English Drama*, ed. John D. Cox and David Scott Kastan (New York, 1997), 441–60.

Reay, Barry, *Popular Cultures in England 1550–1750* (London, 1998).

Redford, John, *Wit and Science*, ed. Arthur Brown (Oxford, 1951).

Rehin, George F., "Harlequin Jim Crow: Continuity and Convergence in Blackface Clowning," *Journal of Popular Culture* 9.3 (winter 1975): 682–701.

Rhodes, Neil, *Elizabethan Grotesque* (London, 1980).

Richardson, W. C., *A History of the Inns of Court* (Baton Rouge, LA, [1975]).

Richman, David, "Shakespeare on Stage: The *King Lear* Quarto in Rehearsal and Performance," *Shakespeare Quarterly* 37.3 (autumn 1996), 374–82.

Robison, William B., "Cawarden, Sir Thomas (*c.* 1514–1559)," in *Oxford Dictionary of National Biography* (Oxford, 2004); available online at www.oxforddnb.com/view/article/37270.

Rosenberg, Marvin, *The Masks of King Lear* (Berkeley, CA, 1972).

Rous, Francis, *The Heavenly Academie: Or the Highest School. Where Alone is that highest Teaching, the Teaching of the Heart* (London, 1638).

Rowley, William, Thomas Dekker, John Ford, *The Witch of Edmonton*, ed. Peter Corbin and Douglas Sedge (Manchester, 1999).

Russell, Jeffrey Burton, *Lucifer, The Devil in the Middle Ages* (Ithaca, NY, and London, 1984).

——, *Satan, The Early Christian Tradition* (Ithaca, NY, and London, 1981).

——, *The Devil: Perceptions of Evil from Antiquity to Primitive Christianity* (Ithaca, NY, and London, 1987).

Saxton, Alexander, "Blackface Minstrelsy and Jacksonian Ideology," *American Quarterly* 27.1 (March 1975): 3–28.

Scott, Kathleen L., *Later Gothic Manuscripts 1390–1490*, A Survey of Manuscripts Illuminated in the British Isles 6, 2 vols (London, 1996)

—— "Limning and Book-producing Terms and Signs *in situ* in Late-Medieval English Manuscripts: A First Listing," in *New Science out of Old Books: Studies in Manuscripts and Early Printed Books in Honour of A. L. Doyle*, ed. Richard Beadle and A. J. Piper (Aldershot, 1995).

Scribner, R. W., *For the Sake of the Simple Folk: Popular Propaganda for the German Reformation* (Cambridge, 1981).

Seaton, Ethel, *Queen Elizabeth and the Swedish Princess: Being an Account of the Visit of Princess Cecilia of Sweden to England in 1565 [1566]* (London, 1926).

Shagan, Ethan, *Popular Politics and the English Reformation* (Cambridge, 2003).

Shakespeare, William, *King Henry VI Part 2*, ed. Ronald Knowles, Arden Shakespeare edition (Walton-on-Thames, 1999).

——, *King Lear*, edited with a theatre commentary by John Russell Brown (New York, 1996).

——, *King Lear*, ed. R. A. Foakes, Arden Shakespeare edition (Walton-on-Thames, 1997).

——, *King Lear: A Parallel Text Edition*, ed. René Weis (London, 1993).

——, *The Norton Shakespeare*, ed. Stephen Greenblatt (New York, 1997).

——, *The Riverside Shakespeare*, ed. G. Blakemore Evans (1974; rpt Boston, 1997).

——, *The Tragedy of King Lear*, ed. Jay L. Halio, The New Cambridge Shakespeare (Cambridge, 1992).

Shakespeare's Plays in Quarto: A Facsimile Edition of Copies Primarily from the Henry E. Huntington Library, ed. Michael J. B. Allen and Kenneth Muir (Berkeley, CA, 1981).

Shepherd, Luke, *Jon Bon and Mast Person*, in *An Edition of Luke Shepherd's Satires*, ed. Janice Devereux (Tempe, AZ, 2001).

Sher, Antony, "The Fool in *King Lear*," in *Players of Shakespeare 2*, ed. Russell Jackson and Robert Smallwood (Cambridge, 1988, 1993), 151–65.

Sherwood, Marika, "Black People in Tudor England," *History Today* (Oct. 2003).

Shuger, Debora K., *Habits of Thought in the English Renaissance: Religion, Politics, and the Dominant Culture* (Berkeley, CA, 1990).

Sibbes, Richard, *Light from Heaven* (London, 1638).

Sidney, Philip, *Apology for Poetry*, ed. H. A. Needham (London, 1931).

Sinden, Donald, "Malvolio in *Twelfth Night*," in *Players of Shakespeare: Essays in Shakespearean Performance*, ed. Philip Brockback (Cambridge, 1985), 41–66.

Sir Thomas More: A Play by Anthony Munday and others; revised by Henry Chettle, Thomas Dekker, Thomas Heywood and William Shakespeare, ed. Vittorio Gabrieli and Giorgio Melchiori (Manchester, 1990).

Sluiter, Engel, "New Light on the '20. and Odd Negroes' Arriving in Virginia, August 1619," *William and Mary Quarterly*, 3d ser., 54 (1997): 396–8.

Smith, Bruce R., *Ancient Scripts and Modern Experience on the English Stage 1500–1700* (Princeton, NJ, 1988).

Southworth, John, *Fools and Jesters at the English Court* (Stroud, 1998).

Stanton, William R., *The Leopard's Spots: Scientific Attitudes Toward Race in America, 1815–1859* (Chicago, 1960).

Stevens, Martin and James Paxson, "The Fool in the Wakefield Plays," *Studies in Iconography* 13 (1989–90): 48–79.

Stone, P. W. K., *The Textual History of* King Lear (London, 1980).

Stow, John, *Survey of London*, ed. C. L. Kingsford, 2 vols (Oxford, 1908), vol. 1.

Strachey, William, *The Historie of Travell into Virginia Britania (1612)* (London, 1953).

Streitberger, W. R., *Court Revels, 1485–1559* (Toronto, 1994).

Strype, John, *Ecclesiastical Memorials, Relating Chiefly to Religion … Under King Henry VIII, King Edward VI, and Queen Mary*, vol. 2 (Oxford, 1822).

Studley, Peter, *Looking-Glasse of Schisme* (London, 1634).

Der Stuttgarter Bilderpsalter Bibl. Fol. 23 Wurrtembergische Landes-bibliothek Stuttgart, 2 vols (Stuttgart, 1965).

Sutcliffe, Matthew, *An Answere to a certaine libel supplicatorie* (London, 1592),

Talbert, E. W., *Elizabethan Drama and Shakespeare's Early Plays: An Essay in Historical Criticism* (Chapel Hill, NC, 1963).

Taylor, Gary, "Monopolies, Show Trials, Disaster, and Invasion: *King Lear* and Censorship," in *The Division of the Kingdoms: Shakespeare's Two Versions of* King Lear, ed. Gary Taylor and Michael Warren (Oxford, 1983), 77–119.

Taylor, John, *A Swarme of Sectaires, and Schismatiques* (London, 1641).

——, *The World Turn'd Upside Down* (London, 1647).

Thomas, Keith, "The Place of Laughter in Tudor and Stuart England," *Times Literary Supplement* 21 (January 1977): 77–81.

——, *Religion and the Decline of Magic: Studies in Popular Beliefs in Sixteenth and Seventeenth-Century England* (1971; rpt New York, 1997).

Thompson, Stith, *Motif-Index of Folk-Literature*, vol. 4: J–K, Indiana University Studies 22 (Sept., Dec. 1934).

Thomson, Peter, "Clowns, Fools and Knaves: Stages in the Evolution of Acting," in *The Cambridge History of British Theatre*: vol. 1, *Origins to 1660*, ed. Jane Milling and Peter Thomson (Cambridge, 2004), 407–23.

——, "Tarlton, Richard (d. 1588)," in *Oxford Dictionary of National Biography* (Oxford, 2004); available online at www.oxforddnb.com/view/article/26971.

Thornton, John K., "The African Experience of the '20. and Odd

Negroes' Arriving in Virginia in 1619," *William and Mary Quarterly*, 3d ser., 55 (July 1998): 421–34.

Three Late Medieval Morality Plays, ed. G. A. Lester (London and New York, 1981).

Three Rastell Plays: Four Elements, Calisto and Melebea, Gentleness and Nobility, ed. Richard Axton (Cambridge, 1979).

Tiffany, Grace, "Puritanism in Comic History: Exposing Royalty in the Henry Plays," *Shakespeare Studies* 26 (1998): 256–87.

Tokson, Eliot, *The Popular Image of the Black Man in English Drama, 1550–1688* (Boston, 1982).

Topsell, Edward, *The Historie of Four-Footed Beastes* (London, 1678).

The Towneley Plays, ed. Martin Stevens and A. C. Cawley (Oxford and New York, 1994), vol. 1.

Tudor Royal Proclamations, ed. Paul L. Hughes and James F. Larkin, 3 vols (New Haven, CT, 1969).

Twycross, Meg, and Sarah Carpenter, *Masks and Masking in Medieval and Early Tudor England* (Burlington, VT, 2002).

Tyler, Royall (ed.), *Calendar of Letters, Despatches, and State Papers. Relating to the Negotiations Between England and Spain*, vol. 10 (London, 1914).

Underdown, David, *Revel, Riot and Rebellion: Popular Politics and Culture in England 1603–1660* (1985; rpt Oxford and New York, 1987).

Urkowitz, Steven, *Shakespeare's Revision of* King Lear (Princeton, NJ, 1980).

Vaughan, Virginia Mason, Othello: *A Contextual History* (Cambridge, 1994).

——, *Performing Blackness on English Stages, 1500–1800* (Cambridge, 2005).

Walker, Greg, *Plays of Persuasion: Drama and Politics at the Court of Henry VIII* (Cambridge, 1991).

Walvin, James, *The Black Presence: A Documentary History of the Negro in England, 1555–1860* (London, 1971).

Warren, Michael, "The Diminution of Kent," in *The Division of the Kingdoms: Shakespeare's Two Versions of* King Lear, ed. Gary Taylor and Michael Warren (Oxford, 1983), 59–74.

Warren, Roger, "The Folio Omission of the Mock Trial: Motives and Consequences," in *The Division of the Kingdoms: Shakespeare's Two Versions of* King Lear, ed. Gary Taylor and Michael Warren (Oxford, 1983), 45–57.

Weimann, Robert, *Authority and Representation in Early Modern Discourse* (Baltimore, MD, 1996).

——, *Shakespeare and the Popular Tradition in the Theater: Studies in the Social Dimension of Dramatic Form and Function* (Baltimore, MD, 1987).

——, and Douglas Bruster, *Shakespeare and the Power of Performance: Stage and Page in the Elizabethan Theatre* (Cambridge, 2008).

Wells, Stanley (ed.), *Shakespeare in the Theatre: An Anthology of Criticism* (1997; rpt New York, 2000).

Welsford, Enid, *The Fool: His Social and Literary History* (1935; rpt Gloucester, MA, 1966).

White, Eugene E., *Puritan Rhetoric: The Issue of Emotion in Religion* (Carbondale, IL, 1972).

White, Paul Whitfield, *Theatre and Reformation: Protestantism, Patronage, and Playing in Tudor England* (Cambridge, 1993).

——, "Theatre and Religious Culture," in *A New History of Early English Drama*, ed. John D. Cox and David Scott Kastan (New York, 1997), 133–51.

Whitworth, C. W. (ed.), *Three Sixteenth-Century Comedies* (New York, 1984).

Wickham, Glynne, *Early English Stages 1300 to 1600*, 3 vols (New York, 1966–1991), vol. 2.

——, "From Tragedy to Tragi-comedy: *King Lear* as Prologue," *Shakespeare Survey* 26 (1973): 33–48.

Wiles, David, *Shakespeare's Clown: Actor and Text in the Elizabethan Playhouse* (Cambridge, 1987).

Wilson, J. Dover, *The Fortunes of Falstaff* (New York, 1944).

Wood, Michael, *Shakespeare* (New York, 2003).

Woodbridge, Linda, *The Scythe of Saturn: Shakespeare and Magical Thinking* (Urbana, IL, 1994).

The Works of Beaumont and Fletcher, ed. Alexander Dyce (London, 1844), vol. 7.

Yachnin, Paul, "Reversal of Fortune: Shakespeare, Middleton, and the Puritans," *English Literary History* 70.3 (2003): 757–86.

Zacha, Richard B, "Iago and the *Commedia dell'Arte*," *Arlington Quarterly* 2.2 (autumn, 1969): 98–116.

INDEX

Abell, William, 195

actor-author collaboration, 22, 156, 157, 181, 188, 189

  Rowley-Middleton, 188–89

A Description of the Coasts of North and South Guinea, 50

aesthetics, 1, 12, 13, 23, 183. *See also* neoclassicism

  trends in, 1, 5, 23, 152, 154–55, 156, 157 n 36, 159, 178–79, 181

Africans. *See also* slavery

  European encounters with, 45–46, 51–53

  and assumed natural folly of, 53

Africanus, Leo, 52

All for Money, 33

Allan, D. G., 112

Anabaptist(s), 111–12

  and "anabaptistical" stereotype, 110, 123, 124, 141

  and irrational/ignorant stereotype, 112, 113

  and Marprelate, 110–11, 113

  and Munzer Commonwealth, 111, 112, 113

  as proto-communist, 124, 125

  conflated with puritans, 111, 112

  Hacket compared to, 113

  rebellion against social order, 111, 112, 113, 114, 123

anachronisms

  in criticism, 7, 12, 13, 20, 64, 100

  in historical analogies, 145

  in stereotypes of sober Protestants and carnivalesque Catholics, 64, 100

anamorphic painting, 63–64

anecdotal historicism, as mystifying, alienating, 7, 8

angels, 29

Anglo, Sydney, 66, 94

anti-Catholicism, 64–65, 67, 103

  against communion, 67

  against processions, 67

  against superstition, 67

  anticlericalism, 67

Antichrist, 72, 81, 88

anti-clericalism, 66, 67

anti-Martinism, 96–98, 100, 106–7, 133. *See also* Bancroft, John; Lyly, John; Marprelate, Martin; May game; Munday, Anthony; Nashe, Thomas; puritan stereotype; Whitgift, John

  An Almond for a Parrot, 111

  and Rabelais, 98

  characterization of opposition, 97–98

  comedies staged, 99

  A Countercuffe given to Martin Junior, 99

  Cutbert Curryknave, 98

  Mar-Martin, 99

  Mar-Martine, 97, 107

  Marphoreus, 98

  Martins Months Mind, 99, 106, 132

  May-game of Martinisme, 98–99, 106, 133

  Pappe with an Hatchet, 106

  Pasquill, 98–99

  puritan response, 97

  Return of Pasquill, 133

  satire of, 100

  Whip for an Ape, 107

anti-papist. *See also* anti-Catholicism, anti-Catholic satire

  misrule, 74, 88

  propaganda, 191

  revels, 74

anti-puritan criticism, 120. *See also* anti-Martinism

  satire, 126, 140

223

Cambridge University
St. John's College, 68, 70, 71, 77–78, 80, 81, 82, 101
Trinity College, 78, 80, 82, 93
and *Anglia deformata and Anglia restituta*, 93
and Cromwellian iconoclasm, 80, 84
and evangelical drama, 72, 78, 83
and misrule, 22, 71–83, 92–93
and reformist tendencies, 79
and visit by Elizabeth, 79, 82 n 90
Cambridge Reformers, 71
Cane, Andrew, 197, 198
Capel, Richard, 117
The Cardinal's Conspiracy, 195
carnival, 58, 76
as character, 76
rarity in England, 76
carnivalesque, 22, 64, 89–90, 94, 110
and Bakhtin, 98
and grotesques, 64, 98
Caroline period, 186, 191, 194
attitudes toward clown, 194
parodies of social types, 194
Cartwright, Thomas, 82, 112
Cartwright, William, 184–5
The Castle of Perseverance, 35
Catholicism,
and anti-papist polemic against super- stition, 103
and feast days, 67–68
and superstition, 67
Cawarden, Thomas, 74
Cecil, William, 24
Cecilia, Princess of Sweden, 24
censoriousness,
in attitudes toward clowns, 10, 183, 196
puritan attitudes toward laughter, 100–101
versus mixing clowns and kings, 195
versus revivals, 195
censorship, 23, 73, 84, 99–100, 144–46, 147 n.11, 169, 183, 191, 196. *See also* Armin, Robert; Interregnum playing; *King Lear*; Red Bull Theatre; Rowley, William
bans on playing, 65, 196
bans on religious playing, 73, 92, 99–100

by Commonwealth government, 196, 197, 198, 199, 202
of iconoclastic misrule, 73–74, 92, 94
of jokes mocking Eucharist, 84
of Martinist Tracts and plays, 96, 99–100
of plays and players, 73, 146, 191
Act to Restrain Abuses, 146
of religious misrule, 73–74
proclamations and bans, 73–74
Chain of Being, 27, 54–56, 62, 97
Chambers, E. K., 75, 99
The Changeling, 183
Chapman, George, 114
The Memorable Masque, 114
character criticism, 149–50
Charles I, 190, 200
Children of Paul's, 41
Cheapside Cross, 87, 89
children's companies. *See also* Children of Paul's, Westminster Grammar School
blackface in plays of, 41, 43
Christmas revels, 76–77, 80, 86
Christmas Lords. See Lord(s) of Misrule
Christopherson, John, 70, 71
Civil Rights Act, 32
classical languages, 118, 121
Clayton, Thomas, 169
clown(s), 1, 3, 4, 10, 19, 20, 23, 24, 64, 100, 144–45, 193–94, 202. *See also* Armin, Robert; Cane, Andrew; cobbler clown stereotype; Ferrers, George; juggler; Kemp, Will; Robins (Robinson); Shakespeare, William, characters; Shank, John; Smith, John; stereotypes; Tarlton, Richard
and carnivalesque persona, 96
and fool type, 143
and puritans, 96–97, 100
and satire, 144, 191, 202
and status of, 132
and stupid puritan type, 102–42
as Mass-priest or "juggler," 89
as rustics, 3, 95
as Vice in clerical gown, 88–89
as "Yoricks," 3, 12
banishment from stage, 185, 193, 196, 198

230

234

235

proto-racism
  ideological foundations of *cont.*
    and invocations of nature, 60
    and simian imperialism, 54
Prynne, William, 101
Psalm 52. See also insipiens
  iconography of, 35, 36, 38 Fig. 2, 48
psalter illuminations, 21, 36
The Puritan, 104
puritans, 82, 112, 118, 120. *See also*
    Marprelate, Martin; misrule;
    puritan clown type
  against Catholic mass, 89, 92, 94, 96
  against holy days, 88
  against humane learning, 119, 120,
    122, 125, 126
  and antipathy to hobby horse, 90–91
  and attitudes toward laughter, 100–101
  and carnival, 96
  and cult of the ear, 139, 140
  and demonic possession and
  and derisive humor, 97
  and dilettantism, 129
  and enthusiasm, 114
  and grotesque caricature, 122, 124
  and ignorant stereotype, 103–5, 112,
    113, 122, 125, 134, 141
  and inspiration, 113,
  and logolatry, 140
  and mockery of dumb ministry, 103
  and preaching ministry, 103
  and prophets and witnesses, 112
  and puritan rhetoric, 124, 133–35,
    138
  and reputation as arrogant, 102–3,
    119, 135, 141
  and "right reason," 118
  and self-promotion as learned, 102–3,
    112, 114
  and spirit, 114
  and stereotypical antipathy to literacy,
    122, 123
  and stupidity, 126,
  anti-intellectualism, 112, 117, 120, 121,
    126
    madness, 34, 112, 114
  as characters/clowns in plays, 90, 101
  as clownish, 134
  as critics of natural, human or
    "humane" reason, 116, 117, 120

  as rebellious, 125
  characters:
    Blurt, Master Constable, 102, 131
    Capriccio, 114
    Dogberry, 131, 135–40
    Hope-on-High Bomby, 90, 91
    Jack Cade, 123, 124, 125, 133n,
      135n, 135, 142
    Jack Straw, 114
    Stupido, 102, 104–5, 121, 126, 138,
      139, 141
    Zeal-of-the Land Busy, 90, 91, 114,
      136
  features of type, 112
  irrationality of, 112
  misterming, 131, 134
  Pilgrimage to Parnassus, 102–5
  stereotype defined, 98, 100, 122
  typed as constables, 131, 135
  typed as puritan magistrate clown,
    130–135
puritan stereotype, 90, 98, 100, 105,
    107–9, 109 Fig. 4, 112, 120, 122,
    125, 134, 140, 141
Rabelais, 98, 118, 165
racism, 5, 25, 37, 40. *See also* proto-
    racism
  and slavery, origins of, 25
  definition of, 54
  history of, 31
  ideological foundations of, 27, 37, 54,
    62
  origins of, 25–27
  pseudo-scientific ideologies of, 27, 51,
    54, 56, 57, 62
  theologies and, 25
Ralph Roister Doister, 19
Ramist rhetoric, logic, and method, 17,
    22, 118, 127, 128, 129, 129 n109,
    130–31 n115, 133, 138, 139, 140.
    See also godly learning, and puri-
    tans; Harvey, Gabriel
  and dialectic, 138
  and dichotomies, 130, 131
  and epitomies, 128
  and logic, 138
  and memorization, 127, 139
  and method, 136, 138
  and numbered lists, 138
  and order, 127, 138, 139